First World War
and Army of Occupation
War Diary
France, Belgium and Germany

42 DIVISION
Divisional Troops
Royal Army Medical Corps
1/3 East Lancashire Field Ambulance
13 March 1917 - 2 April 1919

WO95/2652/3

The Naval & Military Press Ltd
www.nmarchive.com
Published in association with The National Archives

Published by

The Naval & Military Press Ltd

Unit 10 Ridgewood Industrial Park,

Uckfield, East Sussex,

TN22 5QE England

Tel: +44 (0) 1825 749494

www.naval-military-press.com

www.nmarchive.com

This diary has been reprinted in facsimile from the original. Any imperfections are inevitably reproduced and the quality may fall short of modern type and cartographic standards.

© **Crown Copyright**
Images reproduced by permission of The National Archives, London, England, 2015.

Contents

Document type	Place/Title	Date From	Date To
Heading	WO95/2652/3 42 Divn 1/3 E Lancs Field Amb 1917 Mar-1919 Feb		
Heading	42nd Division 1-3rd East Lancs Fld Ambulance Mar 1917-1919 Mar		
Heading	War Diary of the 1/3rd East Lancs, Field Ambulance. from March 11th 1917 to March 31st 1917. (Volume 3)		
Miscellaneous		11/03/1917	11/03/1917
Miscellaneous	Marseilles	12/03/1917	12/03/1917
War Diary	France	13/03/1917	14/03/1917
War Diary	Frucourt	15/03/1917	29/03/1917
War Diary	Campmarly	30/03/1917	31/03/1917
Heading	War Diary of the. 1/3rd East Lancashire Field Ambulance from April 1st 1917. to April 30th 1917. (Volume 4)		
War Diary	Campmarly	01/04/1917	04/04/1917
War Diary	Fontaine Les Cappy	05/04/1917	17/04/1917
War Diary	Doingt	18/04/1917	30/04/1917
Heading	War Diary of the 1/3rd East Lancashire Field Ambulance from May 1st 1917 to May 31st 1917. (Volume V)		
War Diary	Doingt	01/05/1917	20/05/1917
War Diary	Bus	20/05/1917	31/05/1917
War Diary	War Diary of the 1/3rd East Lancashire Field Amb. from. June 1st 1917. to June 30th 1917. (Volume 6)		
War Diary	Bus	01/06/1917	30/06/1917
Heading	War Diary. of the 1/3rd East Lancashire Field Amb. from July 1st 1917. to July 31st 1917. (Volume 7.)		
War Diary	Bus	01/07/1917	09/07/1917
War Diary	Line of March	10/07/1917	10/07/1917
War Diary	Achiet Le Grand	11/07/1917	31/07/1917
Operation(al) Order(s)	1/3 E.L. Field Ambulance Order No. 1	07/07/1917	07/07/1917
Operation(al) Order(s)	1/3rd. East Lancashire Field Amb. Order No. 2	07/07/1917	07/07/1917
Operation(al) Order(s)	1/3rd. East Lancs Field Ambulance. Order No. 3	09/07/1917	09/07/1917
Miscellaneous	1/3rd. East Lancashire Field Ambulance. Scheme of Training for Week Ending Sunday 15-7-1917	15/07/1917	15/07/1917
Miscellaneous	1/3rd. East Lancashire Field Ambulance. Scheme of Training for Week Ending Sunday 22-7-1917	22/07/1917	22/07/1917
Operation(al) Order(s)	1/3rd. East Lancs. Field Ambulance. Order No. 4	25/07/1917	25/07/1917
Operation(al) Order(s)	1/3rd. East Lancs. Field Ambulance. Order No. 5	26/07/1917	26/07/1917
Miscellaneous	1/3rd East Lancashire Field Ambulance. Scheme of Training for Week ending Sunday 29-7-17	29/07/1917	29/07/1917
Heading	War Diary of the 1/3rd C. Lancashire Field Ambulance. from Aug 1st 1917 to August 31st 1917 (Volume 8)		
War Diary	Achiet Le Grand	01/08/1917	21/08/1917
War Diary	Aveluy	22/08/1917	25/08/1917
War Diary	Luna Park	26/08/1917	31/08/1917
Operation(al) Order(s)	1/3rd East Lancs. Field Ambulance. Order No. 6	05/08/1917	05/08/1917
Operation(al) Order(s)	1/3rd East Lancs. Field Ambulance. Order No. 7	06/08/1917	06/08/1917
Operation(al) Order(s)	1/3rd East Lancs. Field Ambulance. Order No. 8	07/08/1917	07/08/1917

Operation(al) Order(s)	1/3rd East Lancs. Field Ambulance. Operation Order No. 1	08/08/1917	08/08/1917
Miscellaneous	O.C., 1/3rd E.L. Fd. Ambulance.	19/08/1917	19/08/1917
Operation(al) Order(s)	1/3rd. East Lancs. Field Ambulance Order No. 9	20/08/1917	20/08/1917
Operation(al) Order(s)	1/3rd East Lancashire Field Amb. Order No. 10	22/08/1917	22/08/1917
Miscellaneous	1/3rd East Lancs. Fld Ambulance. Order No. 11	22/08/1917	22/08/1917
Operation(al) Order(s)	1/3rd East Lancs. Fld. Ambulance. Order No. 12		
Operation(al) Order(s)	1/3rd East Lancs. Field Ambulance. Order No. 13	30/08/1917	30/08/1917
Heading	War Diary. of the 1/3rd East Lancashire Field Amb. from September 1st 17 to September 30th 17 (Volume 9)		
War Diary	Poperinghe	01/09/1917	10/09/1917
War Diary	Ypres.	11/09/1917	18/09/1917
War Diary	Brandhoek	18/09/1917	20/09/1917
War Diary	Winneele	21/09/1917	22/09/1917
War Diary	Coxyde-Ville	23/09/1917	24/09/1917
War Diary	St Idesbald	25/09/1917	30/09/1917
Operation(al) Order(s)	1/3rd East Lancs. Field Ambulance. Order No. 14	02/09/1917	02/09/1917
Operation(al) Order(s)	1/3rd East Lancashire Field Ambulance. Order No. 15	03/09/1917	03/09/1917
Operation(al) Order(s)	1/3rd East Lancs Field Ambulance. Order No. 16	10/09/1917	10/09/1917
Operation(al) Order(s)	1/3rd E. Lancs Field Ambulance. Operation Order No. 17	16/09/1917	16/09/1917
Heading	War Diary 1/3rd East Lancashire Field Ambce. from October 1st 1917 to October 31st-1917 (Volume 10)		
War Diary	St Idesbald	01/10/1917	06/10/1917
War Diary	Coxyde	07/10/1917	31/10/1917
Operation(al) Order(s)	1/3rd East Lancs. Field Ambulance. Operation Order No. 18	05/10/1917	05/10/1917
Miscellaneous	Orders by Lieut Colonel H.H.B. Cunningham Commanding 1/3rd East. Lancs. Fld. Ambulance.	07/10/1917	07/10/1917
Miscellaneous	Orders by Lieut-Colonel H.H.B. Cunningham Commanding 1/3rd East Lancs. Field Ambulance.	08/10/1917	08/10/1917
Miscellaneous	Routine Orders by Lieut-Colonel. H.H.B. Cunningham. Commanding 1/3rd East. Lancs. Field Ambulance.	09/10/1917	09/10/1917
Operation(al) Order(s)	1/3rd East Lancashire Field Ambulance. Order No. 19	28/10/1917	28/10/1917
Heading	War Diary Of 1/3rd East Lancashire Field Ambulance. From:- 1st November, 1917 To:- 30th November, 1917 (Volume XI)		
War Diary	Nieuport	01/11/1917	12/11/1917
War Diary	Coxyde	13/11/1917	19/11/1917
War Diary	Leffrinkouke	20/11/1917	20/11/1917
War Diary	Wormhoudt	21/11/1917	21/11/1917
War Diary	Rietveld	22/11/1917	22/11/1917
War Diary	Oxelaire	23/11/1917	23/11/1917
War Diary	Thiennes	24/11/1917	26/11/1917
War Diary	Bethune	27/11/1917	27/11/1917
War Diary	Mesplaux Farm	28/11/1917	30/11/1917
Miscellaneous	1/3rd East Lancs. Field Ambulance.	01/11/1917	01/11/1917
Miscellaneous	O.C., 1/3rd East Lancashire Field Ambulance.	01/11/1917	01/11/1917
Miscellaneous	1/3rd East Lancs Field Ambulance.	01/11/1917	01/11/1917
Miscellaneous	O.C., 1/3rd East Lancs Field Ambulance.	01/11/1917	01/11/1917
Diagram etc Miscellaneous	A.D.S. Nieuport.		
Map	Map No. 5		
Operation(al) Order(s)	1/3rd East Lancashire Field Ambulance. Order No. 20	15/11/1917	15/11/1917
Operation(al) Order(s)	1/3rd East Lancashire Field Ambulance. Order No. 21	16/11/1917	16/11/1917

Miscellaneous	Addendum to 1/3rd East Lancashire Field Ambulance. Order No. 21	16/11/1917	16/11/1917
Operation(al) Order(s)	1/3rd East Lancashire Field Ambulance. Order No. 22	25/11/1917	25/11/1917
Operation(al) Order(s)	1/3rd East Lancashire Field Ambulance. Operation Order No. 23	26/11/1917	26/11/1917
War Diary	War Diary Of 1/3rd East Lancashire Field Ambulance. From:- December 1st 1917 To:- December 31st, 1917 (Volume XII)		
War Diary	Mesplaux Farm	01/12/1917	31/12/1917
Operation(al) Order(s)	1/3rd East Lancashire Field Ambulance. Order No. 24	07/12/1917	07/12/1917
Miscellaneous	1/3rd East Lancashire Field Ambulance Scale of Diet for Week ending 8-12-1917	08/12/1917	08/12/1917
Map	Map Ref France (Combined Sheet) Bethune		
Operation(al) Order(s)	1/3rd East Lancashire Field Ambulance. Order No. 25	13/12/1917	13/12/1917
Operation(al) Order(s)	1/3rd East Lancashire Field Ambulance. Order No. 26	28/12/1917	28/12/1917
Miscellaneous	1/3rd East Lancashire Field ambce Scale of diet for week ending Decr 29th 1917	29/12/1917	29/12/1917
Miscellaneous	??	16/12/1917	16/12/1917
Heading	War Diary Of 1/3rd East Lancashire Field Ambulance. From:- January 1st, 1918 To:- January 31st, 1918 (Volume I)		
War Diary	Mesplaux Farm	01/01/1918	05/01/1918
War Diary	Mesplaux Fm 5.1.18	05/01/1918	10/01/1918
War Diary	Locon (S)	10/01/1918	31/01/1918
Operation(al) Order(s)	1/3rd East Lancashire Field Ambulance. Order No. 27	08/01/1918	08/01/1918
Operation(al) Order(s)	1/3rd East Lancashire Field Ambulance. Order No. 28 Appendix 41	08/01/1918	08/01/1918
Operation(al) Order(s)	1/3rd East Lancashire Field Ambulance. Ammendment No. 1. to Order No. 28	09/01/1918	09/01/1918
Operation(al) Order(s)	1/3rd East Lancashire Field Ambulance. Order No. 29	10/01/1918	10/01/1918
Miscellaneous	Routine Orders by Lieut-Colonel H.H.B. Cunningham, Commanding 1/3rd East Lancashire Field Ambulance. Appendix 44	18/01/1918	18/01/1918
Miscellaneous	Routine Orders By Lieut-Colonel H.H.B. Cunningham. Commanding 1/3rd East Lancashire Field Ambulance. Appendix 45	20/01/1918	20/01/1918
Miscellaneous	Routine Orders by Lieut-Colonel H.H.B. Cunningham. Commanding 1/3rd East Lancashire Field Ambulance. Appendix 46	21/01/1918	21/01/1918
Operation(al) Order(s)	1/3rd East Lancashire Field Ambulance. Order No. 30 Appendix 47	22/01/1918	22/01/1918
Operation(al) Order(s)	1/3rd East Lancashire Field Ambulance. Order No. 31 Appendix 48	27/01/1918	27/01/1918
Miscellaneous	O.C., 1/3rd East Lancashire Field Ambulance. Appendix 48	27/01/1918	27/01/1918
Operation(al) Order(s)	1/3rd East Lancashire Field Ambulance. Order No. 32 Appendix 49	28/01/1918	28/01/1918
Operation(al) Order(s)	1/3rd East Lancashire Field Ambulance. Order No. 33 Appendix 50	30/01/1918	30/01/1918
Heading	War Diary Of 1/3rd East Lancashire Field Ambulance. From:- February 1st, 1918 To:- February 28th, 1918. (Volume 2)		
War Diary	Locon South	01/02/1918	12/02/1918
War Diary	Labeuvriere	13/02/1918	28/02/1918
Operation(al) Order(s)	1/3rd East Lancashire Field Ambulance. Order No. 34 Appendix 51	03/02/1918	03/02/1918

Operation(al) Order(s)	1/3rd East Lancashire Field Ambulance. Order No. 35 Appendix 52	11/02/1918	11/02/1918
Miscellaneous	A Sec. First Corps Rest Station Appendix 53	16/02/1918	16/02/1918
Miscellaneous	Special Order Of The Day By Lieut-Colonel. H.H.B. Cunningham. Commanding 1/3rd East Lancashire Field Ambulance. Appendix 54	21/02/1918	21/02/1918
Miscellaneous	A.D.M.S., 42nd Division.	26/02/1918	26/02/1918
Heading	War Diary Of 1/3rd East Lancashire Field Ambulance, R.A.M.C. (T.F.) From:- March 1st, 1918 To:- March 31st, 1918 (Volume 111)		
War Diary	Labeuvriere	01/03/1918	24/03/1918
War Diary	Bucquoy	25/03/1918	25/03/1918
War Diary	Monchy	26/03/1918	30/03/1918
War Diary	Bakencourt	31/03/1918	31/03/1918
Operation(al) Order(s)	1/3rd East Lancashire Field Ambulance. Order No. 36	01/03/1918	01/03/1918
Operation(al) Order(s)	1/3rd East Lancashire Field Ambulance. Order No. 37	02/03/1918	02/03/1918
Miscellaneous	'A' Section 1st Corps Rest Station Patients diet sheet for week ending March 3rd 1918 Appendix 58	03/03/1918	03/03/1918
Miscellaneous	1/3rd East Lincashire Field Ambulance Personnel Diet Sheet for week ending March 3rd 1918	03/03/1918	03/03/1918
Miscellaneous	1/3rd East Lancs Field Ambulance Personnel Diet Sheet for week ending March 9 1918 Appendix 59	09/03/1918	09/03/1918
Miscellaneous	1/3rd East Lancs Field Ambulance Patients Diet Sheet for week ending March 9th 1918 Appendix 59	09/03/1918	09/03/1918
Operation(al) Order(s)	1/3rd East Lancashire Field Ambulance. Order No. 38 Appendix 60	18/03/1918	18/03/1918
Miscellaneous	1/3rd East Lancashire Field Ambulance. Order No. 39 App 61	22/03/1918	22/03/1918
Heading	War Diary Of 1/3rd East Lancashire Field Ambulance From:- April 1st, 1918 To:- April 30th, 1918 (Volume IV)		
War Diary	Bavencourt	01/04/1918	01/04/1918
War Diary	Bienvillers	02/04/1918	07/04/1918
War Diary	Henu	08/04/1918	17/04/1918
War Diary	Souastre	18/04/1918	30/04/1918
Operation(al) Order(s)	1/3rd East Lancashire Field Ambulance Order No. 40 Appendix 62	01/04/1918	01/04/1918
Miscellaneous	A.D.M.S. 42nd Division Situation report Appendix 63	02/04/1918	02/04/1918
Operation(al) Order(s)	1/3rd East Lancashire Field Ambulance Order No. 41 Appendix 64	03/04/1918	03/04/1918
Operation(al) Order(s)	1/3rd East Lancashire Field Ambulance Order No. 42 Appendix 65	04/04/1918	04/04/1918
Miscellaneous	A.D.M.S. 42nd Division Appendix 66	05/04/1918	05/04/1918
Operation(al) Order(s)	1/3rd East Lancashire Field Ambulance Order No. 43 Appendix 67	08/04/1918	08/04/1918
Miscellaneous	A.D.M.S. 42nd Division Appendix 68	13/04/1918	13/04/1918
Miscellaneous	Contents Of Section Limber Appendix 68		
Operation(al) Order(s)	1/3rd East Lancashire Field Ambulance Order No. 44 Appendix 69	15/04/1918	15/04/1918
Operation(al) Order(s)	1/3rd East Lancashire Field Ambulance Order No. 45 Appendix 70	16/04/1918	16/04/1918
Operation(al) Order(s)	1/3rd East Lancashire Field Ambce Order No. 46	28/04/1918	28/04/1918
Heading	War Diary Of 1/3rd East Lancashire Field Ambulance. From:- May 1st, 1918. To:- May 31st, 1918 (Volume V)		
War Diary	Souastre	01/05/1918	06/05/1918
War Diary	Pas	07/05/1918	31/05/1918

Operation(al) Order(s)	1/3rd East Lancashire Field Ambulance. Order No. 47 Appendix 72	05/05/1918	05/05/1918
Heading	War Diary Of 1/3rd East Lancashire Field Ambulance. From:- June 1st, 1918 To:- June 30th, 1918 (Volume VI)		
War Diary	Pas	01/06/1918	07/06/1918
War Diary	Louvencourt.	08/06/1918	18/06/1918
War Diary	Gouvencourt	19/06/1918	30/06/1918
Operation(al) Order(s)	1/3rd East Lancashire Field Ambulance. Order No. 48	05/06/1918	05/06/1918
Operation(al) Order(s)	1/3rd East Lancashire Field Ambulance. Order No. 49	08/06/1918	08/06/1918
Miscellaneous	Diet Sheet for the Period ending 10th June 1918 Appendix 75	10/06/1918	10/06/1918
Heading	War Diary Of 1/3rd East Lancashire Field Ambulance. From:- July 1st, 1918. To:- July 31st, 1918 (Volume VII)		
War Diary	Gouvencourt	01/07/1918	04/07/1918
War Diary	Louvencourt	05/07/1918	09/07/1918
War Diary	Gouvencourt	10/08/1918	10/08/1918
War Diary	Gouvencourt	11/07/1918	14/07/1918
War Diary	Louvencourt	15/07/1918	31/07/1918
Operation(al) Order(s) Heading	1/3rd East Lancashire Field Ambulance. Order No. 50 Appendix I	03/07/1918	03/07/1918
Operation(al) Order(s)	1/3rd East Lancashire Field Ambulance Order No. 51	31/07/1918	31/07/1918
Heading	War Diary Of 1/3rd East Lancashire Field Ambulance. From 1st August 1918 to 31st August 1918 Volume VIII		
War Diary	Louvencourt	01/08/1918	14/08/1918
War Diary	Gouvencourt	15/08/1918	31/08/1918
Operation(al) Order(s)	1/3rd East Lancashire Field Ambulance. Order No. 52	01/08/1918	01/08/1918
Operation(al) Order(s)	1/3rd East Lancashire Field Ambulance. Order No. 53 Appendix 80	09/08/1918	09/08/1918
War Diary	War Diary Of 1/3rd East Lancashire Field Ambulance September 1st 1918 to September 30th 1918 Volume IX		
War Diary	Gouvencourt	01/09/1918	06/09/1918
War Diary	Irles	07/09/1918	30/09/1918
Operation(al) Order(s)	1/3rd E. Lancashire Field Ambce. Order No. 54 Appendix 81	19/09/1918	19/09/1918
Miscellaneous	Diet Sheet for the Period ending 25th Sept 1918 Appendix 82	25/09/1918	25/09/1918
Operation(al) Order(s)	1/3rd E. Lancashire Field Ambce. Order No 55 Appendix 83	30/09/1918	30/09/1918
Heading	War Diary Of 1/3rd East Lancashire Field Ambulance. October 1st 1918 to October 31st 1918 Volume X.		
War Diary	Irles	01/10/1918	02/10/1918
War Diary	Ruyaulcourt	03/10/1918	23/10/1918
War Diary	Caudry	24/10/1918	31/10/1918
Operation(al) Order(s)	1/3rd East Lancashire Field Ambulance Order No. 56 Appendix 84	07/10/1918	07/10/1918
Operation(al) Order(s)	1/3rd East Lancashire Field Ambulance Order No. 57 Appendix 85	25/10/1918	25/10/1918
Operation(al) Order(s)	1/3rd East Lancashire Field Ambulance Order No. 58 Appendix 86	30/10/1918	30/10/1918
Heading	War Diary Of 1/3rd East Lancashire Field Ambulance From:- November 1st, 1918 To:- November 30th, 1918 (Volume XI)		
War Diary	Caudry	01/11/1918	17/11/1918

War Diary	Hautmont	18/11/1918	30/11/1918
Miscellaneous	1/3rd East Lancashire Field Ambulance Appendix 87	03/11/1918	03/11/1918
Operation(al) Order(s)	1/3rd E. Lancashire Field Ambce. Order No. 59 Appendix 88	16/11/1918	16/11/1918
Heading	War Diary Of 1/3rd East Lancashire Field Ambulance From:- December 1st 1918 To:- December 31st 1918 (Volume XII)		
War Diary	Hautmont	01/12/1918	10/12/1918
War Diary	Charleroi	15/12/1918	19/12/1918
War Diary	Hautmont	10/12/1918	13/12/1918
War Diary	Charleroi	14/12/1918	31/12/1918
Operation(al) Order(s)	1/3rd East Lancashire Field Ambulance Order No. 60	03/12/1918	03/12/1918
Operation(al) Order(s)	1/3rd East Lancashire Field Ambulance Addendum & Corrigendum No. 1 to Field Ambulance Order No. 61 Appendix 90	11/12/1918	11/12/1918
Miscellaneous	1/3rd East Lancashire Field Ambulance Order No. 61 Appendix 90	11/12/1918	11/12/1918
Heading	War Diary Of 1/3rd East Lancashire Field Ambulance From:- January 1st, 1919 To:- January 31st, 1919 (Volume 1)		
War Diary	Charleroi	01/01/1919	31/01/1919
Heading	War Diary 1/3rd East Lancashire Field Ambulance Vol. II February 1-28th. 1919		
War Diary	Charleroi	01/02/1919	28/02/1919
Operation(al) Order(s)	1/3rd East Lancashire Field Ambulance. Order No. 62 Appendix 91	28/02/1919	28/02/1919
Heading	1/3rd East Lancs F.A Mar 1919 140/3551		
War Diary	Charleroi	01/03/1919	30/03/1919
War Diary	Antwerp	31/03/1919	02/04/1919

WO 95 2652/3

42 DIVN
1/3 E LANCS FIELD AMB
1917 MAR - 1919 FEB

42ND DIVISION

1-3RD EAST LANCS FLD AMBULANCE

MAR 1917 - ~~DEC 1918~~ 1919 MAR

Confidential

War Diary

of the

13th East. Lanc. Field Ambulance.

From March 1st 1917 to March 31st 1917.

(Volume 3)

MARSEILLES	11/3/17	Arrive MARSEILLES.
FRANCE	12/3/17	Entrain for North. MAJOR E.H. COX left K'lake command 2/3 FZ. F.A.M.B.
	13/3/17	On Train
FRANCE	14/3/17	Arrival PONT. REMY & route Billets FRUCOURT. 2 NCO's 10 Men ASC. M.T. own unit Present Strength 9 unit in Billets 80 fficers 202 OR. Horses 15 Riders 37 Draught. Wagons M.T. Transport Establishment

WAR DIARY
or
INTELLIGENCE SUMMARY.

(Erase heading not required.)

Army Form C. 2118.

Instructions regarding War Diaries and Intelligence Summaries are contained in F. S. Regs., Part II. and the Staff Manual respectively. Title pages will be prepared in manuscript.

Place	Date	Hour	Summary of Events and Information	Remarks and references to Appendices
FRUCOURT	15/3/17		Settling into Billets arranging hospital & details of Park duties	205
FRUCOURT	16/3/17		Detention Hospital opened for 127 Bde Area.	65A
FRUCOURT	17/3/17		Routine	65A
FRUCOURT	18/3/17		Inspection of Transport by Div Transport Officer & Vety Officer	65A
FRUCOURT	19/3/17		Routine	20A
FRUCOURT	20/3/17		Routine	65A
FRUCOURT	21/3/17		Inspection of Horses by A.D.V.S. A.D.	65A
FRUCOURT	22/3/17		Routine. Inspection of Horses by V.O.	65A
FRUCOURT	23/3/17		Routine	65A
FRUCOURT	24/3/17		Routine	65A
FRUCOURT	25/3/17		Orders the rupture at 2:15 hr notice	65A
FRUCOURT	26/3/17		Routine	65A
FRUCOURT	27/3/17		Orders ren for transport by road under 127 Bde Transport Officer	65A
FRUCOURT	28/3/17		Transport with equipment & Tents. 10 Officer 34 O.R with 17 vehicles 14 motor Bre Draught	65A
FRUCOURT	29/3/17		Potmil, 10 a 3 O.R by Motor 18 M. Transport & 7 Aux Waggon oxen 2 Motor cycles & road.	65A
			5 Off. 139 other Ranks by rail to CHU—— & G. NOLLES. Camp MARLY. Capt Hankins &	
			10 R. & Men to U.K.	
CAMP MARLY	30/3/17		Setting in taken over, Hospital & cul orders for Div Rest Camp for Div Rest Camp 1st Div.	65A
				65A

WAR DIARY
or
INTELLIGENCE SUMMARY.

(Erase heading not required.)

Army Form C. 2118.

Place	Date	Hour	Summary of Events and Information	Remarks and references to Appendices
CAMP N°1 RLN	31/3/17		Cleaning up of camp routine hospital work	

Ashworth Lt Col
o/c Shawoo I tunl

April 1/17

Confidential.

War Diary
of the
1/3rd East Lancashire Field Ambulance

From April 1st 1917.   To April 30th 1917.

(Volume 4)

COMMITTEE FOR THE
MEDICAL HISTORY OF THE WAR
Date -6 JUN. 1917

WAR DIARY
INTELLIGENCE SUMMARY

Army Form C. 2118

Place	Date	Hour	Summary of Events and Information	Remarks and references to Appendices
CAMP PIMPLEY	1/4/17		Routine. Notice received one complete section to accoust No 1 7? Amb at Athn Corps Rest Statin CERISY.	WA
CAMP PIMPLEY	2/4/17		3 Officers 72 OR including transport to CERISY.	WA
CAMP PIMPLEY	3/4/17		Notify GOC 12 7? Bde. & ADMS 4 2Dn.	
CAMP PIMPLEY	4/4/17		Orders to take over Ambulance Station from 141 ?? Amb. stationed at FONTAINELES CAPPY.	CO?
FONTAINE LES CAPPY	6/4/17		3 Officers, Rank 60 OR. ASC. Horse T. 22 M?ts Tr. G. Animals 29. Motor Cars 5. 2 Motor Cycles. 2 horse amb. 4 G.S. 3 GS limbers, 1 Mach? Cart, 1 Cart Watr, 5 Bicycles. Here on truck & dug outs. Accommodation for Is Patients ready now for reception of 60 other ranks & sick. 1 Officer 2 OR with 1 Car Watr & 2 Motor Amb & 3 Horses left at CAMP MARLY & road to mud 9 1/2 ?? 96 ?? Amb to take over patients there.	6?
FONTAINE LES CAPPY	6/4/17		Routine	7?
FONTAINE LES CAPPY	7/4/17 8/4/17		1 Officer 2? OR returned from CAMP MARLY after bringing over to 1/2 SL ?? Amb. ESR. 10?? Remained with water Cart 2 horses & sick men. Routine	6?

Army Form C. 2118

WAR DIARY
or
INTELLIGENCE SUMMARY
(Erase heading not required.)

Instructions regarding War Diaries and Intelligence Summaries are contained in F. S. Regs., Part II. and the Staff Manual respectively. Title Pages will be prepared in manuscript.

Place	Date	Hour	Summary of Events and Information	Remarks and references to Appendices
FONTAINE LES CAPPY	9/4/17		1 Officer, 30 O.R. rejoined unit from Cyclists Base depot. Two O.R. 3 horses & 1 water cart returned from 1/2 E. L. Fd. Amb.	Ap7
FONTAINE LES CAPPY	10/4/17		Routine	Ap7
FONTAINE LES CAPPY	11/4/17		Routine	Ap7
FONTAINE LES CAPPY	12/4/17		Routine	Ap7
FONTAINE LES CAPPY	13/4/17		Routine	Ap7
FONTAINE LES CAPPY	14/4/17		Routine	Ap7
FONTAINE LES CAPPY	15/4/17		Routine	Ap7
FONTAINE LES CAPPY	16/4/17		Routine	Ap7

WAR DIARY
or
INTELLIGENCE SUMMARY

(Erase heading not required.)

Army Form C. 2118

Place	Date	Hour	Summary of Events and Information	Remarks and references to Appendices
FONTAINE LES CAPPY	17.4.17		Rec'd Operation order No 5 - A.D.M.S. 42nd Div. for two Sections complete to move forward to DOINGT. On 18-4-17 to establish a Corps Rest Station. Surplus Stores to be handed over to 1/2nd E.L. Field Amb. Surplus Stretchers to be retained. 1 officer to proceed to 1/5 Essex Lines Regt - to do temporary duty as M.O. in charge.	AW
DOINGT	18/4/17		Two Sections (2 Off. - 123 O.R. 9 Riding Horses. 21 draught horses 12 H.T. Vehicles - 4 M.T. Vehicles) with complete equipment and Surplus Stretchers left FONTAINE LES CAPPY by march route at 9.15 A.M. Arriving at DOINGT at 2.15 P.M. 1 Horse-artery. Left behind sick - in charge of 2 O.R.	AW
DOINGT	19/4/17		2 O.R. left at FONTAINE LES CAPPY in charge of sick horse reported unit. Horse handed over to 19th Mobile Veterinary Section. 3 Motor ambulances lent on temporarily to 1/2 E.L. Field Amb. Are available men engaged in clearing the ground in prepare Rest Station Site.	AW
DOINGT	20/4/17		1 Officer. 22 O.R. with 1 G.S. waggon. 2 Horse draught. 1 Horse riding. Proceeded to VILLERS BRETONNEUX to take down Adrian huts for Rest Station.	AW
DOINGT DOINGT	21/4/17 22/4/17		L/Col W HOWORTH reported from M Ophr & took command. Clearing of ground for Hospital	AW LSR LSR

Army Form C. 2118

WAR DIARY
or
INTELLIGENCE SUMMARY
(Erase heading not required.)

Instructions regarding War Diaries and Intelligence Summaries are contained in F. S. Regs., Part II. and the Staff Manual respectively. Title Pages will be prepared in manuscript.

Place	Date	Hour	Summary of Events and Information	Remarks and references to Appendices
DOINGT	23/4/17		Holiday began	159
DOINGT	24/4/17		Building Coys Rest (Chalin Ordinis)	159
DOINGT	25/4/17		-	159
DOINGT	26/4/17		Capt. HANNIGAN joined as re-inforcement & replace Major P.N. COX	159
DOINGT	27/4/17		Work proceeding	159
DOINGT	28/4/17		Work proceeding but blocked by delay in delivery of ballast	159
DOINGT	29/4/17		" " " "	159
DOINGT	30/4/17		Present Disposition of Tunb. DOINGT. Officers 4. RMLE 76. ASC(HT) 4 ASC(HT) 20.	I.58 & Map 62C France 1:40000
			VILLERS BRETONNEUX Officers 1. RMLE 60. ASC(HT) 2.	Map France H2M2 1:500000
			CERISY Officers 3. RMLE 53. ASC(MT)3 ASC(HT)9.	G 8/2 H 2
			Orleans. Officer 1. RMLE 25. ASC(HT)3.	
			BC/2 Officer 1. RMLE 5. ASC(MT)6.	
			Total. Officers 10. RMLE 179. ASC(HT) 34. ASC(MT)13.	159
			Deficiencies. RMLE 3. ASC(HT) 2.	
			Wolworth Lt Col.	
			OC/3 Lewes FTunb.	

Confidential

War Diary
of the
1/3rd East Lancashire Field Ambulance

From May 1st 1917 To May 31st 1917

(Volume 3)

COMMITTEE FOR THE MEDICAL HISTORY OF THE WAR
Date 10 JUL. 1917

WAR DIARY or INTELLIGENCE SUMMARY

Army Form C. 2118

(Erase heading not required.)

Place	Date	Hour	Summary of Events and Information	Remarks and references to Appendices
DOING T	1/5/17		Formation of Corps Rest Station (III Corps of Army) proceeding	104
DOING T	2/5/17		"	104
DOING T	3/5/17		Large amount of material came up by train – embodying	104
DOING T	4/5/17		10 bowmen instead of 15" at work – structures – 120 bins brought in to-day	104
DOING T	5/5/17		embodying proceeding	104
DOING T	6/5/17		"	104
DOING T	7/5/17		Nothing	104
DOING T	8/5/17		Nothing continued	104
DOING T	9/5/17		"	104
DOING T	10/5/17		"	104
DOING T	11/5/17		embodying France. Orders to take over Corps Scabies Station received & completed 5.0 pm	104
DOING T	12/5/17		Corps Scabies Station routine – embodying train (trucks) continued	104
DOING T	13/5/17		Routine & embodying train completed	104
DOING T	14/5/17		Orders received to hand over Corps Scabies Station to 7th Amb of 59th Div. by 12.0 noon tomorrow	104
DOING T	15/5/17		7th seron camped in area of Corps Rest Station	104
DOING T	16/5/17		Handed over Corps Scabies Station to 2/Fg NORTH MIDLAND F.A. MB. & resumed work with 42 Div. Rest Station	104
DOING T	17/5/17		Routine Operation Order NO 10 ADMS 42 Div Rec'd	104

WAR DIARY or INTELLIGENCE SUMMARY

Army Form C. 2118

(Erase heading not required.)

Instructions regarding War Diaries and Intelligence Summaries are contained in F. S. Regs., Part II. and the Staff Manual respectively. Title Pages will be prepared in manuscript.

Place	Date	Hour	Summary of Events and Information	Remarks and references to Appendices
DOINGT	18/5/17		Routine	
DOINGT	19/5/17		Amendment Operation Order No 10 issued	
DOINGT	20/5/17	10.30 AM	March for B.U.S. Disposition table as follows: OR. R(MG) OR.ASC(HT) OR.ASC(MT)	Map Reference France 57.C.
			DOINGT — 4 — —	1/40000 O.24 C 58
			LACHAPELETTE — 4 — —	
			CERISY 3 45 8 3	France Army 15/VS/17 2.38rd - 1.10am H.2.
			BUS 3 57 17 5	57C. 1/40000 Q.20 D.2.8
			Adv. D. STATION (METZ) 1 46 4 4	
			DETACHED 2 5 1 —	
			ON LEAVE 1 22 4 1	
			10 183 34 13	
BUS	20/5/17	6.0 PM	Disposition as above. Orders received issued 35 men to F 15° Corps MAIN DRESSING STATN	Map Ref 4th France 57.C. ASK Y 18.C.
BUS	21/5/17		Camp formed	ATI
BUS	22/5/17		Divisional Rest Camp opened	ATI
BUS	23/5/17		Inspection of horses by C.O. & O.C.'s rendered	ASH
BUS	24/5/17		Routine — Operation Order No 11 issued.	ASH
BUS	25/5/17			Am D.

WAR DIARY
or
INTELLIGENCE SUMMARY

Army Form C. 2118

Instructions regarding War Diaries and Intelligence Summaries are contained in F. S. Regs., Part II. and the Staff Manual respectively. Title Pages will be prepared in manuscript.

(Erase heading not required.)

Place	Date	Hour	Summary of Events and Information	Remarks and references to Appendices
BUS	25/5/17		On the night of 25-5-17 the 1/3 East Lancs Field Amb. detachment at METZ handed over to the 136th Field Amb. The evacuation of that portion of our right sector taken over by the 131st Infantry Brigade. This relief was completed by 10 P.M. The evacuation of this part of the line was through the right end Centre Regimental Aid Posts, Wheeled Stretcher were used to evacuate between Regt. Aid Posts + Advanced Dressing Stns. The Snowd Wheel Stuffer heavy were counted to the patients - and easier to manipulate. Steel holes than the large wheeled mod. Up to this date (from 21-5-17 to 26-5-17) 10 wounded. 24 sick. + 2 men gassed (carbon monoxide) passed through the Adv. Dressing Stn. - all of which were transferred to XI CORPS Main Dressing Stn at FINS. See map reference in map in. The detach took place at A.D.S. on 26-5-17, from Same brancheating wound Chest. Owing to the above horrifying relief - 2.3 OR. which 2 ASC(MT) Force trucks Ambulance, rejoined the Head Quarters of Ambulance at BUS on 26-5-17. Nothing of importance to record.	Map Ref. 57c. 1-40,000 Q.30-D.2.5. See Appendix I. Map Ref. France 57c 1/40,000 V.18.a Aus7/Aus7
BUS	27/5/17			
BUS	28/5/17		On the night of 27-5-17 the Advanced Dressing Station at METZ. also the evacuation of that part of the line handed over by 131st Brigade	

WAR DIARY or INTELLIGENCE SUMMARY

Army Form C. 2118

Place	Date	Hour	Summary of Events and Information	Remarks and references to Appendices
BUS	28/5/17		to 177th Infantry Brigade, was handed over to the 2/3rd North Midland Field Amb. (59th Division) This relief was completed by 6 P.M. On this date 7 patients (Six Sick & one wounded) have transferred to Corps Main Dressing Stn at FINS. and on 28/5/17 the remainder of the detachment of this field Amb. (1 Off, 23 OR, 2 M.T. A.S.C. & A.S.C. H.T) returned from METZ to BUS at 12 Noon. In addition to 2 Motor Ambulances & 2 horse Ambulances (accommodation for 16 Stretcher cases) they had the following Medicine & Surgical equipment with them while at METZ:-	

No 1 Field Medical Pannier — 1
Medical Comfort Pannier — 1
Stretchers — 6
Surgical Haversacks — 7
Medical companions — 2
Water bottles — 6
Tent, operating — 1
Axe, felling w- Pick — 1
Butchu Cool J. Kettles Camp — 8
Spades G.S. — 2

AuT

WAR DIARY
or
INTELLIGENCE SUMMARY

Army Form C. 2118

Place	Date	Hour	Summary of Events and Information	Remarks and references to Appendices
BUS	29/5/17		Routine.	Amy
BUS	30/5/17		Three Officers, 56 O.R. with complete Section equipment and Transport (two Officers & two horses having been left behind sick) arrived from C.E.R.I.S. Where they had been for 2 months assisting at 3rd Corps Rest Station. They left CERISY by March route on 29/5-17. Stopping the night of 29th-30th at PERONNE.	Map of AMIENS 17 2nd Ed. 1 - 100,000 Amy
BUS	31.5.17		Present disposition is as follows:-	
			OFFICERS. O.R.(RAMC) O.R.(ASC HT) O.R.(ASC MT)	
			BUS 8 110 30 13	
			DOINGT — 4 — —	
			PERONNE — 4 — —	
			XV CORPS. M.D. STN. — 30 — —	
			DETACHED 1 4 — —	
			LEAVE 1 29 4 —	
			10 181 34 13	
			BUS	

Lieut Colonel, R.A.M.C. (T.F.)
Acting O.C. 3rd EAST LANCS. FIELD AMBULANCE

Vol 5

Confidential

War Diary
of the
1/3rd East Lancashire Field Amb.

From June 1st 1917.   To June 30th 1917.

(Volume 6)

June 1917

WAR DIARY or INTELLIGENCE SUMMARY

Army Form C. 2118

Place	Date	Hour	Summary of Events and Information	Remarks and references to Appendices
BUS	1-6-17		Routine	AW
BUS	2-6-17		Routine	AW
BUS	3-6-17		Capt HANNIGAN. H. posted to Medical charge 1/10 Manchester Regt and reverts from the strength of this unit. Capt SCHOFIELD D. F.W. posted to temporary medical charge of 910th Brigade R.F.A.	AW
BUS	4-6-17		CAPT. HASKINS. N.H.H. posted to temporary medical charge of 1/6 Lanc. Fusiliers. Operation order No 96 read from 126 Infantry Brigade showing situation of units in their Brigade from which we shall collect sick - Intercommunications when necessary have been arranged from this Field Ambulance	AW
BUS	5/6/17		Site chosen at BUS by D.D.M.S. III CORPS & P.D.M.S 42nd Div. for a new III CORPS MAIN DRESSING STN. Ground staked out and "Reserved" notices put upon area 300 x 200 yards.	Map reference France 57d 1-40-000 023-d. AW
BUS	6/6/17		Work commenced at new Corps Main Dressing Site - hourly steel hytes being build up. 30 O.R. assigned unit from present Corps Main	

Army Form C. 2118

WAR DIARY
or
INTELLIGENCE SUMMARY
(Erase heading not required.)

Place	Date	Hour	Summary of Events and Information	Remarks and references to Appendices
BVS	6/6/17		Dressing Stn at FINS. Where they have been employed for past fortnight. Work on DIV. REST STATION proceeding as usual. About 70 patients being in hospital.	AW]
BVS	7/6/17		Routine. All available men at work fixing in shell hole at site of New Corps Main Dressing Stn.	AW]
BVS	8/6/17		Routine.	AW]
BVS	9/6/17		Routine —	AW]
BVS	10/6/17		Sunday — No work today to enable the men to do washing and other odd jobs. Very heavy thunder storm at night which filled up field & remaining shell hole.	AW]
BVS	11/6/17		Work continued. Pump obtained from R.E.s and water pumped from all shell hole. Two motor ambulance roads marked out to site of New Corps M.D. Stn and work on them begun.	AW]
BVS	12/6/17		Work continued. New Stn tent pitched — and hospital NISSEN hut for 9 patients erected. Work on roads proceeding satisfactorily.	AW]

WAR DIARY
or
INTELLIGENCE SUMMARY

(Erase heading not required.)

Army Form C. 2118

Place	Date	Hour	Summary of Events and Information	Remarks and references to Appendices
BUS	13/6/17		Work at new Corps Main Dressing Stn. Continued.	AW7
BUS	14/6/17		Routine	AW7
BUS	15/6/17		Routine - Capt Wilson H. detailed for temp Med. Charge 1/4 Manchester Regt.	AW7
BUS	16/6/17		Routine - Work at Corps Main Dressing Station Continued	AW7
BUS	17/6/17		Routine	AW7
BUS	18/6/17		Routine	AW7
BUS	19/6/17		Routine	AW7
BUS	20/6/17		CAPT SCHOFIELD. F.W. posted for duty to 1/1 x E.L Field Amb &. CAPT HASKINSS N.H.H. rejoined unit from temp Med Charge 1/6 Lancashire Fusiliers. Work proceeding at Corps Main Dressing Stn.	AW7
BUS	21/6/17		Routine	

Army Form C. 2118

WAR DIARY
or
INTELLIGENCE SUMMARY
(Erase heading not required.)

Place	Date	Hour	Summary of Events and Information	Remarks and references to Appendices
BUS	22/6/17		Routine	And
BUS	23/6/17		Routine - Capt. GRAY. E.N.H. RAMC (S.R) posted to this unit for duty.	And
BUS	24/6/17		Routine	And
BUS	25/6/17		Routine	And
BUS	26/6/17		Arrival of Major CUNNINGHAM - H.H.B., R.A.M.C.(T.F) who assumes Command of the unit from this date. Assumption of command under authority DMS Fourth Army P.O/116 and III Corps A.A.&Q.M.G./130/17 of 20/6/17 duly notified ADMS in accordance with Fourth Army Standing Orders.	And / MMK
BUS	27/6/17		Building of CMDS proceeding. 70 patients under treatment in D.R.S.	MMK
BUS	28/6/17		62 patients under treatment in D.R.S.	MMK
BUS	29/6/17		84 patients under treatment. Building of CMDS proceeding, being now completed. Three Armour huts, Prison hut of dispensary, two store tents, Hospital mason hut and nine marquees erected. Cook house + wash house nearing completion. Captain WILSON. H. rejoined unit from temporary detached duty.	MMK
BUS	30/6/17		88 patients under treatment.	

W. Cunningham Major
O.C. 13 F.A.

1875 Wt. W593/826 1,000,000 4/15 J.B.C. & A. A.D.S.S./Forms/C. 2118.

Confidential

War Diary.
of the
1/3rd East Lancashire Field Amb.
From July 1st 1917. To July 31st 1917.
(Volume 7.)

COMMITTEE FOR THE MEDICAL HISTORY OF THE WAR
Date 10 SEP. 1917

Army Form C. 2118.

WAR DIARY
or
INTELLIGENCE SUMMARY.
(Erase heading not required.)

Instructions regarding War Diaries and Intelligence Summaries are contained in F.S. Regs, Part II. and the Staff Manual respectively. Title pages will be prepared in manuscript.

Place	Date	Hour	Summary of Events and Information	Remarks and references to Appendices
BUS	1.7.17	0900	79 patients under treatment in D.R.S	
		1700	Captain E.N.H. GRAY proceeds to 1/4 EAST LANCS Regt for temporary duty as O/food.	
BUS	2.7.17	0900	90 patients under treatment in D.R.S	
		1530	Buildings of new C.M.D.S inspected by D.D.M.S 11th Corps.	
		1200	Transport inspected by A.D.V.S	
BUS	3.7.17	0900	91 patients under treatment	
		1400	Transport of Unit inspected by O.C Divisional Train	
		1430	Isolation compound erected to house sick contacts & Cerebrospinal Meningitis	
BUS	4.7.17	0900	95 patients under treatment	
		0100	RAMC 42nd Division asked No: 13 received 3 50 patients evacuated to C.R.S in emergence	
			S.S.M ROLFE from temporary duty with this Unit returned to Divisional Train	
BUS	5.7.17	0900	29 patients under treatment	
			D.R.S closed down	
BUS	6.7.17	0900	8 patients under treatment in F. Ambulance.	
		0900	Unit heads to route march still order.	
			C.M.D.S completed.	
BUS	7.7.17	0900	39 patients under treatment including several from the wheesy 38th Division	
			C.M.D.S handed on to 2/3 Home Counties Field Ambulance 38th Division	
		0900	Unit handed for route march with skeleton marching order: 2 moved to Captain WILSON copies attached	I 2
			Field Ambulance Index No: 1	
BUS	8.7.17	0900	39 patients under treatment including 34 from 38th Division	
			all 58th Division patients transferred to 2/3 Home Counties Field Ambulance.	
			all D.R.S stores & tentage hence handed on to 2/3 Home Counties Field Ambulance	
BUS	9.7.17	0900	7 patients under treatment	3
			Field Ambulance when No. 3. returns to move on 10th Unit attached	

WAR DIARY
or
INTELLIGENCE SUMMARY.

(Erase heading not required.)

Army Form C. 2118.

Place	Date	Hour	Summary of Events and Information	Remarks and references to Appendices
Line of March	10.7.19	0810	Unit handed in marching order @ BUS. to proceed in brigade group 127 Brigade, in accordance with R.A.M.C. 42nd Division order No.13 & 127 Brigade Operation Order No.36. To ACHIET LE PETIT. all sick in Field Ambulance evacuated to C.C.S. in new area.	
		1345	Unit arrived at new location G.9, C.2 & that France sheet 5 x E no casualties enroute.	
		1700	Advance parties of Field Ambulance & Kent ambulance church. Scheme of Training commenced today, copy attached	
ACHIET LE GRAND	11.7.19		Attended conference of Field Ambulance Commanders at Divisional H.qrs.	
	12.7.19	0800	3 patients under treatment	
		1200	Camp inspected by A.D.M.S.	
		0800	5 patients under treatment	
			Training continued	
"	13.7.19	0800	6 patients under treatment	
			Training continued: all N.C.Os grouped & informed & informed withdrawn & formed into a class under the Sergeant Major & course of instruction. Some corporals & selects private acting as Sgt of R.C.Os	
			Captain HULME returned from leave to U.K.	5.
"	14.7.19	0800	11 patients under treatment	
			Training continued	
	15.7.19	0800	15 patients under treatment	
			Captain E.N.H. GRAY rejoined Unit from temporary medical charge of 1/5 East Lancs Regt.	
"	16.7.19	0800	15 patients under treatment	
			Training continued	
		0730	Orderly Officer taking Sick Parade of 1/5 Manchester Regt.duty temporary	
		0900	Captain HULME taking Sick Parade of VI Corps Hqrs. for 10 days only	
"	17.7.19	0800	15 patients under treatment	
			Training continued	
	18.7.19	0800	10 patients under treatment	
			Training continued	
			37059 Sgt Major F. CARROLL granted commission as Qr./Mr. & Hon. Lieutenant, proceeds today to England for retired & instruction.	

WAR DIARY
or
INTELLIGENCE SUMMARY.

(Erase heading not required.)

Army Form C. 2118.

Place	Date	Hour	Summary of Events and Information	Remarks and references to Appendices
ACHIET-LE-GRAND	19.7.17	0800	15 patients in Hospital. Training continued.	M.M.M.
		1730	Conference of F. Ambulance C.O.s @ Office of A.D.M.S. 42 Division	M.M.M.
do	20.7.17	0800	17 patients in Hospital. Training continued.	M.M.M.
do	21.7.17	0800	18 patients in Hospital. Training continued.	M.M.M.
		1430	S.S.M. ROLFE A.S.C. & nineteen (19) drivers and 22 complete establishment attended a conference @ Office of D.D.M.S. VI. Corps.	M.M.M.
do	22.7.17	0800	21 patients in Hospital. Training continued.	M.M.M.
do	23.7.17	0800	23 patients in Hospital. Training continued.	M.M.M.
do	24.7.17	0800	27 patients in Hospital. 2 N.C.O.s and 8 127 Bde have been instructing the N.C.O.s of this Unit and men in drill.	M.M.M.
	25.7.17	0800	21 patients in Hospital. Training continued.	M.M.M.
		1400	Unit marched to H.Q.S.I. Field Ambulance to contest recreational sports	M.M.M. 6
		1430	Captain J.A. TOMB & two subaltern proceed to duty of 29 County Clearing Station John attacks.	
	26.7.17	0800	16 patients in Hospital. Training continued.	M.M.M.
		1500	Captain A.M. JOHNSON affirmed to be O.C. M.S. 1/Lancashire Fusiliers who attacks Lieutenant S.W. MILNER (T.C.) taken on strength on being of/ordered to duty with the Unit.	
	27.7.17	0800	16 patients in Hospital. Captain E.N.H. GRAY admitted to Hospital transferred to 49 C.C.S. Scheme/Training attacks.	M.M.M. 8

Army Form C. 2118.

WAR DIARY
or
INTELLIGENCE SUMMARY.
(Erase heading not required.)

Instructions regarding War Diaries and Intelligence Summaries are contained in F. S. Regs., Part II. and the Staff Manual respectively. Title pages will be prepared in manuscript.

Place	Date	Hour	Summary of Events and Information	Remarks and references to Appendices
ACHIET LE GRAND	28.7.19	0800	24 patients in Hospital. N.C.Os. proceeded to 149 Bde. for Sunday inspection by 2nd Army. 6th & 7th sections inspected. 2 Patients left on front & visits to 149 Bde. front sectors.	
"	29.7.19	0800	No patients in Hospital.	
"	30.7.19	0800	14 patients in Hospital.	
		0830	2/L N.C.Os. under instruction leave from reporting station return from respective units.	
		1230	Training & N.C.Os. refresher class return from instruction.	
"	31.7.19	0800	28 patients in Hospital. N.C.Os. return today with their sections.	

M. M. [signature], Lt Col.

SECRET

I

1/3 E.L. Field Ambulance
Orders No 1

Reference Map FRANCE   July 7. 1917
1/40,000 Sheet 57C.

1. Captain H. WILSON is detailed as Officer i/c advance Party.

2. He will meet the Staff Captain 127 Bde outside the E.F. Canteen YTRES at 10 am on the 8th inst with reference to billeting the 9th. Under Divisional instructions this Unit will march from BUS on the 10th joining the Bde Group Column on that day.

3. The advance party consisting of one officer and two men carrying two days rations will meet the Staff Captain 127 Bde outside E.F. Canteen YTRES at 9 am on the 9th inst, & proceed on motor lorry to take over the new site for the Field Ambulance at ACHIET LE PETIT.
A guide to B and C echelons the Field Ambulance site will be on arrival of the Unit.

Distribution:
Copy No 1 Capt Wilson
    No 2 War Diary
    No 3 File

M. McConnagh
Lieut.-Colonel, R.A.M.C. (T.F.)
O.C. 1/3rd EAST LANCS. FIELD AMBULANCE

SECRET.   Copy. No. 2.

1/3rd. East Lancashire Field Amb.

Order No. 2.

Reference Map. FRANCE.
1/40,000 Sheet 57.C.

July 7th. 1917.

1. **ADVANCED PARTIES.** Reference Field Ambulance Order No.1 para 3. This paragraph is cancelled and the following substituted:-

    The advance party consisting of one Officer and two men carrying two days rations will meet the Staff Captain 127th. Bde. outside the Town Majors Office BUS at 7-0 a.m. on the 9th. inst, and proceed by motor lorry to take over the new site for the Field Ambulance at ACHIET-LE-PETIT.

    A guide to be sent to conduct the Field Ambulance to its site on arrival of the Unit.

Issued at 6.39 p.

Lieut-Col. R.A.M.C. T.F.
O.C. 1/3rd. East Lancs. Fld. Ambulance

Distribution:-

Copy No.1. Capt. Wilson.
  "   " 2. War Diary.
  "   " 3. File.

SECRET.   Copy No. 3

1/3rd. East Lancs. Field Ambulance.

Order No. 3.

Reference Map. FRANCE.
    1/40,000 Sheet 57 C.
127th. Bde. O.O. No. 36.   July 9th. 1917.

    1. On the 10th July the Field Ambulance with A.S.C. attd will move in accordance with 127th. Bde Operation Order No. 36. from the area O.16.A to the new area at ACHIET LE PETIT.

    2. The Unit will parade at 8-25 a.m. Full marching order. Steel helmets will be worn, service caps slung on right belt hook of tunic, water bottles filled, and unexpended portion of days ration to be carried in haversack.

    3. Blankets and Greatcoats will be handed in at the Quartermaster's Stores by 6-30 a.m.

    4. MARCH DISCIPLINE TO BE STRICTLY MAINTAINED.

    5. L/Cpl. Crosby V. will act as cyclist orderly and will follow in rear of R.A.M.C. The Motor cyclist will accompany the Unit.

    6. The Horse Transport will march in rear of R.A.M.C. and the senior N.C.O. (A.S.C. H.T.) will ride in rear of the Transport.

    7. Motor Transport (A.S.C.) will proceed direct i/c of Sergt. Dobson A.A.S.C. (M.T.)

127th. Bde. duties.

    8. Captain Prestwich F.G. is detailed to accompany the column rearguard. He will decide if men who have fallen out are fit to march of whether they should be carried in the Ambulance Wagons.

    9. Halts will be made at the clock hour for 15 minutes. Packs will be removed:- mounted men will dismount and men will fall out on the right hand side and clear of the Road during halts.

Issued at 4.50 p.m.

Lieut-Colonel, R.A.M.C. T.F.
O.C. 1/3rd. East Lancs. Field Ambulance.

Distribution:-

Copy No. 1. Capt. Prestwich F.G.
 "   " 2. Officers.
 "   " 3. War Diary.
 "   " 4. File.

1/3rd. East Lancashire Field Ambulance.

Scheme of Training for Week Ending Sunday 15-7-1917.

WEDNESDAY.	R. A. M. C.	A. S. C. (H.T.)

WEDNESDAY.
11-7-17.

R. A. M. C.
Reveille   6-0 a.m.
Physical Drill. 6-30 to 7-0 a.m.
Squad Drill.   9-0 " 10-0 a.m.
Lectures.   10-0 " 11-0 "
Company Drill. 11-0 " 12-0
Parade.(2-0 p.m. 4-0 p.m.
(Fld. Ambulance Drill.)

A. S. C. (H.T.)
Reveille.   5-30 a.m.
Stables.   5-45 to 6-45 a.m.
Water & Feed.   6-55 a.m.
Harness &   9-0 a.m. to
Wagon Cleaning. 10-30 a.m.
Stables.   11-15 to 12-15 p.m.
Water & Feed.   12-10 p.m.
Grazing.   1-30 to 3-30 p.m.
Stables.   3-45 to 4-45 p.m.
Water & Feed.   5-35 p.m.

THURSDAY.
12-7-17.

Same programme as Wednesday.

Friday.
13-7-17.

Reveille.   6-0 a.m.
Physical Drill.   6-30 a.m. to)
   "   "   7-0 a.m.)
Squad Drill.   9-0 a.m.
Lectures.   10-0 a.m.
Company Drill.   11-0 to 12-0
Route March.   2-0 " 4-0 p.m.
@ N.C.Os Refresher Course.
see foot note.

Reveille.   5-30 a.m.
Stables.   5-45 to 6-45 a.m.
Water & Feed.   6-55 a.m.
Harness &   9-0 a.m. to
Wagon Cleaning. 10-30 a.m.
Stables.   11-15 to 12-15 p.m.
Water & Feed.   12-10 p.m.
Route March.   2-0 p.m.
Water & Feed.   5-35 p.m.

SATURDAY.
14-7-17.

Reveille.   6-0 a.m.
Physical Drill.   6-30 to 7-0 a.m.
Company Drill.   9-0 a.m.
First Aid Instruction. 10-0 a.m.
Field Ambulance Drill. 11-0 a.m.)
   "   "   "   to 12,0.)

Same programme as
Wednesday.

SUNDAY.
15-7-17.

Reveille.   6-0 a.m.
Camp Fatigue. 6-30 a.m. to 7-15
Kit Inspection. 9-0 a.m.

Reveille.   5-30 a.m.
Stables. 5-45 to 6-45 a.m.
Water & Feed.   6-55 a.m.
Stables. 11-15 to 12-15 p.m.
Water & Feed.   12-10 p.m.
Stables. 3-45 to 4-45 p.m.
Water & Feed.   5-35 p.m.

@. Note.   All N.C.Os of the rank of Corporal and upwards
           withdrawn from duty and formed into a class for
           instruction under the Sergeant-Major. The course
           being continuous for a fortnight, their duties
           being performed by Lance-Corporals and selected
           privates.

[signature]

Lieut-Colonel, R.A.M.C. T.F.
O.C.1/3rd. East Lancs. Field Ambulance.

10-7-17.

1/3rd. East Lancashire Field Ambulance.

Scheme of Training for Week Ending Sunday 22-7-1917.

	R.A.M.C.	A.S.C.(H.T.)
MONDAY. 16-7-17.	Reveille. 6-0 a.m. Tea. 6-15 " Squad drill. 6-30 to 7-0 a.m. Company drill. 9-0 " 10-30 " Lectures. 10-30" 11-15 " Physical drill. 11-15 to 12-0 Fld. Ambce. drill. 2-0 p.m.-4-0	Reveille. 5-30 a.m. Tea. 5-40 " Stables. 5-45 to 6-45 " Water & Feed. 6-55 " Harness & 9-0 to wagon cleaning. 10-30 " Stables. 11-15 to 12-15 p.m. Water & Feed. 12-10 " Grazing. 1-30 to 3-30 " Stables. 3-45 " 4-45 " Water & Feed. 5-35 "
TUESDAY. 17-7-17.	Reveille. 6-0 a.m. Cocoa. 6-15 " Squad drill. 6-30 to 7-0 a.m. Company Drill. 9-0 to 10 " First Aid. 10-30 " 11-15 " Physical Drill. 11-15 to 12-0 Route march. 2-0 p.m. to 4-0	Reveille. 5-30 a.m. Cocoa. 5-40 " Stables. 5-45 to 6-45 " Water & Feed. 6-55 a.m. Harness & 9-0 a.m. to wagon cleaning. 10-30 a.m. Stables. 11-15 to 12-15 p.m. Water Feed. 12-10 " Route march. 2-0 " Water & Feed. 5-35 "
WEDNESDAY. 18-7-17.	Reveille. 6-0 a.m. Tea. 6-15 " Squad drill. 6-30 to 7-0 a.m. Company drill. 9-0 to 10-0 " Relay Instruction. 10-0 to 12-0 Fld. Amb. drill. 2-0 to 4-0 p.m.	Same programme as Monday.
THURSDAY. 19-7-17.	Reveille. 6-0 a.m. Cocoa. 6-15 " Squad drill. 6-30 to 7-0 a.m. Company " 9-0 to 10-0 " Relay Instruction. 10-0 to 12-0 " Route march. 2-0 to 4-0 p.m.	Same programme as Tuesday.
FRIDAY. 20-7-17.	Reveille. 6-0 a.m. Tea. 6-15 " Squad drill. 6-30 to 7-0 a.m. Company " 9-0 to 10-30 " First Aid. 10-30 " 11-15 " Physical drill 11-15 to 12-0 Fld. Amb. Drill. 2-0 to 4-0 p.m.	Same programme as Monday.
SATURDAY. 21-7-17.	Reveille. 6-0 a.m. Cocoa. 6-15 " Squad drill. 6-30 to 7-0 a.m. Company " 9-0 to 10-0 a.m. Relay Instruction. 10-0 to 12-0	Same programme as Monday.

1/3rd. East Lancashire Field Ambulance.

Scheme of Training for Week Ending Sunday 22-7-1917.

Continued.

SUNDAY.
22-7-17.   Reveille   6-0 a.m.   Reveille.   5-30 a.m.
           Camp Fatigue. 6-30 to 7-15.   Tea.   5-40 a.m.
           Kit Inspection. 9-0 a.m.   Stables.   5-45 to 6-45 a.m.
                                            Water & Feed.   6-55 a.m.
                                            Stables. 11-15 to 12-15 p.m.
                                            Water & Feed. 12-10 p.m.
                                            Water & Feed.   5-35 p.m.

Note:- All N.C.Os of the rank of Corporal and upwards withdrawn
       from duty on 13-7-17 and formed into a class for
       instruction under the Sergeant-Major. The course
       being continuous for a fortnight, their duties being
       performed by Lance-Corporals and selected privates.

                                    [signature]
                                    Lieut-Colonel R.A.M.C.T.F
15-7-17.   O.C.1/3rd. East Lancs.Field Ambulance.
J.H.A.

SECRET. Copy No. 2

1/3rd. East Lancs. Field Ambulance.

Order No. 4.

Reference Map. FRANCE.
1/40,000 Sheet 57 C.
A.D.M.S. 42nd Div. M28/54.   July 25th 1917.

1. Capt Tomb J.A. is detailed to proceed in charge of a Tent Sub-Division to GREVILLERS and will report to O.C. 29th Casualty Clearing Station for duty to-day. No Field Ambulance Equipment will be taken.

2. The unexpended portion of day's ration, and one days ration will be taken.

3. The details will parade in full marching order at 2-30 p.m.

4. Transport will be provided for Officers baggage.

5. All documents relating to "A" Section will be handed over to Captain Gray.

H.M. Cunningham
Lieut-Col. R.A.M.C. T.F
O.C. 1/3rd East Lancs. Field Ambulance.

Issued at 12.45 pm

Distribution.-

Copy No. 1. Capt Tomb J.A.
"   2. War Diary.
"   3. File.

SECRET.   Copy No...2...

1/3rd. East Lancs. Field Ambulance.

Order No.5.

Reference Map. FRANCE.
  1/40,000 Sheet 57 C.
  A.D.M.S. 42nd Div. M14/113.   July 26th 1917.

1. Captain Johnson A.M. is appointed Officer in Medical Charge of the 1/5th Bn. Lancs. Fusiliers.

2. He will proceed forthwith and report his arrival to the Officer Commanding that Unit, at GOMIECOURT.

3. Necessary transport will be provided.

                                       [signature]
                                       Lieut-Colonel, R.A.M.C. T.F.
                                       O.C. 1/3rd. East Lancs. Field Ambulance.

Issued at... 12/15pm ...

Distribution:-

Copy No. 1. Capt Johnson A.M.
  "   " 2. War Diary.
  "   " 3. File.

1/3rd East Lancashire Field Ambulance.

Scheme of Training for Week ending Sunday 29-7-17.

MONDAY.
23-7-17.

R.A.M.C.		A.S.C.(H.T.)	
Reveille	6- 0 a.m.	Reveille	5-30 a.m.
Tea	6-15 "	Tea	5-40 "
Squad drill	6-30 to 7-0 "	Stables	5-45 to 6-45 "
Company drill	9-0 "10-30 "	Water & Feed	6-55 "
Lectures	10-30 "11-15 "	Harness and	9- 0 to
Gas drill	11-15 "12-0	wagon cleaning	10- 0 a.m.
Field Ambce.	2- 0 to	Wagon driving &	10- 0 to
drill	4- 0 p.m.	saluting drill	10-30 a.m.
		Stables	11-15 to 12-15 p.m.
		Water & Feed	12-10 "
		Grazing	1-30 to 3-30 "
		Stables	3-45 to 4-45 "
		Water & Feed	5-35 "

TUESDAY.
24-7-17.

Reveille	6- 0 a.m.	Reveille	5-30 a.m.
Tea	6-15 "	Tea	5-40 "
Squad drill	6-30 to 7- 0 "	Stables	5-45 to 6-45 "
Company drill	9-0 "10-30 "	Water & Feed	6-55 "
First Aid	10-30 to 11-15 "	Harness and	9- 0 to
Physical Drill.	11-15 to 12- 0	wagon cleaning	10-30 a.m.
		Stables	11-15 to 12-15 p.m.
C,O's Parade	2-0 to 4- 0 p.m.	Water & Feed	12-10 "
Field Ambulance Drill.		C.O's. Parade	2- 0 "
		Water & Feed	5-35 "

WEDNESDAY.
25-7-17.

Reveille	6- 0 a.m.	Reveille	5-30 a.m.
Coffee	6-15 "	Coffee	5-40 "
Company Training	9- 0 to 12- 0 noon	Stables	5-45 to 6-45 "
		Water & Feed	6-55 "
C.O's. Parade	2- 0 p.m.	Harness and	9- 0 to
Recreational Training.		wagon cleaning	10-30 a.m.
		Stables	11-15 to 12-15 p.m.
		Water & Feed	12-10 "
		C.O's. Parade	2- 0 "

THURSDAY.
26-7-17.

Reveille	6- 0 a.m.	Reveille	5-30 a.m.
Coffee	6-15 "	Coffee	5-40 "
Squad drill	6-30 to 7- 0 "	Stables	5-45 to 6-45 "
Company Training	9- 0 to 12- 0 noon	Water & Feed	6-55 "
		Harness and	9- 0 to
C.O's. Parade	2- 0 p.m.	wagon cleaning	10-30 a.m.
Field Ambulance Drill.		Stables	11-15 to 12-15 p.m.
		Water & Feed	12-10 "
		Grazing	1-30 to 3-30 "
		Stables	3-45 to 4-45 "
		Water & Feed	5-35 "

1/3rd East Lancashire Field Ambulance.

Scheme of Training for Week ending Sunday 29-7-17.

Continued

FRIDAY. 28-7-17.	R.A.M.C.		A.S.C.(H.T.)	
	Reveille	6- 0 a.m.	Reveille	5-30 a.m.
	Coffee	6-15 "	Coffee	5-40 "
	Relay Instruction	9- 0 to	Stables	5-45 to 6-45 "
	and First Aid	12- 0 noon	Water & Feed	6-55 "
	Brigade Sports	2- 0 p.m.	Stables	11-15 to 12-15 p.m.
			Water & Feed	12-10 "
			Water & Feed	5-35 "

SATURDAY. 28-7-17.				
	Reveille	6- 0 a.m.	Reveille	5-30 a.m.
	Tea	6-15 "	Tea	5-40 "
	Squad drill	6-30 to 7- 0 "	Stables	5-45 to 6-45 "
	Lectures	9-0 to 10-0 "	Water & Feed	6-55 "
	First Aid	10-0 " 12- 0 noon	Harness and	9- 0 to
	Bath Parade	3-45 p.m.	wagon cleaning	10-30 a.m.
			Stables	11-15 to 12-15 p.m.
			Water & Feed	12-10 "
			Grazing	1-30 to 3-30 "
			Bath Parade	3-45 " 4-45 "
			Water & Feed	5-35 "

SUNDAY. 29-7-17.				
	Reveille	6- 0 a.m.	Reveille	5-30 a.m.
	Camp Fatigue,	6-30 -7-15 "	Stables	5-45 to 6-45 "
	Kit Inspection	9- 0 "	Water & Feed	6-55 "
			Kit Inspection	9- 0 "
			Stables	11-15 to 12-15 p.m.
			Water & Feed	12-10 "
			Water & Feed	5-35 "

Note :- All N.C.O's. of the rank of Corporal and upwards withdrawn from duty on 13-7-17 and formed into a class for instruction up to 25-7-17. This class will be attached to the Battalions of the 127th Brigade for instruction from 28-7-17 to 29-7-17.

Confidential.

War Diary

of the

1/3rd E. Lancashire Field Ambulance.

From Aug 1st 1917 to August 31st 1917.

(Volume 8.)

Army Form C. 2118

WAR DIARY
INTELLIGENCE SUMMARY
(Erase heading not required.)

Instructions regarding War Diaries and Intelligence Summaries are contained in F. S. Regs., Part II. and the Staff Manual respectively. Title Pages will be prepared in manuscript.

Place	Date	Hour	Summary of Events and Information	Remarks and references to Appendices
ACHIET le GRAND	1/8/17	0800	30 Patients in Hospital.	
		0900	Half the Officers & N.C.Os attended a 3 hour course at the Divisional Gas School	
		1400	Remainder of Officers & N.C.Os attended similar course.	
	2/8/17	0800	28 Patients in Hospital. Continual rain, no Training possible	
	3/8/17	0800	31 Patients in Hospital. Continual wet weather	
	4/8/17	0800	28 Patients in Hospital. Continual wet weather. R.A.M.C. Shots postponed on account of weather.	
	5/8/17	0800	29 Patients in Hospital.	
		1430	Captain E. HULME and 1 Section Tent Subdivision proceed to 29 C.C.S. on relief of Captain T.A. TOMB	2.
	6/8/17	1145	Captain TOMB & half Section Tent Subdivision then arrived on temporary Unit	
		0800	28 Patients in Hospital.	
		1100	Captain T.A TOMB proceed to 1/5 Manchester Regt to duty as O/i/c. Temporary administration. Training continuing.	10.
	7/8/17	0800	30 Patients in Hospital. Training continuing. weather improving	
		1400	Q.M. and the Lieutenant J.E.H. ANDERTON proceeded to Base Depot ROUEN empty for reserve stretch Frame owing to Manœuvres orders attached	11.
	8/8/17	0800	18 Patients in Hospital. Divisional R.A.M.C. Sports held today.	
	9/8/17	0800	16 Patients in Hospital.	
		0900	Field Ambulance took part in 127 Infy Brigade Group manœuvres. R.A.M.C orders attached	12.

WAR DIARY
INTELLIGENCE SUMMARY
(Erase heading not required.)

Army Form C. 2118

Place	Date	Hour	Summary of Events and Information	Remarks and references to Appendices
ACHIET le GRAND	10.8.17	0800	13 patients in Hospital. Field Ambulance divided. Day fine.	MMf
"	11.8.17	0800	22 patients in Hospital. Weather windy with showers.	MMf
"	12.8.17	0800	30 patients in Hospital. Weather as above.	MMf
"	13.8.17	0800	20 patients in Hospital. Proceedings of F.G.C.M. in case of one private R.A.M.C. tried under S.S.8. promulgated, being sentenced to 2 years I.H.L., one year remitted.	MMf
"	14.8.17	0800	33 patients in Hospital. Training continued.	MMf
2	15.8.17	0800	29 patients in Hospital while units antigas apparatus through inspection & gas N.C.Os & units exercised in wearing respirators for one hour.	MMf
1	16.8.17	0800	34 patients in Hospital.	MMf
1	17.8.17	0800	30 patients in Hospital. Fine weather today, Training continued.	MMf
	18.8.17	0800	24 patients in Hospital. W.I. Corps Horse Show. Ambulance wagon & motor ambulance entered.	MMf
	19.8.17	0800	24 patients in Hospital. Captain D. HARDIE 9th M.C. (T.C) from 9th Division reports his arrival on being posted to this unit.	MMf
		1230	Captain H. WILSON appointed O.I/m.c. 1/4 East Lanc. Regt. a strunk of attempt accordingly.	13
		1430	Captain H. HENRY. from O.I/m.c. 1/4 East Lanc. Regt. reports his arrival a taken on strength accordingly.	MMf

WAR DIARY
INTELLIGENCE SUMMARY
(Erase heading not required.)

Army Form C. 2118

Instructions regarding War Diaries and Intelligence Summaries are contained in F.S. Regs., Part II. and the Staff Manual respectively. Title Pages will be prepared in manuscript.

Place	Date	Hour	Summary of Events and Information	Remarks and references to Appendices
ACHIET LE GRAND	19.8.17		Captain N.H.H. HASKINS acting temporarily as D.A.D.M.S. 42nd Division, whilst DADMS on leave.	
"	20.8.17	0800	23 patients in Hospital. Field Ambulance evacuated stores packs ut from teams of mud route tramway before attacks	MMf 14
"	21.8.17	0800	1. Patient in Hospital	MMf
		0830	Unit paraded in full marching order & marched to AVELUY nr. of FRANCE LENS 11. arrived 1345.	
AVELUY	22.8.17	0800	6 patients in Hospital	MMf 15.
		0900	Captain E.N.H. GRAY proceeded by road i/c of the m.t. transport of the Unit less en route. Ambulance 7th Division Hqrs en route for Map sheet 27. L. 22. a. 4. 9.	
		1900	B Section marched up to 60 O.R. proceeded under Captain F.G. PRESTWICH to provide a station, attending to constructing attacks.	
	23.8.17	0800	1. Patient in Hospital	16. MMf
		1100	C Section with details of A section handed over to Captain N.H.H. HASKINS A.S.C. & Transport handed over to Captain H. HENRY according to instructions attached	19 MMf
		1300	Remaining M.T. Ambulance made into 96 proceeded to BEAUCOURT sur ANCRE Trench 8 & O.C. 1/1/E.L. Field Ambulance.	station of entertainment
	24.8.17	0215	Hqrs of Field Ambulance arrived at POPERINGHE along & marked L.15.b.9.1. Sheet 27 Belgium	
	25.8.17	0815	Unit marched to LUNA PARK L.9.b.1.2. Sheet 27 Belgium & took our Field Ambulance site.	
		1800	3 patients in Hospital A.D.M.S. visited Ambulance site.	
LUNA PARK	26.8.17	0800	20 patients in Hospital. A & B Tent subdivisions opened & employed on hospital duty.	

WAR DIARY
INTELLIGENCE SUMMARY

(Erase heading not required.)

Army Form C. 2118

Place	Date	Hour	Summary of Events and Information	Remarks and references to Appendices
LUNA PARK	27.8.17	0800	49. Patients in Hospital	WMcF
		0530	C.O. accompanied A.D.M.S. through YPRES visiting nearer R.A.P.s & A.D.S.	
"	28.8.17	0800	79. Patients in Hospital	WMcF
			Lieutenant M.E. DELAFIELD (T.C.) reported his arrival & taken on strength. Captain E.N.H. GRAY evacuated sick to C.C.S.	
"	29.8.17	0800	96. Patients in Hospital	WMcF
			Captain J.A. TOMB struck off strength on being posted to medical charge of 1/S Manchester Reg.	
"	30.8.17	0800	100. Patients in Hospital	WMcF
		0830	11 R.C.O.s & men Bearers with stretchers carried wheels proceeded to YPRES for duty with 1/1 2nd London Field Ambulance.	
			Training of recruit officers in drill so able for other work under q.m R.C.O.s	
		1730	3 Orderlies as stretcher and 2 Cpls walking wounded collecting post VLAMERTINGHE MILL	Belgian Sht 29
"	31.8.17	0800	109. Patients in Hospital	Map Belgium Sht B 28.
		0600	accompanied Captain HASKINS visited Bearer Aid Post BAVARIA House, A.D.S. POTIJZE, A.D.S. YPRES & Cafe Main Dressing Station	18.
		1030	RED FARM. B. Section. To Staubliniana under C/Com. PRESTWICH and [?] the CLOISTERS POPERINGHE took over the XIX Corps Sector Section	
		1100	Captain HASKINS proceeded to YPRES for duty in advance area	WMcF
		1330	Three Officers proceeded to Cafe Main Dressing Station BRANDHOEK to form a medical Unit today.	
			Captain E.N.H. GRAY struck off strength of Unit on being evacuated to There.	

M McMurray Col
Cmdg 1/3 E.T. Field Amb.

1/9/17

SECRET.   Copy No. 5

1/3rd East Lancs. Field Ambulance.

Order No.6.

Reference Map.FRANCE.
  1/40,000 Sheet 57 C.
A.D.M.S. 42nd Div.M14/115.   August 5th 1917.

1. Captain Hulme E. is detailed to proceed in charge of a Tent Sub-Division to GREVILLERS and will report to O.C. 29th Casualty Clearing Station for duty to-day in ~~relief~~ relief of the Tent Sub-Division in charge of Captain Tomb J.A.
   On completion of this relief Captain Tomb will march his Tent Sub-Division back to Field Ambulance Headquarters.

2. The unexpended portion of day's ration and one days ration will be taken.

3. The details will parade in full marching order at 2-30 p.m.

4. Transport will be provided for Officers baggage.

5.

                                    [signature]
                                    Lieut-Colonel, R.A.M.C. T
                                    O.C.1/3rd. East Lancs. Field Ambulance.

Issued at 1105

Distribution.-

Copy No. 1. Capt. Hulme E.
 "   " 2. Capt. Tomb J.A.
 "   " 3. O.C. 29th C.C.S.
 "   " 4. A.D.M.S. 42nd Div.
 "   " 5. War Diary.
 "   " 6. File.

SECRET.   Copy No. 5.

1/3rd East Lancs. Field Ambulance.

Order No. 7.

Reference Map. FRANCE.
  1/40,000 Sheet 57 C.
A.D.M.S. 42nd Div. M 14/115.

August 6th 1917.

1. Captain J.A.TOMB is detailed as Officer in Medical Charge of the 1/5th Manchester Regt. Temporarily, in relief of Captain CLEGG-NEWTON proceeding for duty to No.6 Stationary Hospital FREVENT.

2. He will report to O.C.1/5th Manchester Regt at ACHIET LE PETIT, to-day.

3. Necessary transport will be provided.

4. On application by Captain CLEGG-NEWTON transport will be provided to take him to FREVENT.

Lieut-Colonel, R.A.M.C. T.F
O.C.1/3rd. East Lancs. Field Ambulance.

Issued.... 10.30 a.m.

Distribution.-

Copy No.1. Capt.J.A.TOMB.
 "   " 2. Capt.CLEGG-NEWTON.
 "   " 3. O.C.1/5th Man.Regt.
 "   " 4. A.D.M.S. 42nd Div.
 "   " 5. War Diary.
 "   " 6. File.

Copy No. 2

1/3rd East Lancs. Field Ambulance.

Order No. 8.

Reference A.A.& Q.M.G.
A.35/514. A.D.M.S. M 33/17.
D.G.,M.S.,G.H.Q. 2nd Echelon.
No.445/1.

August 7th 1917.

Under instructions from 42nd Divisional Headquarters, certified true copy attached, Quartermaster and Hon. Lieut. J. E. H. ANDERTON will proceed forthwith to ROUEN and report himself to O.C. Base Depot.

He will report to the R. T. O. ACHIET LE GRAND for the purpose of proceeding there.

[signature]

Lieut-Colonel, R.A.M.C. T.F.
O.C. 1/3rd. East Lancs. Field Ambulance.

Issued: 1305

Distribution.-

Copy No. 1. Lieut. J. E. H. ANDERTON.
  "   " 2. War Diary.
  "   " 3. File.

Copy No......6. 12

1/3rd. East Lancs. Field Ambulance.

Operation Order No. 1.

Reference 127th Bde. Assault Scheme,
Operation Order No.1.
Special Map "S"

August 8th 1917.

1. 1/3rd Field Ambulance will furnish a main dressing station at MIRAUMONT, an advanced dressing station at L.16.d. and a bearer relay post at L.16.b.3.6 *)
 On ZERO day these stations to be equipped by ZERO hour - 30.

2. At ZERO +140 the bearer relay post at will be re-inforced, becoming a bearer aid post. A relay post will be established at G.10.d.7.8. or as soon after as possible. All casualties will be evacuated by MIDDLE LANE.

3. Officers i/mc Bn. will communicate the location of their Regimental Aid Posts to the Officer i/c Advanced Dressing Stn by ZERO - 30.

*) To the bearer relay post. L.16.b.3.6

4. Officers i/mc L. & M. Bns will communicate the location of their Aid Posts as soon as possible after their Battalions have consolidated the first objective.

5. Officers i/mc O. & P. Bns will communicate to Bearer relay post at G.10.d.7.8 the location of their Regtl Aid Post as soon as possible after their Battalions have consolidated the 2nd & 3rd. objectives.

6. The Officer i/c A.D.S. will establish a soup kitchen and be ready to issue at ZERO hour. Officers i/mc Bns. will arrange for surplus bones from their Units to be forwarded to the Officer i/c A.D.Stn. for the purpose of making soup, the bones to arrive at A.D.S. by ZERO - 30.

Lieut-Colonel, R.A.M.C. T.F.
O.C. 1/3rd. East Lancs. Field Ambulance.

Issued at 10/30 a.m.

Distribution.-
Copy No.1. 127th Bde H.Qrs.
 "   " 2. O i/mc "L" Bn.
 "   " 3.   "   "M" Bn.
 "   " 4.   "   "O" Bn.
 "   " 5.   "   "P" Bn.
War Diary.
File.

O.C., 1/3rd E.L.Fd.Ambulance.

Please direct Captain WILSON to proceed to 1/4th Bn.East Lancs Regt this day for attachment to that unit in relief of Captain H.HENRY, R.A.M.C.

Captain HENRY is posted to your unit on relief.

Captain WILSON will be struck off your strength accordingly.

19/8/17.
B.

C. A. Jones
Colonel,
A.D.M.S., 42nd Division.

1/4 East Lancashire Regt.

Captain H. Wilson is directed to report to you forthwith in compliance with above minute.

M. M. Yemmich
O.C. 1/3rd EAST LANCS. FIELD AMBULANCE.

SECRET. Copy No. 6

1/3rd. East Lancs. Field Ambulance.
Order No.9.

Reference Map. FRANCE.
LENS 11. 1/100,00
42nd Div R.A.M.C. Orders No.14.
127th Bde. Order No.37. August 20th 1917.

1. The Unit will move by march route from ACHIET LE GRAND to AVELUY area with the 127th Bde Group on 21-8-17.

2. The Unit will be prepared to entrain after midnight 21/22 probable entraining station AVELUY.

3. The advanced party consisting of Captain D.HARDIE M.C. and 2 other ranks will report to R.T.O. ACHIET LE GRAND 2-O p.m. at 9.15 on 20-8-17, and will take 3 days rations with them. Station of detrainment HOPOUTRE.

4. The Unit will parade at 8-30 a.m. Full Marching Order Steel helmets will be worn, service caps sling on right belt hook of tunic, water bottles filled, and days ration will be carried in haversack.

5. MARCH DISCIPLINE TO BE STRICTLY MAINTAINED.

6. The Horse Transport will march in rear of R.A.M.C. under the command of the Warrant Officer A.S.C. who will detail a N.C.O. to march in rear.

7. Motor Transport A.S.C. will proceed direct i/c of Sergeant Dobson A. A.S.C.(M.T.)

127th Bde. duties.
8. Captain H.HENRY is detailed to accompany the column rearguard. He will decide if men who have fallen out are fit to march or whether they should be carried in the Ambulance Wagons.

9. Sergeant Roberts E. will report to the Acting Staff-Capt at 127th Bde. Headquarters at 5-30 a.m. on 21-8-17 and will proceed to AVELUY to be allotted billets.

10. Halts of 10 minutes will be made at 9-55 a.m., 10-55 a.m. 11-55 a.m. etc.

11. Captain E.N.H.GRAY will hand over the Camp to Town Major and obtain certificate of cleanliness prior to departure.

Issued at 12/50 p.m.
Distribution.-
Copy No.1. C.O.
"   No.2. Capt Prestwich
"   No.3. Capt Henry.
"   No.4. Capt Hardie.M.C.
"   No.5. S/SM.Rolfe.
"   No.6. War Diary.
"   No.7. War Diary.
"   No.8. File.
"   No.9. Capt E.N.H.GRAY;

Lieut. Colonel. R.A.M.C. T.F.
O.C. 1/3rd. East Lancs. Field Ambulance.

Secret.   Copy No. 2

1/3rd East Lancashire Field Amb.
Order No. 10.

Reference Administrative Instruction
Number 2 issued on 127th Bde Operation Order No. 37.

August 22nd 1917.

1. Captain F.G. PRESTWICH will proceed in charge of "B" Section which will be made up to total strength of 1 Officer and 60 Other Ranks, by train No. 11. departing from AVELUY at 10/11 pm 22/8/17

2. Marching out states in triplicate will be sent down and handed to R.T.O. 4 hours before train is due to leave.

3. The section will arrive at the station complete 3 hours before departure of the train. Entrainment must be complete 1/2 an hour before the Scheduled time of departure of the train when it will be removed from the loading siding.

4. The O.C. train is Lieut-Colonel T.D. CRONSHAW 17th MAN. REGT.

5. The section will load as much as possible of the surplus baggage already at the station on to flats. The Guard will proceed with this. A guard of 2 men will be found by "A" Section to take charge of the remainder. No personnel or stores will be loaded in Brake vans at each end of the train.

6. Rations for the 23/24 will be distributed prior to the section marching off and water bottles will be filled.

7. The O.C. Train will detail an Officers piquet at each end of the train and will prevent men leaving the train without orders at the various stops.

8. There are 3 Entrances to the entraining station, the middle one is the entrance for troops. No men are to go to the canteen until entrainment is finished and the canteen will be cleared one hour before departure of train.

Issued 22/8/17
Distribution
Copy No 1 Capt Prestwich
" " 2 war diary
" " 3 war diary
" " 4 file.

W. M. Kenmir
Lieut Colonel.
O.C. 1/3rd EAST LANCS. FIELD AMBULANCE.

SECRET.   Copy No 2

13th East Lancs Fd. Ambce.
Order No 11

Ref. Administrative Instruction   August 22/7
No 2 issued on 127. Bde. Operation Order No 37.

1. Captain N.H.H. HASKINS will proceed in charge of "C" Section and details of "A" Section by train No 23, departing from AVELUY at 2-11 p.m. on 23/8/7.

(2) Marching out states in triplicate will be handed to R.T.O. 4 hours before train is due to leave.

3. The detachment will arrive at the station complete 3 hours before departure of the train. Entrainment must be complete ½ an hour before the scheduled time of departure of the train when it will be removed from the loading siding.

4. The O.C. train is Major A.C. LINGS/8th Manr. Rgt.

5. The unconsumed portion of the rations of the 23rd will be carried on the man's rations for the 24th. on supply wagon, water bottles will be filled. The men to have a hot meal prior to leaving camp.

6. The O.C. train will detail an Officers Picquet at each end of the train and will prevent men leaving the train without orders at the various stops.

7. There are 3 Entrances to the entraining station the middle one is for entrance of troops. No men are to go to the canteen until entrainment is finished and the canteen will be cleared one hour before departure of train.

8. The Transport will proceed by the same train in charge of Captain H. HENRY.

9. A rear party of 1. N.C.O and 8 men to be detailed to clean up the camp and rejoin unit on completion of this duty.

Issued at ___
Distribution
No 1 Capt HASKINS.
" 2 WAR DIARY
" 3 WAR DIARY
" 4 FILE

W.W. Jennings
Lieut Col.

O.C. 13th EAST LANCS. FIELD AMBULANCE

SECRET.   Copy No 4.

1/3rd East. Lancs. Fld. Ambulance.
         Order No 12.
Ref. Administrative Instructions.
No 2 issued on 127th Bde. O. Order No 37

1. Captain H. HENRY will proceed in charge of the whole Field Ambulance Transport less Motor Transport by train No 23 departing on the 23rd inst. from AVELUY at 2/11 p.m.

2. Accomodation on each train is as follows.

   1. Officers carriage — 30 Officers
   30 Trucks
                          • 40 Other Ranks. or 8 light draught or 6 heavy draught animals.
   17 Flats
                          • Nominally 4 axles to flats but owing to various sizes. 1. G.S. Wagon + half limber can be rolled on.

3. No personnel or stores will be loaded in Brake Vans at each end of the trains.

4. The Transport will arrive complete at the station 3 hours before departure of the train. Entrainment must be complete half an hour before the scheduled time of departure of the train when it will be removed from the loading siding.

5. Breast ropes for Horse Trucks must be provided by each unit. There are no staples to secure horses to as in the English trucks. Picketing ropes or drag ropes can be used for this purpose. Ropes for lashing vehicles on the Flat trucks will be provided by the Railway Coy. Care must be taken that the loads on all vehicles are thoroughly secured.

6. Harness will be removed and stacked in the trucks with the animals; sacks should be used if obtainable.

7. Supply Wagons will entrain loaded.

                                              (Continued)

Continued. /3rd E. Lancs. Field Ambulance   Copy No. 4.
Order No. 12

8. All animals will be watered prior to entrainment and will carry a feed for the journey. At each station or its vicinity there is a watering point for watering of animals.

9. Water Carts will be filled prior to departure.

10. O.C. /8th Man. Regt. will detail from the Company leaving on train No 23, One Officer and 50 Other Ranks to report to R.T.O. at 7.0 a.m. to clean trains and for horse ramps.

11. There are 3 entrances to the entraining station, the Southern entrance nearest AVELUY village is for wheeled traffic which will be parked along this entrance in double columns up to loading ramp. Horses will be unhooked and immediately taken to water unless they have already been watered before arrival.
The water point is east of the station opposite the middle entrance. Horses will be entrained on their return from watering.

Issued at:- 7.15 p.m.
Distribution
Copy No 1. Capt. HENRY.
" " " 2 " HASKINS.
" " " 3 S/S.M. ROLFE.
" " " 4 War Diary
" " " 5 War Diary
" " " 6 File.

W. Cammish
Lieut-Col.
O.C. /3rd EAST LANCS. FIELD AMBULANCE

SECRET.   Copy No. ...1...

1/3rd East Lancs. Field Ambulance.

Order No. 13.

Reference Map BELGIUM & FRANCE.
1/40,000 Sheets 27 & 28.
R.A.M.C. 42nd Division Order No. 17
of 29-8-1917.

August 30th 1917

1. No. 354)80 Sergeant Ashton J.H. and 10 O.R. will proceed by march route at 8-30 a.m. on 30-8-17 to YPRES, taking the seven stretcher wheeled carriers with them and report to O.C., 1/1st E.L.F.Amb. & the Prison.

2. "B" Section Tent Sub-division with "B" Section Transport will parade at 10-30 a.m. on 31st inst. and proceed by march route to the "CLOISTERS" POPERINGHE and take over the XIXth Corps Scabies Section. The Quartermaster-sergeant will proceed with this party.

3. The Bearer Sub-divisions "B" and "C" Sections made up to full strength, will parade at 5-30 a.m. on 1-9-17 in skeleton marching order under Capt. Haskins and proceed by march route to YPRES and report to O.C., 1/1st E.L.F.Amb. Move to be completed by 10-0 a.m. Transport will be provided to carry packs and rations.

4. The Field Ambulance less two Tent Sub-divisions and two Bearer Sub-divisions will parade at 10-30 a.m. on 1-9-17 in full marching order and proceed by march route to the "CLOISTERS" POPERINGHE.

5. "A" Section Tent Sub-division under Captain H. HENRY will remain i/c of LUNA PARK, until relieved by 59th Division.

6. MARCH DISCIPLINE TO BE STRICTLY MAINTAINED.

7. The Horse Transport less 1 Ambulance Wagon, 1 Water Cart and 1 Limber G.S. remaining at LUNA PARK, will march in rear of R.A.M.C. under the command of the Warrant Officer A.S.C. who will detail a N.C.O. to march in rear.

8. Three Daimler Cars will proceed i/c Corpl. Clements to REDFARM on 30-8-17 and report to O.C., 1/2 E.L.F.Amb Move to be completed by noon.

9. The Motor Transport less four Daimler Ambulance Cars will proceed direct to POPERINGHE. One Daimler Ambulance Car will remain at LUNA PARK under the orders of Captain H. HENRY.

10. The Quartermaster will arrange for the daily issue of rations to personnel and patients at LUNA PARK, of Medical Stores and Comforts required, and also for handing over stores on relief. Patients fit for discharge from LUNA PARK will be sent to the "CLOISTERS" POPERINGHE for forwarding to their Units.

11. Communication between LUNA PARK and Field Ambulance Headquarters will be maintained by cyclist orderly.

Issued at ...
Distribution :-
No. 1. O. i/c "B" Section.
" 2. Capt. Haskins.
" 3. Capt. H. Henry.
" 4. Quartermaster.
" 5. S.S.M. Rolfe.
" 6 & 7. War Diary.
" 8. File.

Lieut.-Colonel, R.A.M.C. T.F.
Comdg., 1/3rd East Lancs. Field Ambulance.

Confidential

War Diary
of the
1/3rd East Lancashire Field Amb.

From September 1st 17 To September 30th 17.
(Volume 9)

COMMITTEE FOR THE
MEDICAL HISTORY OF THE WAR
Date — 5 NOV. 1917

WAR DIARY
or
INTELLIGENCE SUMMARY

(Erase heading not required.)

Army Form C. 2118

Instructions regarding War Diaries and Intelligence Summaries are contained in F.S. Regs., Part II. and the Staff Manual respectively. Title Pages will be prepared in manuscript.

Place	Date	Hour	Summary of Events and Information	Remarks and references to Appendices
POPERINGHE	1/9/17	1100	Unit arrived at the Cloisters, less detachment at YPRES under Captain HASKINS and "A" Section T&S Subdivision remaining at LUNA PARK.	That Belgium Civil 2/9,3/9,2/9
		1200	43rd Field Ambulance having handed over patients & notes marched out	
		1200	193. Patients in Hospital.	
		1400	Lieut MILNER proceeded to BRANDHOEK as member of Medical Board assembling there	
?	2/9/17	0500	192 Patients in Hospital	
		0830	Officers told off to assist all able bodied patients employed in cleaning up premises	19.
			Whole of personnel + all all bodied patients employed in cleaning up premises	
		0830	A/Sister T&S Subdivision handed in LUNA PARK to 2/3 N. MIDLAND F. Ambulance + rejoined Hqrs	
		1400	Lieut MILNER proceeded to temporary medical charge 1/10 Manchesters when attached	
		1630	A.D.M.S. inspected Hospital	
			No 357,020 Serj Roberts attached acting sergeant Major (authority D.G.M.S.) enemy aeroplanes active firing with Lewis guns during night	
,	3/9/17	0800	197 Patients in Hospital	
			still cleaning up Hospital site debris of all kinds & much equipment found	
		1315	Lieut DELAFIELD i/c a detail 19 strong marched out to 33rd C.C.S. @ BRANDHOEK for temporary duty	
			Enemy aeroplanes active during night, 6 bombs thrown about midnight	
,	4/9/17	0500	1 officer 213 OR patients in Hospital.	
			Enemy aeroplanes very active all night (3) firing on POPERINGHE with machine guns, & bombing. Several casualties occurred quite close to Units ABC lines	
,	5/9/17	0800	242 Patients in Hospital	
			Enemy aeroplanes again attacks town during night. Three Lewis mounted including Tres goods	

Army Form C. 2118

WAR DIARY
or
INTELLIGENCE SUMMARY
(Erase heading not required.)

Instructions regarding War Diaries and Intelligence Summaries are contained in F.S. Regs., Part II. and the Staff Manual respectively. Title Pages will be prepared in manuscript.

Place	Date	Hour	Summary of Events and Information	Remarks and references to Appendices
POPERINGHE	6/9/17	05:00	243 Patients in Hospital	WMF
"	7/9/17	06:00	C.O. proceeded up to Bearn and post Znie + hay forward, visited BAVARIA HOUSE, A.D.S. POTIZJE, + YPRES. Captain PRESTWICH proceeded up at same time in relief of Captain HASKINS who returned to Hqrs with C.O.	Met BELGIUM Sheet 28 N.W.
"	"	08:00	296 Cases in Hospital	WMF
"	8/9/17	"	4 P.B. men arrived. Jook the place of 4 A.S.C. Category "A" drivers who has proceeded to H.T. Base. left Jown shelled + attacked by aeroplanes (bombs, machine gun) during night	WMF
"	9/9/17	08:00	323 Patients in Hospital. a draft of 15 privates arrived. Complete establishment A.D.M.S. visits Field Ambulance.	WMF
"	"	05:00	314 Patients in Hospital Lieutenant DELAFIELD and details returned to Hqrs from temporary duty @ 32 C.C.S. 2.O.R. admitted wounded (slightly)	WMF 21. WMF
"	10/9/17	08:00	290 Patients in Hospital. Received orders to relieve 1/2 E.L. Field Ambulance in line.	WMF
"	"	19:30	Final details moved out in advance with Field Ambulance also started 20:16.	
"	"	18:00	C.O. proceeded to YPRES.	
YPRES	11/9/17	12:00	Relief as detailed in Field Ambulance orders 20/16 duly carried out + Command of Forward evacuating and manning of C.O. Shelling fairly continuous. A.D.S. YPRES. C.O. Captain HARDIE Captain EVANS Mc.W. I.F.F.A. Captain TURVIS 1/2 I.F.F.A. B-C. Distributor A.D.S. POTIZJE Captain PRESTWICH + DELAFIELD a section tent subdivision, A.D.S. BAVARIA HOUSE Captain HASKINS, RAILWAY WOOD Captain Henry + section tent subdivision Bearer of SQUARE FARM, BAVARIA HOUSE + RAILWAY WOOD, remainder @ YPRES	Met BELGIUM Sheet 28 N.W.
"	12/9/17	03:00	C.O. proceeded with Captain HARDIE M.C. to POTIZJE and dfferent owing to shelling, gradually the bearer communicating dumps, as A.D.S. and had to be carried on in gas proof shelters all ranks wearing respirators from A.D.S. C.O. proceeded with H. DELAFIELD to BAVARIA House, returning to YPRES with Captain HASKINS.	WMF
"	"	09:00	Distribution I Officer YPRES. C.O. Captain CAMPS 1/2 I.F.F.A., BRANDHOEK Captain HASHIM	

1875 Wt. W593/826 1,000,000 4/15 J.B.C. & A. A.D.S.S./Forms/C. 2118.

WAR DIARY or INTELLIGENCE SUMMARY

Army Form C. 2118

Place	Date	Hour	Summary of Events and Information	Remarks and references to Appendices
YPRES	12.9.17		2nd PRESTWICH POTIZE Captain HARDIE MC & PURVIS 1/2 E.L.F.A. RAILWAY WOOD Captain HENRY, BAVARIA H0, 2nd DELAFIELD, A section Tent ambulance @ POTIZE B section tent ambulance @ YPRES, C section tent ambulance at YPRES till 6pm when at BRANDHOEK, Beaver @ YPRES. Shelling at intervals during the day night - but C.O. visits details HQ at BRANDHOEK	1/M
		1500		
"	13.9.17	0900	Early morning shelling around HDS YPRES. Distribution YPRES, Captain HASKINS & PRESTWICH, Lewy CAMPS 1/2 E.L.F.A. - BRANDHOEK Lieut DELAFIELD POTIZE and 12th BAVARIA H0 Captain HENRY, RAILWAY WOOD Captain EVANS 1/1 E.L.F.A.	1/M
"	14.9.17	0900	Quiet night little shelling. visited yesterday 8 ADMS 59th Division, PRESTWICH, today 8 ADMS 39 Division. Distribution YPRES (Lieut ... PRESTWICH, ...) LEWY CAMPS, POTIZE Captain WEBSTER 1/2 E.L.F.A (now ...) BRANDHOEK Lieut DELAFIELD ... 1/1 E.L.F.A, RAILWAY WOOD Captain EVANS. 1/3 E.L.F.A. BAVARIA ...	1/M
	15.9.17	0900	Very quiet day. Captain PRESTWICH proceeded on outlying duty, & Captain HARDIE returned to Hqrs. Distribution normal on route to BRANDHOEK CMDS equipment sent aide at BRANDHOEK handed over to 27th Field Ambulance.	2/M
"	16.9.17	0900	Distribution normal. Captain PRESTWICH proceeded to XIV Corps Hqrs as evidence at a G.C.M. Captain HENRY & DELAFIELD proceeded on outlying duty. 1/2 E.L.F.A. leaves on outlying attachment of 1/1 E.L.F.A leaves on new attachment their Field Ambulance Hqrs @ POPERINGHE. Captain EVANS MC 1/1 E.L.F. Ambulance when rejoined his F. Ambulance Hqrs.	3/M
"	17.9.17	0900	Distribution as above on attack, Orders 2/17. Captain HENRY on relief from DIVMARIA H0 proceeded to BRANDHOEK to take command of F.A details. Captain WEBSTER on relief from POTIZE rejoined his F. Ambulance Hqrs (1/2 E.L.F. Amb.) Captain CAMPS rejoined Hqrs 1/1 E.L.F. Ambulance The O.C. 28th Field Ambulance arrived at YPRES	22
		1680		
"	18.9.17		Reliefs proceeding on as order 2/17. Considerable shelling during night. Considerable shelling during early morning.	1/M

1875 Wt. W593/826 1,000,000 4/15 J.B.C. & A. A.D.S.S./Forms/C. 2118.

WAR DIARY
or
INTELLIGENCE SUMMARY

Army Form C. 2118

(Erase heading not required.)

Instructions regarding War Diaries and Intelligence Summaries are contained in F.S. Regs., Part II. and the Staff Manual respectively. Title Pages will be prepared in manuscript.

Place	Date	Hour	Summary of Events and Information	Remarks and references to Appendices
BRANDHOEK	18.9.17	0500	Command of unit evacuating area handed over to O.C. 38th Field Ambulance.	
		0900	Relief completed & details departed in all YPRES.	
		1000	Field Ambulance received at BRANDHOEK.	
		1030	Captain HASKINS proceeded to Divisional Hqrs facing on D.A.D.M.S. Temporary. Unit bivouaced in grounds of 44 C.M.D.S. Rested on 15 lines	
"	19.9.17	1130	Field Ambulance marched out of BRANDHOEK & proceeded to LEE CAMP L.10.c.8.2. Arrived at Divisional night	Ref. Belgium Sheet 24,
	20.9.17	0810	Field Ambulance marched out of LEE CAMP & proceeded by road route via WATOU, to WINNEZEELE J.16. central, arriving about 1.30 p.m. Unit party billetted & hastily encamped.	Ref Belgium Sheet 27,
WINNEZEELE	21.9.17	1310	All M.T. A.S.C. Transport of Unit less 1 water cart proceeded by road route under Captain HARDIE M.S. and Brigade Transport officer under Bde Transport officer to a new destination.	
"	22.9.17	0700	C.O. proceeded to COXYDE to view new area & ascertain disposition of Bivouacs being relieved & obtain billets for Personnel & Transport.	
		0810	R.A.M.C. under Captain HENRY marched out & went to tenders and 500 yds from Camp where whole personnel was entrained, & reached their destination at 2.30 p.m.	
COXYDE-VILLE	23.9.17	0030	Transport arrived safely. Unit remaining in billets.	
"	24.9.17	1515	In accordance with R.A.M.C. (W3rd) Indn. 1023. The Field Ambulance marched out to S. IDESBALD. Captain HENRY with A Section Tent subdivision less 9 O.R. proceeded to STEENKERKE & took over the clearing station from a detachment of 7th 9/2 I. Lowe Field Ambulance.	
S! IDESBALD	25.9.17	1000	The station & duties was from 9/2 I. Lowe Field Ambulance. Division being notified about the relief was completed by this hour.	
"	26.9.17		Second advanced Dd. tactical absorration & larkus staff of stand Canteen reopened. Brigade headquarters visited & arrangements made for collection of sick no news.	
		1500	Lieut MILNER reported his arrival in relief from 7th 1/10 Manchester Reg. Lieut MILNER reported his departure for Temporary duty to 36 C.C.S.	

1875 Wt. W593/826 1,000,000 4/15 J.B.C. & A. A.D.S.S./Forms/C. 2118.

WAR DIARY or INTELLIGENCE SUMMARY

Army Form C. 2118

(Erase heading not required.)

Place	Date	Hour	Summary of Events and Information	Remarks and references to Appendices
St IDESBALD	27.9.17		Men not employed on hospital duties fatigues under R.E.O.P.	
"	28.9.17	11.00	One Ford Ambulance on half damaged & shell fire. Captain Dr HARDIE M.C. to MDSPhis departure on termination of his contract & procedure of his office.	
"	29.9.17		Routine Hospital duties	
"	30.9.17		Routine Hospital duties. All men not employed on these duties training.	

M Humphries Capt

SECRET.   Copy No. 3.

1/3rd East Lancs. Field Ambulance.
Order No. 14.

Reference Map BELGIUM & FRANCE.
1/40,000 Sheet 28.
A.D.M.S. 42nd Division M14/132.

2nd September, 1917.

1. Lieut. S. W. MILNER is detailed as Officer in Medical Charge of the 1/10th Bn. Manchester Regt. temporarily, in relief of Capt. H. HANIGAN, proceeding to U.K. on leave.

2. He will report to 126th Brigade Headquarters at I.8.d.1.7. today.

3. Necessary transport will be provided.

[signature]
Lieut.-Colonel, R.A.M.C. T.F.
Comdg., 1/3rd East Lancs. Field Ambce.

Issued at 12.40 p.m.

Distrubution :-

Copy No. 1. Lieut. S.W. Milner.
  "   " 2. War Diary.
  "   " 3. War Diary.
  "   " 4. File.

SECRET.   Copy No. 2

1/3rd East Lancashire Field Ambulance.

Order No. 15.

Reference Map FRANCE & BELGIUM.
1/40,000 Sheet 28
A.D.M.S. 42nd Division 32/14/17.

3rd September, 1917.

1. Lieut. M. E. DELAFIELD is detailed to proceed in charge of a Tent Sub-division to BRANDHOEK and will report to O.C., 32nd Casualty Clearing Station for duty today. No Field Ambulance Equipment will be taken.

2. The unexpended portion of day's ration and one day's ration will be taken.

3. The details will parade in full marching order at 1-0 p.m.

4. Transport will be provided for Officer's baggage.

                                    [signature]
                                    Lieut.-Colonel, R.A.M.C. T.F.,
                                    Comdg., 1/3rd East Lancs. Field Ambulance

Issued at 12.50 p.m.

Distribution :-

Copy No. 1. Lieut. M.E. Delafield.
  "   " 2. War Diary.
  "   " 3. War Diary.
  "   " 4. File.

SECRET   Copy No. 6

1/3rd EAST LANCS FIELD AMBULANCE
Order No. 16

Reference Map BELGIUM
1/40000 Sheet 28 N.W.   10th September 1917
R.A.M.C. 42 Division Order No. 30.

1. (a) A Section tent subdivision less 9. O.R
   (b) B Section tent subdivision less 9. O.R
   (c) 3 O.R. from C Section
   Will parade @ 5.30 p.m. & taking such equipment as is specially detailed and one days rations, will proceed by march route to YPRES & report to O.C. 1/1 E.L.F. Ambulance,

2. (a) forming the night duty staff at A.D.S. POTIJZE
   (b)   "   "   "   "   YPRES
   (c)   "   a relief at Railway wood.
   These details will take over the A.D.S. at these sites respectively & will relieve the day staff by 9. p.m. 10.9.17

3. Captains HENRY & HASKINS will report to O.C. 1/1 E.L.F. Amb. YPRES by 7 p.m. 10.9.17, in order to relieve one officer each at RAILWAY WOOD & BAVARIA HOUSE, by 6 a.m. respectively.

4. Lt. Colonel CUNNINGHAM will proceed to YPRES on the evening of 10.9.17

5. Captain HARDY. M.C. remaining in command of the Unit at POPERINGHE will hand over the Corps Scabies Station to the 1/1 East Lancs Field Ambulance, & march the Unit to YPRES, less the Quartermaster Sergeant & 7 details, & will arrive there by 9. a.m. 11.9.17

6. The Quartermaster Sergeant & details will proceed to BRANDHOEK by march route, after handing over area stores, but taking with them all surplus stores & technical equipment on charge of this Unit. Movement to be completed by 12 noon. 11.9.17.

7. The whole of the Horse Transport will proceed by march route to BRANDHOEK & take over site vacated by 1/1 E.L. Field Ambulance movement to be completed by 12 noon.

8. The remainder of the reliefs at YPRES, POTIJZE, BAVARIA HOUSE, SQUARE FARM, & RAILWAY WOOD will be completed on morning of 11.9.17 by 12 noon.

9. The command of the Forward Evacuating area will pass to O.C. 1/3 E.L.F. Ambulance at 12 noon 11.9.17

10. Motor Ambulance cars will continue as at present distributed

11. 1 officer & 2 bearer subdivisions 1/1 E.L.F. Ambulance and 1 officer & 2 bearer subdivisions 1/2 E.L.F. Ambulance will be attached to 1/3 E.L. Field Ambulance

Issued at 4.30 p.m.
Distribution:
Copy No. 1. O.C. 1/3 E.L.F. Ambulance
         2. Captain Henry
         3.   "   Haskins
         4.   "   Hardie
         5. Quartermaster
         6. War diary
         7. War diary
         8. file.

                                          M. Cunningham Lt.Col.
                                          Comdg 1/3 E.L.F.Amb.

SECRET   22   Copy No. 5.

13th C. James Field Ambulance.
Operation Order No. 1.

References Maps Belgium & France
1/40,000 Sheets No. 20 & 28.
42nd Divl. R.A.M.C. Order No. 21.

September 16th 1917.

1. The 28th Field Amb. will take over the evacuation of the front line, and A.D.Stns from the 13rd C. James Fd Amb. Relief to be completed by 5 am 18th inst.

2. The bearers of the 1/3rd C. James Fd. Amb. will rejoin their Unit to-day.
   The bearers of the 1/2nd C. James Fd Amb on relief on the morning of the 17th will rejoin their Unit.

3. A half Tent Sub division representing the day staff of the 28th Fld. Amb. will arrive at POTIJZE 10 pm on the 16th inst in relief of day staff of the 13rd C. James Fd Amb who will return to YPRES.
   The night staff 13rd C. James Fd Amb will be relieved on the 17th inst.

4. One Officer of the 28th Field Amb. will arrive for duty at A.D.S. POTIJZE on the evening of the 16th inst, in relief of a bearer Officer 1/2nd C. James Fd Amb who will rejoin his Unit.

5. Captain M.E. DELAFIELD will hand over the A.D.S. POTIJZE on relief to the remainder of a Tent Sub division 28th Fd Amb. He will be responsible for the return to YPRES of all Field Ambulance equipment and obtain receipts for the stores handed over.

6. The 1/2nd C. James Fd Amb bearers at SQUARE FARM., BAVARIA HOUSE and RAILWOOD WOOD, will be relieved on the morning of the 17th inst, by 13rd C. James Fd Amb bearers less 10 men each place, the 28th Fd Amb finding these bearers.

Continued

/13th L'pires Fld. Ambulance
Operation Order No. 17. continued

7. Each bearer post will send in guides to POTIJZE by 4/30 am 18th inst to guide the bearers from the 28th Field Ambulance to these posts in relief of the 13th L'pires Fld Amb bearers who will then proceed to YPRES.

8. A.D.S. YPRES will be handed over to the 28th Field Ambulance by 5. am 18th inst., all Field Ambulance equipment being withdrawn and receipts obtained for stores handed over.

9. On relief the 13th L'pires Field Ambulance will proceed to BRANDHOEK.

W. Mummight
Lieut-Colonel R.A.M.C.
Comdg 13th L'pires Field Ambulance.

Issued at 8/0 pm
Distribution:-
Copy No. 1. A.D.S. YPRES.
" No. 2. A.D.S. POTIJZE.
" No. 3. 28th Field Amb.
" No. 4. O i/c Fld Ambulance DETAILS BRANHOEK.
" No. 5 & 6. War Diary
" No. 7. File.

Confidential

War Diary

1/3rd East Lancashire Field Ambce.

From ~~September~~ October 1st 1917. To October 31st 1917.

(Volume. 10.)

COMMITTEE FOR THE
MEDICAL HISTORY OF THE WAR
Date -8 DEC. 1917

WAR DIARY or INTELLIGENCE SUMMARY

Army Form C. 2118

Place	Date	Hour	Summary of Events and Information	Remarks and references to Appendices
St IDESBALD	1.10.17		Routine Hospital duties & Training. No 39160 Sjt ASHTON & No 5633 Pte RATCLIFFE & 334,199 Cpl HERBERT awarded Military Medal each, for gallantry E. of YPRES 6.9.17.	DRO 674. 9.9.17 MM
			No 337,100 Sjt DOWLING received a congratulatory certificate from the G.O.C. 41 Division on honours today E of YPRES 6.9.17	MM
	2.10.17		Weather still during fine. Weekly gas drill & Rifle along first aid with & warning reads. & ABC, stable similar attire	MM
	3.10.17		Stables being repaired by unit, whilst not fully vacated by DH & 94 units. Actual attack stands & new inmates. Using Dug Out 25 army sand shoes made. Previous of hickory	
			motor cycle N. unit trails in Tents.	MM
			Tailors, shoemakers, forming & harness staff all working now. Canteen open. & washer (Nugent) but is now of [?] org'n - on relief Room dispensary, barbers shop. QM's, sub-prescriptions, M.I. room, orderlies mess, an ambulance wag'n	MM
		1410	DMS 4th Army inspected the Field Ambulance & was pleased with what he saw. saying it was the [?] quarters. those & harness & conveniences.	MM
	4.10.17		A number of gas cases passing through, many RFA men from YPRES wounded. Sharing Railway.	MM
		11.15	Visited FA/B's 4/51 Division who were called out of Field Ambulances.	
	5.10.17	18.30	In main, & even all Tents struck & stretchers. Captain HENRY whilst away having seen relieved of his KAPELLE.	MM 23
	6.10.17	08.30	Unit commenced to entrain & ambulance with orders copy attached; en route to COXYDE.	MM
		10.00	Unit relieved the 90th Field Ambulance & took over station from this Unit	
Coxyde	7.10.17		C.O. visited 126 & 129 Bde Hqrs to make arrangements & the evacuation of their sick. also visited a detached post at WULPEN held by other Units.	MM

WAR DIARY
or
INTELLIGENCE SUMMARY

(Erase heading not required.)

Army Form C. 2118

Instructions regarding War Diaries and Intelligence Summaries are contained in F.S. Regs., Part II. and the Staff Manual respectively. Title Pages will be prepared in manuscript.

Place	Date	Hour	Summary of Events and Information	Remarks and references to Appendices
COXYDE	8.10.17	9.00	Whole unit less of section detailed yesterday on trenches duty) on fatigue loading wagons with R.E. iron shelving personnel & stables for horses. Shoemakers, tailors & barbers shops fitted up. Canteen in working order.	
		10.00	Camp visited by A.D.M.S. who inspected all the various establishments. Camp duties as laid down in attached copies of Field Standing Orders. Captain HENRY visited the Royal M.Os of the 127, 128 Bdes & of the 126 & obtained numbers and names through the O.C.S.	
	9.10.17		Work on new stables & shelter for horses being pressed on. A.D.M.S. held a medical board in Camp. Visit of A. Section's horses in billeting area stables. Sick of area passing through Field Ambulance and great in number, average number detained at midday 12, admission being about 20 a day.	
	10.10.17	10.00	C.O. attended a conference of A.D.M.S. officers. An order of admission of cases issued. 2 R.C.Os returned from a 4 days course at Divisional Gas School. N.C.Os classes to junior N.C.Os under Sergeant Major ?? was commenced & got continued. Number of sick admitted during day 24.	
	11.10.17		Work on dug-out & stables continued. N.C.Os class continuing daily. Meeting of Q.Ms & Staff. Number of cases admitted during day 25.	
	12.10.17		Captain HASKINS returned from leave. Number of patients passing through about average. Now ambulance was to substitute death? In area notice in form & one of for emergencies. Number of cases admitted during day 22.	
	13.10.17		Gas drill of whole unit under Gas Officer continued. Football Cup Tie commenced ??. Number of cases admitted during day 24.	
	14.10.17		C.O. visited Army Headquarters. Number of cases admitted during day 19.	

Army Form C. 2118

WAR DIARY
or
INTELLIGENCE SUMMARY
(Erase heading not required.)

Instructions regarding War Diaries and Intelligence Summaries are contained in F.S. Regs., Part II. and the Staff Manual respectively. Title Pages will be prepared in manuscript.

Place	Date	Hour	Summary of Events and Information	Remarks and references to Appendices
COXYDE	15.10.17	1000	Motor Bus with CO as passenger left on reconte to commence an Indian Army N.C.Os class of instruction continues	MW/
		1500	ADMS Pell Copas society inspected now on the Field Ambulance	MW/
		1500	CO delivered first of series of lectures to the N.C.Os entitled "Tactics" Details of cases admitted to Field Ambulance during day 25.	MW/
	16.10.17		Work on Personnel dug outs (shelters non-existent and bays 2 deep in water) continued with umber prepared and of portable concrete.	MW/
		1500	C.O. took 8 parts to 126 sta. Hypt. for interview as candidates for CO Tent Sub. Captain HENRY lectures N.C.Os on organisation + equipment 26 Cases admitted to Field Ambulance during day.	
	17.10.17	1500	Work on dug-outs being pushed forward. 41 Cases admitted to Field Ambulance Captain PRESTWICH lectures N.C.Os on Topography	MW/
	18.10.17		Work on shelters continuing	MW/
		1500	44 Cases admitted to Field Ambulance Captain DELAFIELD lectures N.C.Os on Military Law	
		0930	Captain PRESTWICH proceeds to 1/5 East Lancs Reg. for temporary duty as O/Spec.	
	19.10.17	1000	Work on shelters continuing. O.C. Divisional Train inspected transport of Unit	MW/
		1500	41 Cases admitted to Field Ambulance Captain HASKINS lectures N.C.Os on Military History	
	20.10.17	1000	A.A.+Q.M.G. + Division inspected Camp including Horse Lines	MW/
		1040	ADMS inspected site of Camp including Horse Lines. Old Censor start No 1912 destroyed being a new one being received in lieu. Work of shelters continues	

1875 Wt. W593/826 1,000,000 4/15 J.B.C. & A. A.D.S.S./Forms/C. 2118.

PASSED BY CENSOR No. 1098

WAR DIARY
or
INTELLIGENCE SUMMARY
(Erase heading not required.)

Army Form C. 2118

Instructions regarding War Diaries and Intelligence Summaries are contained in F.S. Regs., Part II. and the Staff Manual respectively. Title Pages will be prepared in manuscript.

Place	Date	Hour	Summary of Events and Information	Remarks and references to Appendices
COXYDE	20-10-17		A. Section 28 men C. Section 2 all H.T.A.S.C., 1 N.C.O. 19.7 O.R.'s posted us in charge and establish. Lieutenant Col LINER relieves N.C.Os. 20 Cases admitted to Field Ambulance	MMA
	21.10.17	1700	C.O. Took on hand to H Army HQ in to enable him to change his arms & also overtiremens. A. Section Exempting inspects of Section Commander. 12 Cases admitted to Field Ambulance	MMA
	22.10.17	10.00	Work in Personal shelter continued) B Section transfer inspects of Section Commander	MMA
		11.10	DADVS inspects motor all ranks. 25 Cases admitted to Field Ambulance	
	23.10.17		Rainy. Hard, work continuing	MMA
		12.40	Captain PRESTWICH returns from Temporary medical charge of 115 Tour Leaves Regt. G.O.C Division inspects camp. 30 Cases admitted to Field Ambulance	
	24.10.17		Cold & windy weather work continuing	MMA
		12.00	ADMS visited camp. Wood arrives for hut-ment of Staffs camp. 29 Cases admitted to Field Ambulance. Captain HASKINS proceeds to temporary medical charge of 311 Bde R.F.A.	
	25.10.17		Very weather. Shelter & shelter proceeding. Dining hut for men now in use. 23 Cases admitted to Field Ambulance	MMA
	26.10.17		Work continuing. 29 Cases admitted to Field Ambulance	MMA

WAR DIARY
INTELLIGENCE SUMMARY

Army Form C. 2118

Place	Date	Hour	Summary of Events and Information	Remarks and references to Appendices
COXYDE	24/10/14	0930	Work continuing. C.O. visits 1/3 Z.F. Ambulance in view of R.A.M.C. 421 Sent later Pg 24	
		1430	Field Ambulance proceeds and visits to D.H.Q. where Military Medical Inspector and friends & Sergt ASHTON 3rd HERBERT & P. RADCLIFFE by the G.O.C. H.B. Division who asked about the work was made being rendered by the AA&Q.M.G. The Field Ambulance Horse and Well & new compliments to the G.O.C. on being of Ambulances. 22 Cases admitted to Field Ambulance.	
	28/10/14	0930	C.O. proceed to A.D.S. NIEUPORT to ascertain details of arrangements of A.D.S. and to look in shelters & states containing	
		1745	letter for men of Field Ambulance issued. 15 cases admitted to Field Ambulance.	
	29/10/14	1500	Work continuing. Fixing details under Captain PREST which proceeded to NIEUPORT in small batches. A.D. took in O.R. to shirts for interment of C.R.E. with a view to Commission in ZARE. 29 Cases admitted to Field Ambulance.	
	30/10/14		Work continuing. Further details proceed to NIEUPORT. 1st Cases admitted to Field Ambulance	
	31/10/14	1400	Work in state continuing not completed. Tomorrow & Frogs have been almost completed. Replace of the shelter proceed complete for whole proceed. Captain DELAFIELD proceed to A.D.S NIEUPORT	
		1630	Nursing detail proceed to X 13, Z.3.0. separate details on duties from 1/3 Z.F. Ambulance. Lieutenant MILNER proceed taken over Field charge M.I. Room	

31/10/14

M.M.Cunningham Col.
Cmdt 1/3 S. Lancs Field Ambulance

SECRET.   Copy No. ...6......

1/3rd East Lancs. Field Ambulance.

Operation Order No. 18.

Reference Coast Administrative Map 1/100,000
Special Maps Nos. 4 & 5 1/10,000.
42nd Divisional R.A.M.C. Order No.26.

October 5th, 1917.

1. The 1/3rd E. Lancs. Field Ambulance will be relieved by an Ambulance of 41st Division on the morning of the 6th instant.

2. The 1/3rd E. Lancs. Field Ambulance will relieve the 92nd Field Ambulance of 32nd Division at X.7.c.8.7. on the 6th instant.

3. "C" Section with its transport will parade in full marching order at 8-30 a.m. on 6th instant, and proceed by march route.
"B" Section with its transport will parade in full marching order at 9-0 a.m. on 6th instant, and proceed by march route.
"A" Section with its transport will parade in full marching order at 9-30 a.m. on 6th instant, and proceed by march route.

4. On arrival in the new area, O.C. "C" Section will take over from 92nd Field Ambulance. All stores and billets must be carefully checked before being signed for.

5. O.C. "A" Section is responsible that the occupied site is perfectly clean before marching off. He will leave a guard if necessary for any stores which have not been removed at the time the Section marches out, and will be responsible for receipts being obtained of all area stores and surplus stores handed over.

6. Motor Transport (A.S.C.) will proceed direct in charge of Cpl. Clements.

7. March Discipline to be strictly maintained.

Issued at 3.50 pm

Distribution :-

Lieut.-Colonel, R.A.M.C., T.F.,
Commanding, 1/3rd East Lancs. Field Ambulance.

Copy No. 1. O.C. "A" Section.
"   "   2. O.C. "B"   "
"   "   3. O.C. "C"   "
"   "   4. O.C. 92nd Field Ambulance.
"   "   5. O.C. 139? Field Ambulance.
"   "   6 & 7. War Diary.
"   "   8 File.

Orders
by
Lieut Colonel H. H. B. Cunningham,
Commanding 1/3rd East Lancs. Fld. Ambulance.

24

Sunday 7-10-17.

Officer on Hospital Duty.   Capt. H. Henry.
Orderly Officer.   Capt. F. J. Prestwich
Orderly Sergeant.   Sgt. S. Fearing
Next for Duty.   Sgt. J. H. Ashton.

Duties. The Officer on Hospital Duty will take charge of M.I. Room and Wards during his tour of duty.

The Orderly Officer will visit the Personnel huts and Shelters daily, see the personnel meals, see the Horse lines, and take stables as far as time permits, and will superintend Camp Fatigues.

Duty will be from reveille to reveille.

R.A.M.C.		A.S.C.	
Reveille	6 a.m.	Reveille	6-0 a.m.
Breakfast	7-30 a.m.	Stables	6-15 am to 7-15 am
Orderly Room	8-30 a.m.	Breakfast	7-30 a.m.
Fatigues	9-0 a.m.	Orderly Room	8-30 a.m.
Lunch	12-30 p.m.	Fatigues	9-0 a.m.
Fatigues	2-0 p.m.	Stables	11-0 a.m.
Dinner	5-0 p.m.	Lunch	12-30 p.m.
Supper	8-0 p.m.	Fatigues	2-0 p.m.
		Stables	4-0 p.m.
		Dinner	5-0 p.m.
		Supper	8-0 p.m.

Winter Time. Winter time will come into use on 7th October at 1 a.m. Summer time on that date the clocks will be put back one hour.

Action at Transport lines during Shelling or Bombing.

C.R.O. 838. When transport lines are shelled the senior officer present will decide whether the men are to stand to their horses or not. In the absence of orders to turn out and stand to the horses, all ranks will remain under cover until the raid is over.

During an air raid all ranks in transport lines will remain under cover until the raid is over.

Air Raids. When air raids are in progress all ranks
C.R.O. 841. are to take advantage of such cover as is available unless their duties necessitate their remaining in the open.

continued.

Field Ambulance orders continued.

__Respirators__ Box Respirators will be worn by all ranks.

__Pay.__ The Field Ambulance will parade for pay under Sectional Arrangements at 4-15 p.m.

__Strength__ The undermentioned proceeded on furlough to U.K. on 6-10-17.

    354405 Pte. J. Evans.
    T4/111308. Dvr. D. B. Brooks.
    T4/037330. " J. Clayton.

The undermentioned reported their arrival from furlough in U.K. on 6-10-17.

    T/627. Dvr. T. S. Ward.
    354455. Pte. E. J. Fever.

The undermentioned proceeded as shown for one month's attachment as candidate for R.A. commissions.

    354436. Pte. J. Stretching. C/210 Bty. Wagon lines
    354070. " A.W. Horrocks C/211 Bty. Wagon lines
    T/4/247933. Dvr. D. Humphreys C/211 Bty. Wagon lines.

In the Field.
6-10-17.

                          Lieut-Colonel.
                    Cmdg. 13th East. L. Fld. Ambce.

ORDERS
by
Lieut-Colonel H.H.B.Cunningham,
Commanding 1/3rd East Lancs. Field Ambulance.

Monday 8-10-1917.

Officer on Hospital Duty   Capt. F. G. Prestwich.

Orderly Officer.   Capt. M. E. Delafield.

Orderly Sergeant.   Sergt. J. H. Ashton.
Next for Duty.   Sergt. T. Coan.

R.A.M.C.		A.S.C.	
Fatigues	9- 0 a.m.	Stables	6-15 a.m.
Fatigues	2- 0 p.m.	Harness Cleaning	9- 0 "
Guard Mounting	6- 0 "	Stables	11- 0 "
First Post	8-15 "	Stables	4- 0 p.m.
Last Post	8-45 "	Stables Picquet	
Lights Out	9- 0 "	Mounting	6- 0 "
		First Post	8-15 "
		Last Post	8-45 "
		Lights Out	9- 0 "

Fire and Convoy Picquet.

    One N.C.O. and 8 men of "A" Section will be detailed as Fire and Convoy Picquet. Their tour of duty will be for 72 Hours commencing at reveille on the first day the 8th inst.
    They will carry out ordinary duties in camp but may not leave camp whilst on picquet. In the event of fire they will immediately fall in and deal with the fire under instructions from the Orderly Officer.
    On arrival of patients or discharge of patients, they will fall in at the M.I.Room on the bugle sounding the Pioneer Call. They will then act under instructions of the Officer on Hospital duty.

Duties.   The Hospital duties will be found by "C" Section, viz:-
    Day Wardmaster   1 Sergeant. Night Wardmaster 1 Sergeant
    Nos 1 2 & 3 Wards and M.I.Room:-
       Day   1 Nursing Orderly   )per
            1 General Duty Orderly)ward
      Night M.I.Room & No. 3 Ward 1 Nursing Orderly each.
        Nos 1. & 2 Wards   1 General Duty Orderly each.
The Wardmasters will not leave their duties without permission from the Officer on Hospital Duty, and when not in the wards will remain in the M.I.Room.
The Wardmasters are responsible that the orderlies do not leave their duties and at meal times only half the orderlies are away at a time.

Guard   The Sergeant Major or in his absence a Staff Sergeant detailed
Mounting by him will invariably parade the guard for inspection by the Orderly Officer. The Orderly Sergeant's duties consist in taking any notes of instructions given by the Orderly Officer or the Sergeant Major.

Strength The undermentioned proceeded for duty at the Divisional Baths.
       354002 Sgt. J. C. Cowan.

      The undermentioned reported their arrival from furlough on 7-10-17
        354020 S.M.E.Roberts   354355 Pte. W. C. Brigg
        354464 Pte T. Taylor   29196 " T. Sharrocks
        354420 " J. Bradshaw   39470 " J. Roper.

                              Lieut.-Colonel, R.A.M.C. T.F.
In the Field   Commanding 1/3rd East Lancs.Field Ambulance.
7-10-1917.

Routine Orders
by
Lieut-Colonel. H. H. B. Cunningham,
Commanding 65th East. Lancs. Field. Ambulance.

Tuesday 2-10-17.

Officer on Hospital Duty.   Capt. A. E. Delafield.
Orderly Officer.   Capt. L. Henry.
Orderly Sergeant.   Sgt. T. Soar.
Next for Duty.   Sgt. T. Fearing.

R.A.M.C.

Fatigues	9-0 a.m.
Fatigues	2-0 p.m.

A.S.C.

Stables	6-15 a.m.
Harness Cleaning	9-0 a.m.
Stables	11-0 a.m.
Wagon Cleaning	2-0 p.m.
Stables	4-0 p.m.

Duty. The Orderly Officer will visit the guard and stable piquet at least once by night after lights out.

Censorship.
G.R.O. 2666. Distinguishing signs which have been adopted by units and formations, and the signs authorized by certain transport vehicles, are secret, and must not be disclosed in correspondence.

Oil Drums.
G.R.O. 2645. All empty Oil Drums, whether considered fit for further use in their original capacity as oil containers or not, will be returned to the Base immediately they become available. Sufficient drums are being handed over at the bases to provide stoves and braziers.

Haircutting Charges.
G.R.O. 2676.
1. The total charges in any one month to cover the payment to barbers and the cost of implements must not exceed 10 centimes per man whose hair is cut.
2. In Army Areas, C.O.s may claim a monthly sum equivalent to 10 centimes per man whose hair is cut. They may use their discretion in managing details of expenditure, provided that no portion of the fund is applied to purposes other than those connected with haircutting.

Sand Colic.
D.R.O. 702. The following procedure will be carried out to prevent animals from getting their heads to the ground when standing in a normal position:- Pass a stirrup-leather strap over the top of the neck, six inches behind the poll, and buckle round the rear portion of the nose band of head collar under the jaw.

Rum
D.R.O. 705. A daily issue of rum is approved until further notice.

continued.

Field Ambulance orders ctd:-

Winter Clothing
D.R.O. 794.
Reference G.R.O. 2621 - one pair only of drawers woollen will be issued, another being held by Corps Baths for necessary change. Bands body will be issued on the scale of 10% of strength, as it has been noticed that they are rarely worn. Should, however, a unit require more they can be obtained.

Hotels and Estaminets - La Panne.
C.R.O. 842.
The following Hotels are reserved for Officers only:-
 HOTEL TERLINK.
 GRAND PATISSERIE DU PHARE.
 HOTEL CONTINENTAL.
The following hotel is reserved for W.O's only:-
 HOTEL DE L'HORLOGE.
The following Estaminets are reserved for Warrant Officers and Sergeants:-
 HOTEL PATISSERIE MER DIGNE.
 HOTEL DE LA DIGNE. Avenue de la Mer.
 HOTEL COSMOPOLITE. Junction of Rue d' Chateau and Avenue de la Mer.
These hotels and Estaminets are out of bounds at all times to other ranks below the rank of Sergeants. W.O's and Sgt's are not forbidden to use hotels and estaminets other than those reserved to them.

Detachment Duty.
The undermentioned proceeded to 2nd E.L.F. Amb. on 8-10-17 for detachment duty.
 M2/265271. Pte. A. W. Froud.
 354095. " G. W. Harvey.

N.C.O's Class
An N.C.O's class will assemble for instruction under the Sergeant-Major at 9am.

In the Field
8-10-1917
 Lieut-Colonel.
 Cmdg. 15th East L. Fld. Ambce:

Notice

Attention is drawn to Field Ambulance Orders dated 5-10-17. calling for the names of men with a knowledge of dispensing.
Also for names of additional buglers and drummers.

SECRET.   Copy No. 8
                1/3rd East Lancashire Field Ambulance.

                         Order No. 19.

42nd Divisional Routine Order No.27 d/26-10-17.
Reference Map 1/40,000 Provisional Issue.
         Special Sheets 4 & 5.
                                                October 28th, 1917.

1. The 1/3rd East Lancs. Field Ambulance will relieve the
   1/2nd East Lancs. Field Ambulance in the NIEUPORT Sector
   on the nights 30/31st October, and 31st October /
   1st November 1917.
   Field Ambulance Rear Headquarters will move to X.13.b.3.0.
   at 12 noon 1-11-17.

2. O.C. "B" Section will detail one Officer, half tent sub-
   division and 32 bearers to proceed to A.D.S. NIEUPORT on
   29-10-17, hour will be notified later.
   O.C. "B" Section will detail one Officer to proceed
   31-10-17 the tent sub-division less half and bearer sub-
   division less 32 bearers to proceed to A.D.S., NIEUPORT
   on 30-10-17.
   O.C. "A" Section will detail necessary personnel to
   complete "B" Section tent sub-division to establishment
   and bearers to complete bearer sub-division proceeding
   on 30-10-17 up to 32 other ranks.

3. O.C. "A" Section will detail a N.C.O. to take charge of
   Trench Foot Centre at WHITE HOUSE.

4. O.C. "C" Section will detail half tent sub-division to
   take over the Dressing Station at X.13.b.3.0. on 1-11-17.
   The A.& D. Book will close at 12 noon at the present site
   and re-open the same hour at X.13.b.3.0.
   He will also detail the N.C.O. i/c Canteen to proceed to
   A.D.S. 31-10-17 and take over canteen there.

5. "B" Section will load their mobilization equipment on
   29-10-17.
   "A" and "C" Section will load their mobilization equipment
   on 31-10-17.

6. The Mechanical Transport and Horse Transport less horses
   will move to X.13.b.3.0., but the horses will remain
   stables on the present standings until further orders.

7. The Quartermaster will arrange to move surplus stores
   on 1-11-17.

8. Os. C. Sections will notify Field Ambulance Headquarters
   completion of their movements.

9. Os.C. Sections will see that all stores and billets taken
   over are carefully checked before being signed for, and
   receipts obtained for all stores handed over by them
   before moving to new area.

10. Os.C. Sections will hand in the A.Fs.B.122 of their
    sections to Field Ambulance Headquarters before moving.

11. No maps or important documents will be taken beyond the
    A.D.S., NIEUPORT.

12. The O.C. Field Ambulance will move to A.D.S., NIEUPORT
    on 1-11-17.

Issued at 5-457
Distribution :-
Copy No.1. Capt. H. Henry.
  "   " 2. Capt. N.H. Haskins   Lieut.-Colonel,
  "   " 3. Capt. J.G. PRESTWICH.   Comdg. 1/3rd East Lancs. Fld. Ambce.
  "   " 4. "   M.E. DELAFIELD. No 6. QUARTERMASTER. No 8/9 WAR DIARY No 10. FILE.
  "   " 5. LIEUT. S.W. MILNER.   " 7. A.S.C. W.O.

WAR DIARY

OF

1/3rd EAST LANCASHIRE FIELD AMBULANCE.

FROM :- 1st November, 1917   TO :- 30th November, 1917.

(VOLUME X/)

Army Form C. 2118

WAR DIARY
or
INTELLIGENCE SUMMARY
(Erase heading not required.)

Instructions regarding War Diaries and Intelligence Summaries are contained in F. S. Regs., Part II. and the Staff Manual respectively. Title Pages will be prepared in manuscript.

Place	Date	Hour	Summary of Events and Information	Remarks and references to Appendices
NIEUPORT	1.11.17	0600	Command of A.D.S. handed to O.C. 1/3 E. Lanc Field Ambulance	Capt FURNES proceeded
		0900	C.O. proceeded to NIEUPORT & assumed charge of A.D.S., Captains PRESTWICH & DELAFIELD being on duty at this post.	
		0900	Captain HENRY i/c Rear Headquarters proceeded to X 13.6, 3.0.	
		0900	Captain HASKINS proceeded to Corps Hqrs for interview of DDMS with a view to Regular commission	
			Captain MANSON T.C. taken on strength as from 31.10.17.	
	2.11.17	0530	25 Casualties passed through ADS. inclusive of sitting down.	
			C.O. accompanied by Captain PRESTWICH proceeded around all bearer posts examining forms from the ADS ground very much cut up & shell fire, in several places no trenches at all, & in some places very soft & muddy. Most advance distribution at ADS & bearer post attached	28
			Captain MANSON proceeded to 41st Division as ??? ??? & instructed w/steng. & nos attached	26
			Lieutenant MILNER proceeded to 41st Division as a ??? ??? ??? also proceeded to 41st Division.	87
			Staff Sergeant & 2 Privates ??? ??? ??? ??? ??? S. Staff & reno' returns of ADS completed.	
			"NEW POST" ??? hut now completed. Dining room for people of ADS completed. I'm Coen passed through ADS.	
	3.11.17		Bearers of Field Post withdrawn to Redan, Fishen being nearly nearly over Isabel Pier, & no Trenches leading up to it now from it.	
			2 men poisoned by ??? ??? ??? late ??? by night ADS every tent being sandbagged & gas proofs, regard.	
			??? ??? ??? ???	
			Bearers ??? out by my Posts helping this morning.	
			8 Cases being killed died from wounds this morning.	
			Lath & retain clean baths.	
		1215	C.O. proceeded to New Hqrs "COXYDE" & then with Captain HENRY & ADMS @ John & attend a conference	
		1845	returning to ADS via FURNES "WULPEN" giving talks now through post DUNKERQUE being heavily shelled on Route these wounded & 4 wounds at duty	
			A.D.S. heavily shelled during evening; 8 shells hit being made.	
			28 Cases passed through ADS.	
	4.11.17	0100	Bosch still shelling ADS	
		0545	C.O. visited NEW POST at the REDAN, Captain DELAFIELD visited other posts on ??? ??? of ??? also South Redan & Trench fog centre, including Lot Hitchen & Trench Pert centre	

1875 Wt. W593/826 1,000,000 4/15 J.B.C. & A. A.D.S.S./Forms/C. 2118.

Army Form C. 2118

WAR DIARY
or
INTELLIGENCE SUMMARY

(Erase heading not required.)

Instructions regarding War Diaries and Intelligence Summaries are contained in F.S. Regs., Part II. and the Staff Manual respectively. Title Pages will be prepared in manuscript.

Place	Date	Hour	Summary of Events and Information	Remarks and references to Appendices
NIEUPORT	4.11.17	1400	Heavy Shelling ADS entrance of forty yd damaged, one motor ambulance & one motor bicycle smashed. Direct of ambulance now on way up to ADS hit amongs the big car etc. One 200 shells of about 5.9 calibre been fired by enemy Dixmuide railway destroyed rather & damaged ADS, & approach to ADS where used by ambulance cars pitted with shell holes. Several direct hits on roof of ADS sustained. Foul air which came up in evening broke its last cake in shell holes. 26 cases passed through ADS.	MM
	5.11.17	0500	Roof of ADS & approaches being repaired. Also sand bag walls of gas guard being renewed. Daily work of ADS continues.	MM
		1540	Captain PRESTWICH proceeds to rear headquarters. CORPS DE being relieved by Captain HASKINS. 14 cases passed through ADS. An new headquarters at CORPS DE work being carried on in elephant shelter & pierced	MM
	6.11.17	0530	C.O. accompanied by Captain HASKINS went around all R.A.P.s & horse posts. Visits the new R.A.P. & horse post under construction in the REDAN. Repair work on the A.D.S.'s being continued. Medicine from the small column have removed the broken Ford car, & chassis & engine of Daimler, which was destroyed by shell fire etc. 20 cases passed through A.D.S.	MM
	7.11.17	0530	Captain DELAFIELD proceeds round the horse posts visiting the R.A.P.s Raining today. Foul guns so far had any cases use in. Some heavy shelling a short distance away from the ADS. Several cases coming in now.	MM
		1220		
		1600	C.O. visits Bde. H.qrs. to arrange about R.A.P.s & horse foot centre.	
		1930	25 cases passed through ADS.	
	8.11.17	0530	Captain HASKINS proceeds round the horse posts & R.A.P.s after work continued at ADS post, latrines, gas ward etc. while washing of R.A.P.s continuing.	MM
		0930	C.O. visits A/P section seat kitchen & Horse foot centre. Now transfer mud from X, Y & 8.9. to GROOTE KWINTE FARM taking staple route. 1, 1/2 E Lewis Field Ambulance	

1875 Wt. W593/826 1,000,000 4/15 J.B.C. & A. A.D.S.S./Forms/C. 2118.

Army Form C. 2118

WAR DIARY
or
INTELLIGENCE SUMMARY
(Erase heading not required.)

Instructions regarding War Diaries and Intelligence Summaries are contained in F. S. Regs., Part II. and the Staff Manual respectively. Title Pages will be prepared in manuscript.

Place	Date	Hour	Summary of Events and Information	Remarks and references to Appendices
NIEUPORT	8.11.17	1630	ADMS visited ADS & issued sundry instructions. 13 Cases passed through ADS.	
"	9.11.17	1000	Considerable amount of hostile shelling, as usual mainly in the vicinity of the ADS with frequency at (ADS & RAPs) which was all being withstood. Roof of ADS being strengthened also protection of Sandbags & attacks to them. Captain DELAFIELD proceed to rear Hqrs. being relieved by Captain PRESTWICH. Horse 21 near Hqrs. being stiffed, still a little repair work going on there. 15 Cases passed through ADS.	
"	10.11.17 0530 0600		Captain PRESTWICH visited RAPs & these posts. New beach post in the REDAN cleared & at noon this was one. ADMS on returning from trenches visited ADS, dug was unable to see what was & had sorry to shelling. Heavy shelling of ADS vicinity during afternoon & evening. Three attempts to remove casualties failed for this reason, shells being dug heavy calibre of "front 9". In this one shelter occupied 8 16 men (wounded in 8 dead of 2), no casualties. Narrow escape of one bearer party returning to ADS, a shell exploding along 3 yds from them, when about 15 yds from entrance to ADS, splitter mud and canteen, damaging 8 rifles & a Lewis gun. Heavier bombardment of posts & bearers returning from Redan, the last we nearing the bridge being shortly over. First ambulance can able to reach ADS through fire not reach 24.15. Cases evacuated after this.	
	11.11.17 0500 1030 1430		Repair & roof of anneurising boy carried on. CO proceeded to near Hqrs. under convoy. Captain HENRY relieving him at the ADS. CO attended a conference as ADMS office, & remained 28 cases ADS.	
"	12.11.17 1300		Preparations being made to collect surplus stores as and stores them in in view of our infantry more clearing of horse latrines. 23 hours having been shifted. Painting of waggons & repairing of harness continued. Visit of ADS again this afternoon today. No single store of white course throw from port 4.9 entire particularly taken in the Redan on the 13th An advanced French Ray pasto was established in the ADS by Captain DELAFIELD Captain HASKINS relieved & ADS by Captain DELAFIELD. A Bugle hand found in the Ruins, by volunteers from the RAMC personnel.	

Army Form C. 2118

WAR DIARY
or
INTELLIGENCE SUMMARY
(Erase heading not required.)

Place	Date	Hour	Summary of Events and Information	Remarks and references to Appendices
COXYDE	13.11.17		Commenced made in returning surplus stores to store. Four wagon loads being brought down from A.D.S. during day. A difficult procedure owing shelling in vicinity of A.D.S. Clothing of house being continued. Ordnance, R.E., & medical surplus stores being returned to respective depots.	WMY
"	14.11.17		Two ambulance car loads of medical stores sent back to Adv. base medical stores. Several G.S. wagon loads of ordnance & R.E. stores returned to their respective dumps. Two G.S. wagon loads of others returned from A.D.S. in evening. Clothing of horses continued. Painting & painting of wagons unit cars etc continued. At A.D.S. whitewashing of fixtures continued, & repairs to roof & annexe.	WMY
"	15.11.17		Repairs & painting of wagons continued. Clothing of horses completed.	WMY
		15.45	Commenced returning R.E. stores @ Hqs hand S with clerks. Similar return for more received.	29.
		20.50	Two G.S. wagon loads of stores returned from A.D.S. in evening. Field Ambulance orders for movements on and up to 18th issued (No. 30) at A.D.S. while washing of interior & repairs outside continued.	
"	16.11.17		Stores received from A.D.S. being returned to Ordnance dumps. Repairs & painting of wagons continued.	
		10.35	Field Ambulance orders for relief issued (No. 31)	30.
		11.15	French officers today on Thursdays visits Field Ambulance today	31
		20.00	Field Ambulance orders for movements of "C" Section issued (No. 31)	
"	17.11.17	10.00	Attended S.O. Officer of A.D.M.S. in accordance with instructions. Surplus medical stores sent to C.M.D.S. All mobilization equipment loaded on wagons	

1875 Wt. W593/826 1,000,000 4/15 J.B.C. & A. A.D.S.S./Forms/C. 2118.

WAR DIARY
or
INTELLIGENCE SUMMARY
(Erase heading not required.)

Army Form C. 2118

Instructions regarding War Diaries and Intelligence Summaries are contained in F.S. Regs., Part II. and the Staff Manual respectively. Title Pages will be prepared in manuscript.

Place	Date	Hour	Summary of Events and Information	Remarks and references to Appendices
COXYDE	14.11.17	1400	French relieving Units arrived, & is bivouacking at GROOTE QUINT FARM for the night	1/4020 FURNES Provincial map
"	18.11.17	0800	C Section Transport & cars left new camp Furnes & returned for more stores	
		1000	Headquarters moved from X.13.b.3.0. to X.4.c.8.7. & bivouaced for night being joined by details from NIEUPORT as they were relieved by French troops.	
"	19.11.17	0330	Orders received for ADS at X.13.b.3.0.	
		0645	A & B Section RAMC parties in motor lorries & motor bus under command of Captain HENRY en route of ADINKERKE enlarging them to LEFFRINCKOUKE I.29.b.5.8.	S.log.B.19
		0800	Transport & horse driven parties under Captain DELAFIELD & marched to LEFFRINCKOUKE these sections being marching with 135 Bde group to follow Army Area.	
			C Section under Captain HASKINS being detailed to rendezvous at X.13.b.3.0. under R.V. "C." officer	
		1305	RAMC Transport & cars at Billets	
		1610	C.O. visited Bde Hqrs to ascertain if any medical services were required	
LEFFRINCKOUKE	20.11.17		13 aid collected from Bde group & evacuated. To Quin Alexandria Hospital Major Les Burns	
		0900	Field Ambulance (less C Section detached as Coxyde) marched via LES-MOERES - HOYMILLE eastern outskirts of BERGUES - FAULQ du CASSEL to WORMHOUDT, reaching its billet @ 1435 Captain PRESTWICH & motor ambulance, each of Captain DELAFIELD i/c Transport on arrival, all personnel went to baths to dry bath, followed by foot inspection. & I O'cas kits of en route	
WORMHOUDT	21.11.17	1000	12 sick collected from Bde group & evacuated to 13 C.C.S. ARNEKE Field Ambulance marched out of WORMHOUDT along roads (CASSELS) to billets @ C.28.d.4.b. & found the G.O.C. Division en route, who complimented the Unit on their turn out, both men & transport inspected by the Band. He also pointed out on this main defects to Commanders. Captain DELAFIELD i/c motor ambulance sect., & Captain HENRY i/c Transport	8½.log.29

1875 Wt. W593/826 1,000,000 4/15 J.B.C. & A. A.D.S.S./Forms/C. 2118.

WAR DIARY
or
INTELLIGENCE SUMMARY

(Erase heading not required.)

Army Form C. 2118

Place	Date	Hour	Summary of Events and Information	Remarks and references to Appendices
RIETVELD	22.11.17	0845	Unit paraded, Captain PRESTWICH i/c Transport & Captain HENRY i/c sick & motor ambulances, & marched along WORMHOUDT - CASSEL road, then through L'ANGE, WEMAERS-CAPPEL, ZUYTPEENE, BAVINGHOVE to billets @ O.34.2. arriving @ 1245. Only 2 cases being picked up en route. Misty weather, ground very muddy.	Sket 39A.
		0915	Sick cases evacuated to 13 C.C.S. @ ARNEKE	
		1530	C.O. proceeded to AIRE & reported location of Unit to A.D.M.S.	
OXELAIRE	23.11.17	1000	Unit paraded Captain DELAFIELD i/c Transport & Captain PRESTWICH i/c sick & motor ambulances, & marched by ROMAN Road to THIENNES arriving at 1335. No cases picked up en route. Fine cold weather, ground very muddy & bad in places. Unit in billets, accommodation for horse poor, & medical inspection room & staff & J.A. section	
		1075	3 cases evacuated to 13. C.C.S @ ARNEKE	
THIENNES	24.11.17	0900	Detailed disinfection of personal Sectional mobilization equipment checked Personal clothing being overhauled, cleaned & repaired. Personal kit under sectional arrangements laid out by cutting carried out all day. 4 cases evacuated to 39 Stationary Hospital	
"	25.11.17	09.00	Repairing of personal clothing continued Overhauling of weapons continued	Mr 36A.
		15.00	O.C. visits ADMS @ JHQ AIRE & then proceeded to 127 Bde Hqrs @ LAMBRES 1st Lieutenants LONG & DOUGLASS U.S.A. O.M.R.C. arrived having been posted to the Unit as reinforcements Orders for move with 127 Bde Hqrs received.	BETHUNE 1:20000
	26.11.17	0730	Captain HENRY, a quartermaster sergeant & 14 O.R. proceed q motor lorry as advance party to MESPLAUX Farm	32
		0800	Unit paraded & proceeded by march route via TANNAY, HAVERSKERQUE, S¹ VENANT, ROBECQ @ BETHUNE Orders for march attached (F. Ambulance letter 22.)	
		1545	Arrived @ BETHUNE, & billeted for night in Barracks.	

WAR DIARY
or
INTELLIGENCE SUMMARY

(Erase heading not required.)

Army Form C. 2118

Place	Date	Hour	Summary of Events and Information	Remarks and references to Appendices
BETHUNE	27.11.17	0900	Unit paraded & proceeded by march route via ESSARS to MESPLAUX Farm X.14.a.9.7.	1875 BETHUNE
		1030	arrived at destination & relieved 99th Field Ambulance as detailed in F. Ambulance Orders No. 23	33
			Captain HENRY i/c ADS TUNING FORK F.S.C.S.9. Captain DELAFIELD i/c ADS. LONE FARM A.M.d.0.3	MMM
			Captain PRESTWICH i/c M.I. Room & MDS. 1st Lieutenant DOUGLASS i/c Wards & MDS.	
			24 cases transferred from 99th Field Ambulance.	
MESPLAUX Farm	28.11.17	1100	Barber, Tailors, shoemakers shops & Canteen reopened, also gramophone.	MMM
			C.O., Sergeant Major inspected both ADS & all RAPs in sector	
		1500	1st Lieutenants LONG & Seguard ALSOP proceeded 1st Army School Instruction to BETHUNE.	
	29.11.17		10 cases admitted to Field Ambulance.	MMM
			Whilst weather continuing work commenced of 99th Field Ambulance commenced. Not much constructive work required with ADS & MDS owing to the amount of work done by previous Field Ambulance.	
			weather fine & mild	
			23 cases admitted to Field Ambulance	
	30.11.17	1000	Lt. Col accompanied ADMS to LONE FARM ADS. RAPs of 1/4 Manchester 1/4 Lanc Fusiliers & 1/5 Manchester	MMM
			& went round trenches in forward area returning to MDS at 4 pm.	
		1800	A. Sutton under command Captain HASKINS arrived as MDS	
			23 cases admitted to Field Ambulance	

MMMurray Lt Col
Comdg 1/3 E. Lancs Field
Ambulance

Appendix 26

Copy No. 2.

1/3rd East Lancs. Field Ambulance.

Reference A.D.M.S., N.14/146.
dated 1/11/17.

November 1st 1917.

1. Under instructions from 42nd Divisional Headquarters, certified true copy attached Capt. Manson will proceed as reinforcement for 41st Division on the morning of 2nd November 1917. to report to A.D.M.S., 41st Division at ROSENDAEL.

2. Necessary transport will be provided.

Howard Henry.
Captain.R.A.M.C. T.F.,
for O.C., 1/3rd East Lancs. Field Ambulance.

Issued at.... 8/30 pm

Distribution.-

Copy No.1.Captain.Manson.
"   " 2.War Diary.
"   " 3.File.

O.C.,
   1/3rd East Lancashire Field Ambulance.

   Captain Manson, R.A.M.C., T.C., will be taken on your strength from 31/10/17.

   Captain Manson and Lieut. S.W. Milner will proceed as reinforcements for 41st Division on the morning of 2nd November 1917, and are to be struck off your strength accordingly.

   They are to report to A.D.M.S., 41st Division at ROSENDAEL, near office of D.M.S., Fourth Army.

M.14/146   (sd) Geo. Dalziel, Captain,
1/11/17.   D.A.D.M.S., 42nd Division.

Certified true copy

Howard Henry, Capt.
for O.C. 1/3rd E. Lancs Field Ambce

27

Copy No. 2.

1/3rd East Lancs. Field Ambulance.

Reference A.D.M.S.M.14/146.
dated 1/11/17.

November 1st 1917.

1. Under instructions from 42nd Divisional Headquarters, certified true copy attached, Lieut. S.W.Milner will proceed as reinforcement for 41st Division on the morning of 2nd November 1917. to report to A.D.M.S., 41st Division at ROSENDAEL.

2. Necessary transport will be provided.

Howard Henry
Captain. R.A.M.C.T.F.,
for O.C.,1/3rd East Lancashire Field Ambce.

Issued at 8.30pm.

Distribution.-

Copy No.1.Lieut.S.W.Milner.
 "   " 2/3 War Diary.
 "   " 4.File.

O.C.,
   1/3rd East Lancashire Field Ambulance.

   Captain Manson, R.A.M.C.,T.C., will be taken on your strength from 31/10/17.

   Captain Manson and Lieut.S.W.Milner will proceed as reinforcements for 41st Division on the morning of 2nd November 1917, and are to be struck off your strength accordingly.

   They are to report to A.D.M.S.,41st Division at ROSENDAEL, near office of D.M.S.,Fourth Army.

M.14/146   (sd) Geo.Dalziel, Captain,
1/11/17.   D.A.D.M.S., 42nd Division.

Certified true copy

Howard Harry, Capt.
for. O.C. 1/3rd E. Lancs. Fld. Ambce.

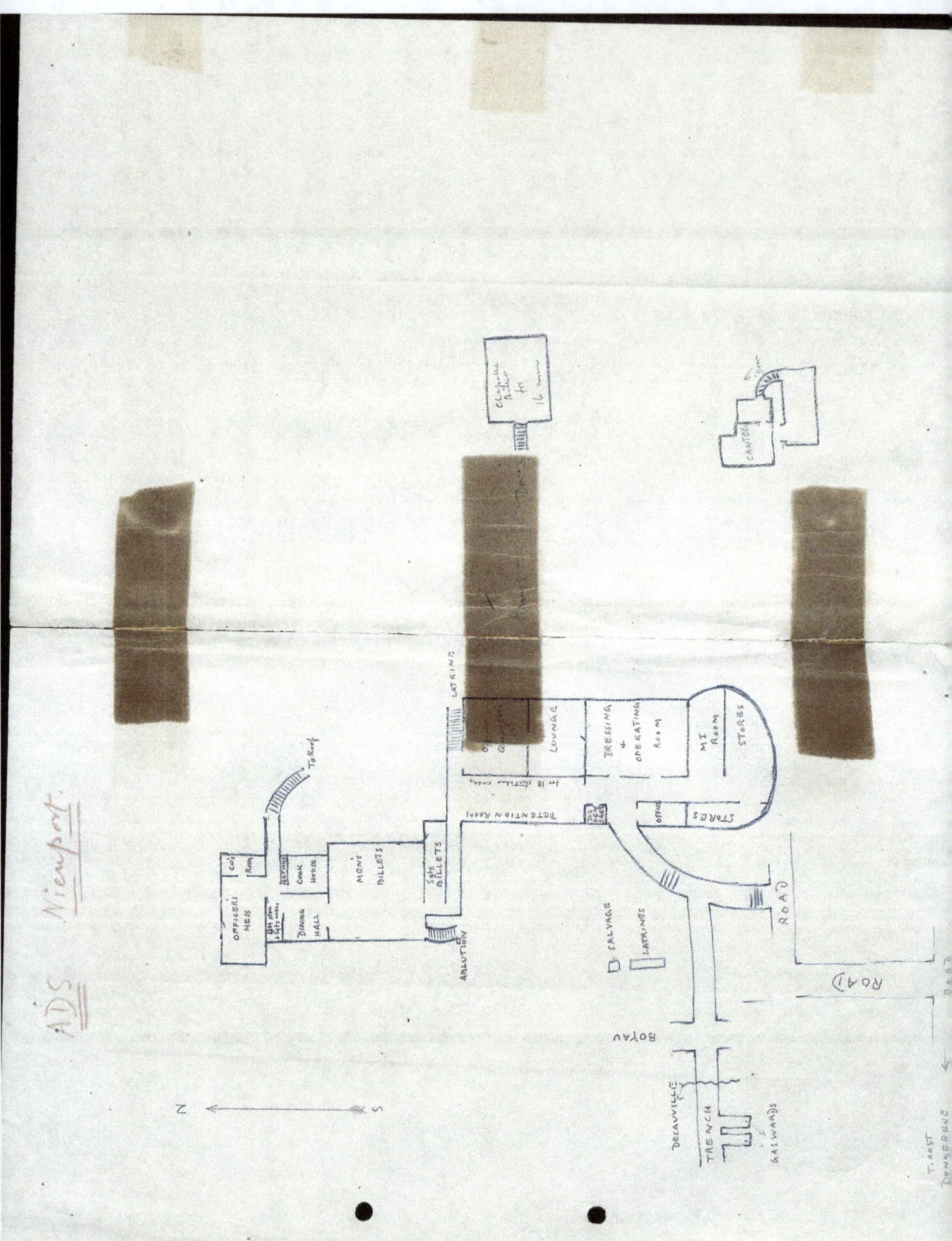

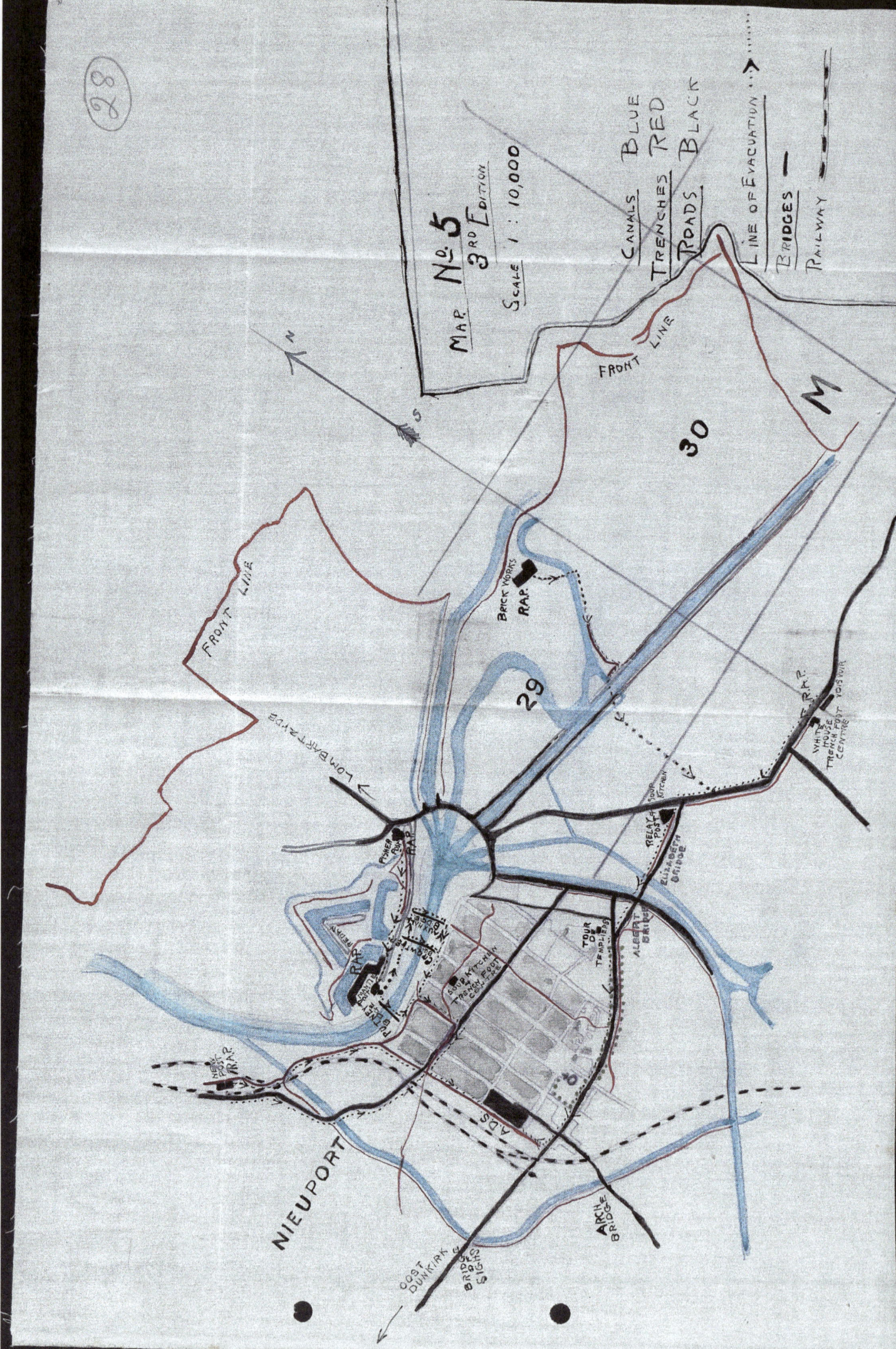

SECRET Copy No. 8

1/3rd East Lancashire Field Ambulance.

Order No.20.

R.A.M.C. 42nd Divisional Order No. 28.
Reference Map 1/40,000 Provisional Issue.

November 15-1917.

1. The Headquarters of the 1/3rd East Lancs.Field Ambulance will move from its present site to site at X.7.c.8.7. evacuated by the 1/2nd East Lancs.Field Ambulance on the morning of the 18th November.

2. On the 16th inst.,

    All wheeled stretcher carriers on charge of the 1/1st and 1/2nd East Lancs.Field Ambulance will be returned to Headquarters.

    The O.C., A.D.S. will return all surplus Sectional equipment to Headquarters.

3. On the 17th inst.,

    Sectional mobilization equipment (less that at A.D.S.) will be loaded on transport.

    Wheeled stretcher carriers on charge of 1/1st and 1/2nd East Lancs.Field Ambulance will be returned to their units.

    Surplus drugs, dressings, and medical comforts at Headquarters will be sent to XV C.M.D.S.

    The Motor Ambulance Car of 1/2nd East Lancs.Field Ambulance attached to 1/3rd East Lancs.Field Ambulance will rejoin its unit in the evening.

4. On the 18th inst.,

    R.A.M.C. personnel will parade at 10 a.m. and proceed by march route to new camp. Dress Marching Order.
    The guard at GROOTE KWINTE FARM will be withdrawn in time for this parade.
    Sanitary orderlies will form rear party to clean up.

    "A" Section Horse Transport will parade complete at 10 a.m., "B" Section at 10-15 a.m., "C" Section at 10-30 a.m. Transport will proceed immediately to destination, taking over the horse lines on arrival.

    Mechanical Transport will proceed independently at 10 a.m.

    The Quartermaster will arrange for surplus baggage to be conveyed to new site by 11 a.m.

    The stables at GROOTE KWINTE FARM and billets at COXYDE will be handed over to the Town Major, COXYDE, by Captain N.H.H.HASKINS on completion of move.

Issued at 8.30 p.m.
Distribution :-
Copy No.1. O.C., "A" Section.
Copy No.2. O.C., "B" Section.
" " 3. O.C., "C" Section.
" " 4. Quartermaster.
" " 5. Staff Capt. 125 Bde.

Lieut.-Colonel,
Comdg.1/3rd East Lancs.Field Ambulance.

Copy No.6. A.S.C., W.O.
" " 7. Sgt.Dobson. A.S.C., M.T.
" " 8/9. War Diary.
" " 10. File.

SECRET   Copy No. 10

1/3rd East Lancashire Field Ambulance.

Order No. 21.

R.A.M.C. 42nd Divisional Order No.28.
Reference Maps 1/100,000 Sheets 1A & 5A.
            1/40,000 Sheets 11, 12, 19, 20.

November 16th, 1917.

1. The 42nd Division is being relieved by the 133rd French Division, and moves out of the XVth Corps Area to the First Army Area via WORMHOUDT.

2. The 1/3rd East Lancs. Field Ambulance will march with the 125th Brigade.

3. Ambulance Cars of 1/1st East Lancs. Field Ambulance will rejoin their Unit at 10 a.m. on morning of the 19th inst.

4. Trench Maps will be handed over on relief.

5. The A.D.S. and bearer posts will be relieved by the French on the night 18th/19th, also personnel at Soup Kitchens and Trench Foot Centres.
R.A.M.C. personnel, sectional equipment and medical comforts will be conveyed to Headquarters in Ambulance Cars.
Lists of Ordnance Stores left behind will be prepared in duplicate, showing locality, one copy being handed to Headquarters, 125th Brigade, for transmission to O.C., Rear Party.
Drugs, Dressings, and Reserve Rations will be handed over to the French, receipts being obtained.

6. The Field Ambulance will parade in Marching Order on the 19th, at an hour to be notified later, and proceed by march route to ADINKERKE, and thence proceed by barge to TETEGHEM.

7. The Horse Transport in charge of Capt. DELAFIELD, will proceed by march route, under orders from G.O.C., 125th Bde.

8. The Mechanical Transport will proceed independently under orders of O.C., Field Ambulance.

9. "C" Section will hold itself in readiness to proceed independently if so ordered.

10. All surplus stores will be loaded on a lorry on the morning of the 19th, at an hour to be notified later, a baggage guard of one N.C.O. and 2 men accompanying this lorry. 2 days' rations to be carried.

11. The Soup Kitchens will be maintained in working order on the night 18th/19th, free issues of cocoa and Oxo being made to all troops.

12. Supplies will be drawn from 125th Brigade dump daily. Site of dump will be notified to Unit.

Issued at 10:35 am
                                                  Lieut.-Colonel,
                                       Commanding 1/3rd East Lancs. Field Ambce.

Distribution :-
Copy No. 1. O.C., "A" Section.
  "   " 2. O.C., "B" Section.
  "   " 3. O.C., "C" Section.   Copy No. 7. French Medical Unit.
  "   " 4. Capt. Delafield.   "   " 8. A.S.C, W.O.
  "   " 5. Quartermaster.   "   " 9. Sgt. Dobson, A.S.C., M.T.
  "   " 6. Staff Capt., 125th Bde.   "   " 10/11. War Diary.
                                            "   " 12. File.

SECRET.   Copy No. ..6..
                        Addendum to
            1/3rd East Lancashire Field Ambulance Order No.21.

Reference Order No.21. para.9.

                                                November 16th, 1917.

    1. "C" Section is detailed to move under orders
       of C.R.A.

    2. O.C., "C" Section will report to Staff Captain
       R.A. Headquarters COXYDE BAINS on 21st instant
       for orders.

    3. The Section will be rationed under Regimental
       arrangements up to and for the 22nd instant.
       Subsequently they will be rationed by 428th
       Coy., A.S.C.

    4. The Section will proceed as strong as possible
       with horse transport, mobilization equipment,
       and Motor Ambulances.
       Application is being made to Headquarters, R.A.,
       for extra transport for surplus baggage and stores

    5. They will collect and evacuate sick from the
       group with which they march.

                                                [signature]
Issued at ..8pm......
                                                Lieut.-Colonel,
Distribution :-   Commanding 1/3rd E.Lancs. Fld. Ambce.

Copy No.1. O.C., "C" Section.
  "   " 2. Quartermaster.
  "   " 3. 428th Coy., A.S.C.
  "   " 4. A.S.C., W.O.
  "   " 5. Sgt.Dobson, A.S.C.,M.T.
  "   " 6/7.War Diary.
  "   " 8. File.
  "   " 9. Capt.Delafield.

SECRET.   Copy No. ...9...

1/3rd East Lancashire Field Ambulance.

Order No. 22.

R.A.M.C. 42nd Division Order No.29.
Reference Maps 1/40,000 Sheets 36.A.
           and BETHUNE Combined Sheet.

November 25th, 1917.

---

1. The 42nd Division relieves the 25th Division in the GIVENCHY and Canal Sectors on 27th and 28th instants.

2. The 1/3rd E.Lancs. Field Ambulance (less one section) will march to the new area with and under orders of 127th Inf. Brigade and will take over the evacuation of the GIVENCHY Sector from an Ambulance of 25th Division with Headquarters at MESPLAUX FARM X.14.a.9.7. on 27th instant.

3. The Field Ambulance will parade in marching order at 8-0 a.m and proceed by march route to BETHUNE, where it will billet for the night. Water bottles will be filled.

4. Halts for 5 minutes at 25 past the hour and for 10 minutes at 10 to the hour will be made. Also a mid-day halt for 1 hour and ten minutes at 11-50 a.m.; the Quartermaster will arrange for hot tea and a meal at this hour, and horses will be watered.

5. An advance party of 12 N.C.Os. and men in charge of Capt. HENRY will proceed by lorry at 7-30 a.m., and report to O.C. Field Ambulance at MESPLAUX FARM. Two days' rations will be carried.

6. A guard of 1 N.C.O. and 2 men will be detailed for surplus stores, which will be loaded on the lorry on arrival. Two days' rations will be carried.

7. All wagons will be packed on 25th instant, all hospital equipment being returned to wagons.

8. No.354002 Sgt. J.C.Cowan will proceed on bicycle at 7-0 a.m. and report to Town Major, BETHUNE, for billets which have already been allotted.

9. Rations will be loaded by 7-30 a.m. 26th instant on Train wagon which will report on 25th instant.

10. Mechanical Transport will proceed independently under Capt. DELAFIELD, who will arrange to collect sick and stragglers on the march.

Issued at 8.35 p.m.

Distribution :-

Copy No. 1. Capt. H.Henry.
  "   " 2. Capt. F.G.Prestwich.
  "   " 3. Capt. M.E.Delafield.
  "   " 4. Quartermaster.
  "   " 5. 25th Div. Field Ambce.
  "   " 6. W.O., A.S.C.
  "   " 7. 125th Brigade.
  "   " 8. 127th Brigade.
  "   " 9/10. War Diary.
  "   " 11. File.

Lieut.-Colonel,
Commanding 1/3rd E.Lancs. Field Ambce.

SECRET. Copy No: ....7....

1/3rd East Lancashire Field Ambulance.

Operation Order No: 23.

Reference Map France.
BETHUNE. Ed.6. 1/40,000.   November 26th 1917.

1. The 1/3rd East Lancashire Field Ambulance will relieve the 77th Field Ambulance in the line at MESPLAUX FARM X.14.A.9.7. marching from BETHUNE at 9a.m. on 27/11/17.

2. O.C. "A" Section will detail one Officer, one N.C.O., one Clerk, 2 Nursing Orderlies, one Cook, eight bearers, and one Batman for duty at TUNING FORK A.D.S.
   One Daimler and two wheeled stretchers will be taken with this party, also necessary section equipment.

3. O.C. "B" Section will detail one Officer, one N.C.O., one Clerk, 2 Nursing Orderlies, one Cook, twelve bearers, and one Batman for duty at LONE FARM A.D.S.
   One Daimler, ~~one Water Cart~~ and four wheeled stretchers will accompany this party, also necessary section equipment.
   O.C. "B" Section will detail one Officer, necessary personnel and equipment for duty at the Main Dressing Station.

4. The Disposal of urgent cases will be to No. 33 Cas. Clearing Station BETHUNE, ordinary cases will be sent to Nos. 51 & 54 Casualty Clearing Stations, MERVILLE.

5. The Mechanical Transport will proceed independently, in charge of the N.C.O. A.S.C.M.T. to X.14.A.9.7. on 27/11/17.

6. On arrival at Main Dressing Station MESPLAUX FARM the Train wagon will be unloaded and sent back to D.H.Q., and two days rations will be drawn by the Driver.

7. D.A.D.O.S. will be at LOCON on the 28th inst.

8. The Field Cashier's Office will be at LES LOBES.

9. Leave parties will proceed from BETHUNE. They will be accommodated at the Wing at FERHY-DU-ROY the day previous to entrainment.

Issued at...7.10pm....
Distribution:-
Copy No. 1. O.C. "A" Section
  "   " 2. O.C. "B" Section.
  "   " 3. Quartermaster.
  "   " 4. N.C.O. 1/c A.S.C.M.T.
  "   " 5. 127th Brigade.
  "   " 6. 77th Field Ambulance.
  "   " 7. & 8 War Diary.
  "   " 9. File.

Lieut-Colonel R.A.M.C.T.
Cmdg. 1/3rd East Lancs. Fld. Ambulance.

WAR DIARY

OF

1/3rd EAST LANCASHIRE FIELD AMBULANCE.

FROM :- December 1st 1917   TO :- December 31st, 1917.

(VOLUME XII)

WAR DIARY
or
INTELLIGENCE SUMMARY
(Erase heading not required.)

Army Form C. 2118

Place	Date	Hour	Summary of Events and Information	Remarks and references to Appendices
MESPLAUX Farm	1/12/17	1000	C.O. accompanied A.D.M.S. to Tuning fork A.D.S. Thence to R.A.P. of 1/8 Manchesters & up to front line of trenches.	
		1500	1st Lieutenant DOUGLASS proceeded to LONE FARM for duty there as additional officer. 21 cases admitted to Field Ambulance	
"	2/12/17	0500	Orders received to relieve 25th Field Ambulance at HARLEY STREET A.D.S. A. 20. d. 27. Section under Captain HASKINS proceed & moved units in this duty.	Capt Bethume joined
		0900	C.O. visited HARLEY STREET A.D.S. & arranged details of relief	
		1300	C.O. attended conference at Allied A.D.M.S.	relief completed 12 noon
		1600	26 cases admitted to Field Ambulance	
"	3/12/17		1st Lieutenant DOUGLASS returned to M.D.S. for duty. After much of surgery extra being carried out off M.D.S. fine trestle ridges being cleared & refixed. 3 additional motor ambulances reported for duty at M.D.S. as attached to the Field Ambulance. 4 cases admitted to Field Ambulance	
"	4/12/17	0915	C.O. visited A.D.S. HARLEY STREET & proceeded to HERTFORD Rd R.A.P. & front line Trenches with A.D.M.S. & Captain HASKINS. On journey to LONE FARM & TUNING FORK A.D.S., relieved by personnel from M.D.S. MESPLAUX. Relief work at M.D.S., A.D.S.s & R.A.Ps continues. 29 cases admitted to Field Ambulance.	
"	5/12/17	1500	White washing & repairing of R.A.P.s, A.D.Ss & M.D.S. continues. RELAY POST being thoroughly cleaned & white washed. C.O. attended a lecture by D.M.S. 1st Army @ HOUDAIN (Army Hygiene) 12 cases admitted to Field Ambulance.	
"	6/12/17	0900	White washing & repairing being continued - an already oven being built in cookhouse	
		0945	D.M.S. 1st Army, D.D.M.S. XV Corps & A.D.M.S. Division visited the M.D.S., then proceeded to	

Army Form C. 2118.

WAR DIARY
or
INTELLIGENCE SUMMARY.
(Erase heading not required.)

Instructions regarding War Diaries and Intelligence Summaries are contained in F. S. Regs., Part II. and the Staff Manual respectively. Title pages will be prepared in manuscript.

Place	Date	Hour	Summary of Events and Information	Remarks and references to Appendices
MESPLAUX FARM	6/12/17		The ADSs & RAPs. C.O accompanied the inspection during the morning mostly LONE FARM ADS & RAPs & trenches in connection. The D.M.S. expressed his satisfaction with several places. 21 cases admitted to Field Ambulance.	MM
	7.12.17	1530	Repair work continued at ADSs & RAPs. Some party lost three days leave in lieu of. Adm. issued an order to Pay M Duty to Field Ambulance held 20 24 was 30 cases admitted to Field Ambulance.	MM App 34
	8.12.17	1000	White working 2 MDS cl. ADS & several RAPs being carried out now over hill at MDS & kitchen range at ADS LONE FARM improved refitting of Windy Corner RAP continued.	MM
			C.O. proceeded 1st Army School of Instruction @ BETHUNE to attend Field Lectures Course & addresses by DMS, & various students trained last DMS. 1 Lieutenant LONG & one N.C.O. returned to Field Ambulance after the. Drill also for week ending 8th to round of several of Wind Attacks 25 Cases admitted to Field Ambulance	App 35
	9.12.17	1030	White working on fair work at all ADS, RAPs continued. C.O. visited HARLEY STREET ADS. attached Naval RAPs at ROBERTSONS ALLEY and HERTFORD St. & gave them instructions several and stretcher places. 29 Cases admitted to Field Ambulance.	MM
	10.12.17	1045	C.O. made entire round of all several grounds, patients quarters & Transport lines. White working on fair work continued @ RAPs & ADSs.	MM
	11.12.17	0500	Wire received from 126 Bde stating about 50 gas casualties. 20 MACs CCS & Bde communicated a service of cars a 30 minute interval away from MDS MESPLAUX to LONE FARM ADS, & arrangements made to send 20 to 51 CCS, Captain HASKINS made fresh arrangement & an additional Room set to train for HARLEY STREET ADS, Captain PRESTWICH proceeded from LONE FARM ADS. One case died at	MM

Army Form C. 2118.

WAR DIARY
or
INTELLIGENCE SUMMARY.
(Erase heading not required.)

Instructions regarding War Diaries and Intelligence Summaries are contained in F. S. Regs., Part II. and the Staff Manual respectively. Title pages will be prepared in manuscript.

Place	Date	Hour	Summary of Events and Information	Remarks and references to Appendices
NESPLAUX FARM	11.12.17	10-00	LONE FARM A.D.S. "on" an M.D.S., but all cases requiring collects & examined. C.O. made up to the A.D.S. & visited the trenches where the casualties occurred, & saw that evacuation was working satisfactorily. 80 Cases admitted to Field Ambulance (which report passed through LONE FARM A.D.S. Captain J.A. CRAIG reports his arrival in being posted to this Unit.	Appendix
"	12.12.17	15.00	Rain went to A.D.S.S. & R.A.P.s continues himself in the direction of the gas curtains. C.O. attended lecture at 1st Army Headquarters by D.A.Q.M.G. on "A Staff duties". Major attached doing his administration by this Unit. Viz:- M.D.S. at MESPLAUX FARM (X.14.a.9.3.) A.D.S at TUNING FORK (F.S.A.S.O.) LONE FARM (A.7.d.1.1.3) "HARLEY STREET (A.20.d.1.3.7.) with R.A.Ps at A.2.b.4.9., A.8.d.4.4.3, A.8.c.8.4, GORRE A.27.a.6.9., A.21.a.5.7.3, A.14.d.2.1.3 LE PREOL, & Bear Relay Posts @ A.1.b.33, & A.14.a.9.8. A motor ambulance being stationed at each A.D.S. Case being brought to TUNING FORK & LONE FARM A.D.S. by motor ambulance within during the day & on a trolley on the Decauville railway by night cases in heavy from HERTFORD STREET R.A.P. to HARLEY STREET A.D.S. & travel manuvered & from ROBERTSONS ALLEY R.A.P., & hard (stretcher) during the day & Decauville by night. Urgent surgical & medical cases evacuated direct from A.D.S. to C.C.S., all others to M.D.S. 110 cases admitted to Field Ambulance.	Appendix 36
	13.12.17		Captain CRAIG & one NCO proceeded to Divisional Gas school for a four days course. A party of ... officers of the American Medical Corps visited the M.D.S. & went round the whole place taking himself & Thanks for granted, & expressed their pleasure with the organisation. Rain went to R.A.P.s continues the relief HARLEY STREET A.D.S. by the #2 2 F. Ambulance. 34 cases admitted to Field Ambulance. Colin P.O. 25.	Appendix 37
	14.12.17		Rain went of gas curtain continues. 30 cases admitted to Field Ambulance.	

WAR DIARY
or
INTELLIGENCE SUMMARY

(Erase heading not required.)

Army Form C. 2118

Place	Date	Hour	Summary of Events and Information	Remarks and references to Appendices
NESPLAUX FARM	15.12.17	0930	O.R. at TUNING FORK A.D.S. relieved. C.O. visited TUNING FORK A.D.S. & BARNTON Rd R.A.P., also some f.p.s. trenches. 19 Cases admitted to Field Ambulance	
"	16.12.17	0900	1st Lieutenant LONG took parade of Heavy Artillery & ZELOBES daily.	
		1300	Captain HASKINS & details rejoined Field Ambulance after relief by the 1/1 2nd Field Ambulance at HARLEY STREET A.D.S.	
		1400	C.O. attended conference at Office of A.D.M.S.	
			17 Cases admitted to aid Ambulance	
	17.12.17	1000	1st Lieutenant DOUGLASS proceeded to TUNING FORK A.D.S. in relief of Captain HENRY who in turn proceeded to LONE FARM in relief of Captain DELAFIELD who in turn rejoined H.Q.	
		1415	Captain PRESTWICH proceeded to TUNING FORK A.D.S. in relief of 1st Lieutenant DOUGLASS.	
		1515	1st Lieutenant LONG proceeded to temporary medical charge 210 Bde R.F.A.	
		1530	1st Lieutenant DOUGLASS proceeded to temporary medical charge 1/1 Lewis Fusiliers	
			15 Cases admitted to Field Ambulance	
	18.12.17	1045	C.O. visited TUNING FORK A.D.S. Ration Corner RELAY POST, R.A.P.s @ HARTZ REDOUBT, PONT FIXE & WINDY CORNER & A.D.S. LONE FARM. Captain CRAIG returned from course of Gas School, FESTUBERT for opening of the station at NESPLAUX 4 G.S. wagon loads of bricks brought in. Timber trench floor of wagon park almost completed. 2 2 Cases admitted to Field Ambulance	
	19.12.17		clearing up & reconstruction work at RATION CORNER Relay Post commenced. repair work of stables carried on. Further loads of A.S.C. with rations arrived. Topology improved.	
		1400	C.O. accompanied A.D.M.S. to TUNING FORK A.D.S. & RATION CORNER Relay Post	
		1415	19 Cases admitted to Field Ambulance	

WAR DIARY
or
INTELLIGENCE SUMMARY
(Erase heading not required.)

Army Form C. 2118

Place	Date	Hour	Summary of Events and Information	Remarks and references to Appendices
MESPLAUX FARM	20.12.17		Refusal states continued.	M.M.H.
		11.00	Quarterly balancing of mens accounts & forwarding pay.	
		13.40	C.O. visited 2nd N.E. FARM ADS. C.O. visits ADMS on several points relating to Ration Corner & Lone Farm.	
		14.20	Captain HENRY returns to Hqrs on being relieved at LONE FARM by Captain CRAIG.	
		19.00	14 cases admitted to Field Ambulance. On N.C.O. + 20 men reported to T.M.B. officer @ PONT FIXE for fatigue intervening @ 4.00.	
	21.12.19		C.O. proceeded on leave to U.K. The command during his absence devolving on Captain H. HENRY.	M.M.H.
			Refuse fatigues continued. Reconstruction work at Relay Post Ration Corner continued. 10 cases admitted to Field Ambulance.	M.M.H.
		17.00	On N.C.O. + 20 men report to T.M.B. officer at PONT FIXE for fatigue. RELAY POST RATION	
	22.12.17	10.30	Capt HENRY (acting C.O.) visited LONE FARM A.D.S. CORNER & TUNING FORK A.D.S.	M.M.H.
		14.00	Capt HENRY attended conference at office of A.D.M.S.	
			On N.C.O. + 20 men report to T.M.B. officer at PONT FIXE for fatigue.	
		17.00	10 cases admitted to Field Ambulance.	
	23.12.17		Work at RELAY POST. RATION CORNER completed till R.E. are ready to begin work. Refuse fatigues continued. 8 patients admitted to Field Ambulance.	M.M.H.
		17.00	On N.C.O. + 20 men report to T.M.B. officer at PONT FIXE for fatigue.	
	24.12.17		Refuse fatigues continued.	M.M.H.
		15.00	R.A.M.C. 4th Divisional Orders No.31 received re Gas attack.	
		14.30	O/C ADSs instructed to arrange para availability & instructed re disposition of patients at LONE FARM A.D.S. for the night.	

Army Form C. 2118

WAR DIARY
or
INTELLIGENCE SUMMARY
(Erase heading not required.)

Place	Date	Hour	Summary of Events and Information	Remarks and references to Appendices
MESPLEUX FARM	24.12.17	1900	Bufton HASKINS proceeded to LONE A.D.S. A second DAIMLER CAR detailed to LONE FARM A.D.S. for the night.	144.
		1930	Two Bambu bars from 1/1 F.Amb. told that reported there arrived. A second Motor Ambulance from D.A.M.C. for the night.	
		2.00	1st LIEUT. LONG returned from temporary medical charge of 210th Bde. R.F.A. 13 patients admitted to the Field Ambulance.	
"	25.12.17	17.30	1st Lieut DOUGLAS returned from temporary medical charge of 4/7 Lanc. FUSILIERS and reported to TWINING FORK A.D.S. in relief of 2/Lt PRESTWICH who returned to HQrs. 23 patients admitted to Field Ambulance.	144.
"	26.12.17	10.30	1st Lieut. LONG proceeded to LONE FARM A.D.S. in relief of 2/Lt GRAIG who returned to HQrs. Reported at Relay Posts + R.APs. relieved from HQrs PARIS.	144.
		11.00	2/Lt PRESTWICH proceeded on 4 days leave to PARIS.	
		17.30	Bufton HASKINS proceeded to LONE FARM A.D.S.	
		17.00	10 patients admitted to Field Ambulance. 1 N.C.O. + 20 men report to T.M.B. officer at PONTIFIXE for fatigue.	
"	27.12.18	1700	Work on stables continued. Two G.S. wagons reported to 425 Field Coy R.E. 1 N.C.O. + 20 men report to T.M.B. officer at PONTIFIXE for fatigue. 25 patients admitted to Field Ambulance.	144.
"	28.12.18	1700	Work on stables continued. Two G.S. wagons reported to 425 Field Coy R.E. 1 N.C.O. + 20 men report to T.M.B. Officer at PONTIFIXE for fatigue. 13 patients admitted to the Field Ambulance. Orders received for an officer to proceed on unmounted duty. Field Ambulance Order No 26 issued.	144. Appendix 32.

Army Form C. 2118

WAR DIARY
or
INTELLIGENCE SUMMARY

(Erase heading not required.)

Instructions regarding War Diaries and Intelligence Summaries are contained in F.S. Regs., Part II. and the Staff Manual respectively. Title Pages will be prepared in manuscript.

Place	Date	Hour	Summary of Events and Information	Remarks and references to Appendices
MESPLEUX FARM	29.12.17	0800	1 NCO & 12 men reported to RE for work on new ADS at RATION CORNER.	
		1030	Capt CRAIG returned. LIEUT DOUGLASS at TUNING FORK ADS	
			Lieut DOUGLASS proceeded to temporary Medical charge of 1/6 Manchester Regt.	1 Aff
		12.15	DDMS 1st CORPS with ADMS 42 Div visited MDS. & expressed his satisfaction with arrangements	
		15.00	2 PS began report to RE at KANTARA DUMP.	Appendix 39.
			26 patients admitted to the Field Amb.	
			Diet sheet for week ending 29th inst. issued to personnel attached	
"	30.12.17	0830	1 NCO & 12 Men report to RE for work on new MDS RATION CORNER	
		0900	Two Cars 1/1 E.L.F.Amb. reported with 9 cases of Scabies.	1 Aff
		10.00	Two Cars 1/1 E.L.F.Amb. & 2 Cars 1/3 E.L.F.Amb. proceeded to XV Corps Skin Depot MERVILLE + brought back 12 Scabies + Impetigo cases. The Scabies cases were admitted to the Isolation Wards	
			were sent in cars of 1/1 E.F.Amb. to 161st FOUQUIERES	
		15.00	2 PS began report to RE at KANTARA DUMP.	
			44 cases (total) admitted to Field Ambulance	
			Reported ADS LONE FARM that RAP HERTS REDOUBT was seriously damaged by shellfire. RE advise asked for.	
"	31.12.17	0830	1 NCO + 12 men report to RE for work on new ADS. RATION CORNER.	1 Aff
		15.00	3 PS began report to RE at KANTARA DUMP.	
			Divn Gas OFFICER inspected MDS with reference to protection against gas.	
			Our RE officer with Cpl HASKINS visited RAP HERTS REDOUBT & arranging to repair the damage.	
			17 Patients admitted to the Field Amb.	

31/12/17.

Howard Henry
Capt.
for O/c 1/3 E. Lanc Field Ambulance

SECRET. Appendix 34   Copy No ......4......

1/3rd East Lancashire Field Ambulance.

Order No. 24.

Reference Map BETHUNE Combined
Sheet A.13.c.1.8.
A.D.M.S. 42nd Division.

December 7th, 1917.

1. Instructions have been received from A.D.M.S. 42nd Division for Captain HALE, M.O.R.C., U.S.A., Officer in Medical Charge 1/6th Lancashire Fusiliers to be relieved forthwith.

2. 1st Lieutenant R.A. DOUGLASS, M.O.R.C., U.S.A., will proceed forthwith to Harley Street Advanced Dressing Station, and report to O.C. Advanced Dressing Station, who will provide a guide to lead him up to the Regimental Aid Post at Hertford Street.

3. 1st Lieutenant R.A. DOUGLASS will then report to O.C., 1/6th Lancashire Fusiliers that he has arrived in relief of Captain HALE, M.O.R.C., U.S.A.

4. Necessary transport will be provided.

Lieut.-Colonel,
Commanding 1/3rd E. Lancs. Field Ambulance.

Issued at 3.30pm

Distribution :-

Copy No. 1. O.C., 1/6th Lancs. Fus.
 "   " 2. O.C. A.D.S. Harley Street.
 "   " 3. 1st Lieut. R.A. Douglass.
 "   " 4. War Diary.
 "   " 5. War Diary.
 "   " 6. File.

1/3rd East Lancashire Field Ambulance.

Scale of Diet for Week ending 8-12-1917.

	Sunday.	Monday.	Tuesday.	Wednesday.	Thursday.	Friday.	Saturday.
Breakfast 7.30.a.m.	Tea Quaker Oats Bread Fried Bacon	Tea Bread Fried Bacon	Tea Porridge Bread Fried Bacon	Tea Bread Fried Rissoles	Tea Porridge Bread Fried Bacon	Tea Bread Fried Bacon	Tea Porridge Bread Toasted Cheese
Lunch 12-30 p.m.	Tea Bread Butter Cheese Jam	Tea Bread Butter Brawn Jam	Tea Bread Butter Cheese Jam	Tea Bread Butter Cheese Jam	Tea Bread Butter Toasted Cheese Jam	Tea Bread Butter Cold Beef Jam	Tea Bread Butter Boiled Ham Jam
Dinner 5.0.p.m.	Irish Stew Boiled Onions Boiled Potatoes	Stewed Steak Beans Boiled Potatoes Rice Pudding	Grilled Steak Stewed Steak Boiled Onions Boiled Potatoes	Irish Stew Boiled Potatoes Rice Pudding	Boiled Beef Roast Beef Beans Boiled Potatoes	Irish Stew Beans Boiled Potatoes Rice Pudding	Grilled Steak Boiled Onions Boiled Potatoes
Supper 8.0.p.m.	Tea Bread. Jam.	Tea Biscuits Cheese	Tea	Tea Biscuits.	Tea Biscuits	Tea	Tea Biscuits

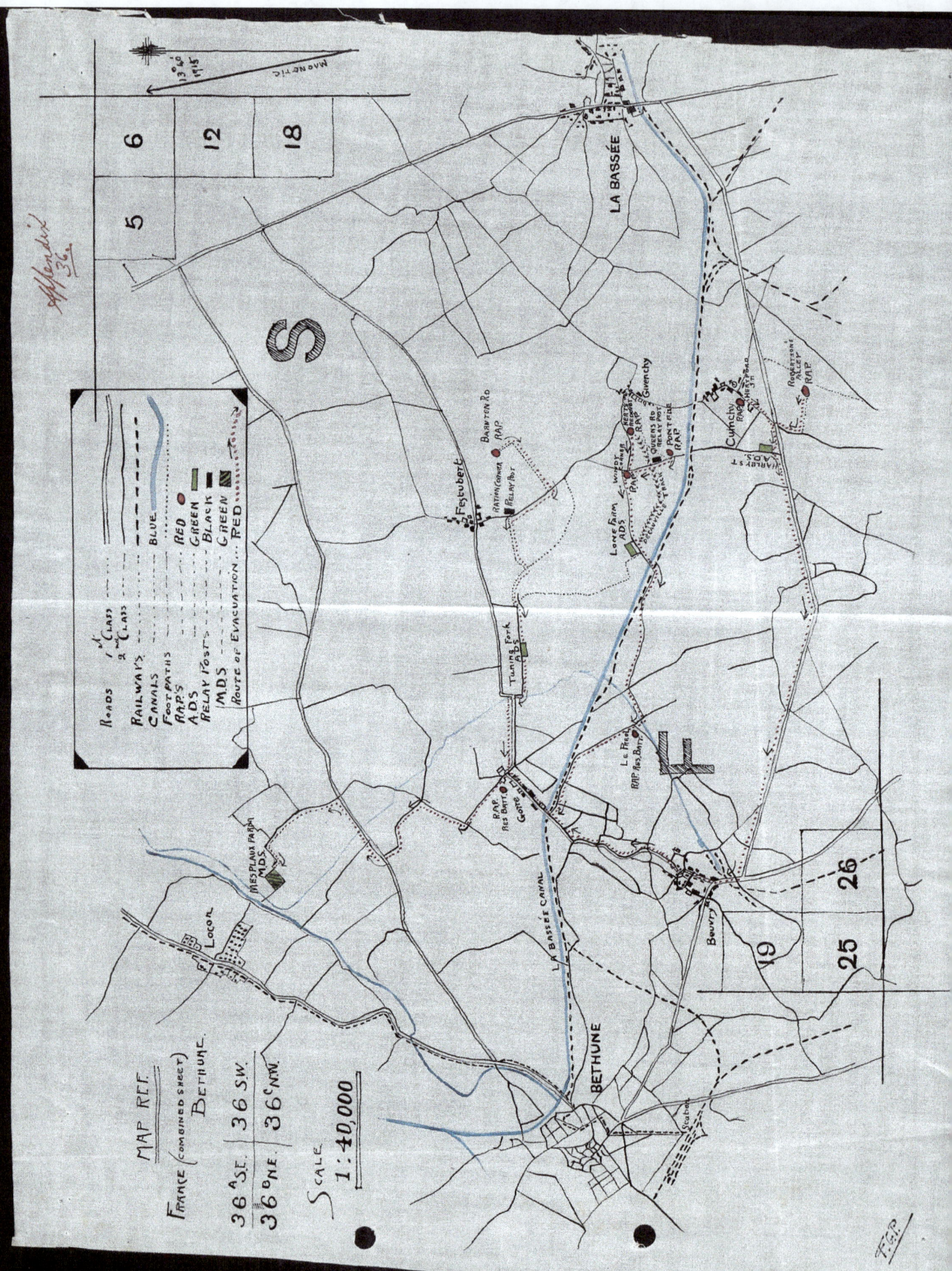

SECRET   Copy No. 3

1/3rd East Lancashire Field Ambulance.

Order No. 25.

Reference Map 1/40,000 BETHUNE Combined Sheet.
 1/10,000 Sheet 36.C. N.W.1.
 R.A.M.C. 42nd Division Order No.30.

December 13, 1917

1. The 1/1st East Lancs. Field Ambulance on 16th instant will take over from 1/3rd East Lancs. Field Ambulance the Advanced Dressing Station HARLEY STREET (A.20.d.3.9.) and evacuation of the line south of the Canal.

2. Headquarters, 1/1st East Lancs. Field Ambulance will be at the Main Dressing Station, ECOLE CATORIVE, BETHUNE. (E.5.c.5.8.)

3. O.C., Advanced Dressing Station, HARLEY STREET will arrange direct with O.C. 1/1st East Lancs. Field Ambulance for the relief.

4. On completion of the relief, the personnel will march by the shortest route to rejoin Field Ambulance Headquarters at MESPLAUX FARM.

5. All Field Ambulance equipment will be collected at A.D.S. prior to relief, and then sent back to Headquarters by Mot or Ambulance Cars. Area Stores only being handed over, the usual receipts being obtained.

                                        W.M. Cunningham
                                        Lieut.-Colonel,
                                        Commanding 1/3rd East Lancs. Field Ambulance.

Issued at 2 p.m.

Distribution :-

Copy No. 1. O.C. A.D.S., Harley Street.
 "   "   2. O.C. 1/1st E.Lancs. Field Ambce.
 "   "   3. War Diary.
 "   "   4. War Diary.
 "   "   5. File.
 "   "   6. 126 Bde Headquarters.

SECRET.   Copy No. 3

<u>1/3rd East Lancashire Field Ambulance.</u>

<u>Order No. 26.</u>

Reference Map BETHUNE Combined Sheet.
A.D.M.S. 42nd Division.

December 28th, 1917.

1. 1st Lieutenant R.A.DOUGLASS, M.O.R.C.,U.S.A., is detailed for duty as Officer in Medical of the 1/6th Battalion Manchester Regiment in relief of Lieut. J.D.LAIDLAW, proceeding to England on expiration of contract.

2. He will report to Officer Commanding 1/6th Battalion Manchester Regiment on 29th instant.

3. Necessary transport will be provided.

Howard Henry
Captain,
<u>Commanding 1/3rd East Lancs. Field Ambulance.</u>

Issued at 9/0 a.m.

Distribution :-

Copy No. 1. 1st Lieut. R.A.Douglass.
"   " 2. O.C. 1/6th Manchester Rgt.
"   " 3. War Diary.
"   " 4. War Diary.
"   " 5. File.

1/3rd East Lancashire Field Co.

Scale of rations for week ending Dec 29th 1914

	Sunday	Monday	Tuesday	Wednesday	Thursday	Friday	Saturday
Breakfast 7.30 am	Tea, Bread, Frying, Fried Bacon	Tea, Bread, Frying, Fried Bacon	Tea, Bread, Porridge, Fried Bacon, Toasted Cheese, Jam	Tea, Bread, Fried Bacon, Frizzy/Puddg	Tea, Bread, Porridge, Fried Bacon	Tea, Bread, Fried Bacon	Coffee, Biscuits, Fried Bacon
Lunch 12.30 pm	Bread Butter, Cheese, Jam	Bread Butter, Boiled Ham, Jam	Dinner:- Soup, Roast Beef, Sausage, Three Vegetables, Plum Pudding & White Sauce, Dessert, Coffee, Biscuits	Tea, Bread Butter, Cheese, Victoria Cake, Jam	Tea, Bread Butter, Cheese, Jam	Tea, Bread Butter, Toasted Cheese, Jam	Tea, Biscuits, Butter, Cheese, Jam
Dinner 5.0 pm	Grilled Steak, Stewed Steak, Beans, Boiled Potatoes, Rice Pudding	Irish Stew, Onion, Boiled Potatoes	Tea:- Cold Beef, Custard & Fruit, Cake	Irish Stew, Bread, Boiled Potatoes	Roast Mutton, Grilled Chops, Beans, Boiled Potatoes, Rice Pudding	Irish Stew, Onion, Boiled Potatoes, Boiled Potatoes	Irish Stew, Fried Rissole, Onion
Supper 8.0 pm	Tea, Biscuits	Tea	Tea, Biscuits & Cheese	Tea	Tea	Tea	Tea

19

No. of Pack in Store..............

Inventory of Articles in possession of No._____ Corps_____
on his admission into the _____ Hospital at _____
Date of Admission _____ Date of Discharge, Transfer or Death _____

	Number				For use only in the Field on Active Service.	No.	Articles retained by the Patient for use in the Ward.	No.
	New	Good	Worn	Bad				
Cloak or Great Coat and Cape					Ammunition, rounds		Blacking, Tin	
*Drawers, pairs					Apron, Kilt		Books, Devotional	
*Frock with badges					*Bandolier		*Boots or Shoes pairs, with laces	
*Gaiters, pairs					Bayonet and Scabbard		*Braces	
Garters, Highland, pairs					Belts { Pouch / Waist		Brushes { Blacking / Hair / Polishing / Shaving / Tooth	
*Gloves, pairs								
*Handkerchiefs					Binoculars			
Haversack					Bottle, Water			
Head-dress, complete					Brassard			
Hose-tops, pairs					Cutters, Wire		*Cap with badge	
*Jacket, with badges					Dirk and Scabbard		Comb, Hair	
Jersey or Waistcoat, Cardigan					Disc, Identity		Helmet (at Tropical Stations)	
Kilt					Dressing, Field		Razor in Case	
Plaid					Fork			
Purse and Belt, Highland					Haversack			
Putties, pairs					Holdall		**Articles sent to the Laundry.**	
*Sash					Housewife			
Scarf					Implements, intrenching		*Drawers, pairs	
Shirts, Flannel					Iron ration and cover		Handkerchiefs	
*Socks, pairs					Knife, clasp		Shirts, Flannel	
Spurs, pairs					„ table		*Socks, pairs	
*Stockings, pairs					Mineral Jelly, Tin		Stockings, pairs	
Titles, metal					Pullthrough		Towels	
Towels					Pistol		*Vests	
*Trousers, Trews, Pantaloons, or Breeches					Rifle, complete			
					Sling, rifle			
Tunic with badges					Spoon		Date sent......................	
*Vests					*Straps			
Valuables :—					Sword or Claymore and Scabbard			
					Tin, Mess, and Cover		Initials of person receiving articles to be washed	
					Web Equipment			
					Belt, waist			
					Braces			
					Carriers { Water bottle / Cartridge / Intrenching tool		Date returned........................	
					Frog			
					Haversack		Initials of Pack Store Keeper	
					Pack			
					Straps, supporting			
					Whistle			

* Insert Description.

Signature of patient or other person
   handing kit into Store _____

Signature of Pack Store Keeper _____

Countersignature of Sister or N.C.O.
   of Ward (if patient is unable to sign) _____

Issued from Store on _____

Received by _____

WAR DIARY OF

1/3RD EAST LANCASHIRE FIELD AMBULANCE.

FROM :- January 1st, 1918   TO :- January 31st, 1918.

(VOLUME I)

Army Form C. 2118

WAR DIARY
INTELLIGENCE SUMMARY
(Erase heading not required.)

Instructions regarding War Diaries and Intelligence Summaries are contained in F.S. Regs, Part II. and the Staff Manual respectively. Title Pages will be prepared in manuscript.

Place	Date	Hour	Summary of Events and Information	Remarks and references to Appendices
MESPLEUX FARM	1.1.18	0830	1 N.C.O. & 12 men report to R.E. for work on return to MDS at RATION CORNER.	NA
		1030	Capt HASKINS returned from LONE FARM to MDS.	
		1430	Capt DELAFIELD proceeded to LONE FARM ADS in relief of LIEUT LONG who returned to MDS.	
		1500	2 G.S. wagons report to R.E. KANTARA DUMP.	
		1530	Capt PREST WICH returned from short leave to PARIS.	
			13 patients admitted to Field Ambulance.	
"	2.1.18	0830	1 N.C.O. & 12 men report to R.E. for work on new ADS at RATION CORNER.	NA
		0900	2 G.S. wagons report to 429 Field Coy R.E.	
			Capt HENRY proceeded on leave to U.K. His command devolve on Capt HASKINS.	
			1 patient admitted to Field Amb.	
	3.1.18	0900	1 G.S. wagon to 429 Coy R.E.	NNNA
		0900	O/O.C. (Capt Haskins) accompanied ADMS 42nd Div. to TUNING FORK & LONE FARM ADS. returned to MDS at LONE FARM. 7 officers - 3 O.R. all men of this wounded by MUSTARD GAS	
		1200	Evacuation of GAS cases complete.	
		1700	20 SCABIES transferred to 1st Casualty Clearing Stn Dt.	
			32 patients admitted to Field Amb.	
	4.1.18	0900	3 G.S. wagons to R.E.	NNNA
		1400	2 G.S. wagons to R.E.	
			31 patients admitted to Field Amb.	
	6.1.18	0900	1 Wagon (G.S.) to R.E.	NNAA
		1000	O/O.C. (Capt Haskins) proceeded to TUNING FORK A.D.S. and visited new A.D.S. at RATION CORNER. 1 N.C.O. & 12 men have been reporting regularly each morning to R.E.	

WAR DIARY
INTELLIGENCE SUMMARY
(Erase heading not required.)

Army Form C. 2118

Place	Date	Hour	Summary of Events and Information	Remarks and references to Appendices
NEDONJX TH.	5.1.18		18 patients admitted to Field Amb.	
do.	6.1.18	0900	G.S. wagon to R.E.	
		1600	Capt PRESTWICH relieved Capt CRAIG at TUNING FORK A.D.S.	
			29 patients admitted to Field Amb.	
	7.1.18	0900	G.S. wagon to R.E.	
			17 patients admitted to Field Amb.	
	8.1.18		Lt Colonel CUNNINGHAM returns from leave & resumes command. Orders for relief of Unit by 1/2 E. Lanc Field Ambulance received. 25 patients admitted to Field Ambulance.	Appendix
	9.1.18	0900	Captain CRAIG proceeds to temporary medical charge of 1/2 Lanc Fusiliers (Field Ambulance orders No. 24)	Appendix 40.
		0915	Captain PURVIS & details from 1/2 E.L. Field Ambulance head 7th/of M.D.S. en route for 1/2 E Lanc A.D.S.'s relief - they moved down with our main party.	Appendix 41.
		1400	Captain NEAME & 1/2 E.L. Field Ambulance arrive & take over Hospital station of the M.D.S., in relief of this Unit as per Field Ambulance orders No. 28	
		1700	LONE FARM & TUNING FORK A.D.S's relieved by 1/2 E.L. Field Ambulance. Instructions for details to proceed to No.18 C.C.S cancelled (Field Ambulance orders No. 28). Instructions to proceed to No.18 C.C.S cancelled (Field Ambulance orders No. 21.)	Appendix 42.
	10.1.18	1000	Field Ambulance marched out & proceeded to billets in LOCON SOUTH area. Captain PRESTWICH proceeded on leave to U.K. Unit camped in section, each section being in a separate Farm, the A.S.C. & Transport & Workshops & ADM Stores & equipment also in a separate Farm. No sanitary arrangements, so latrine accommodation arranged for each with O.C. Sanitary Section for each billet.	

WAR DIARY
INTELLIGENCE SUMMARY
(Erase heading not required.)

Army Form C. 2118

Place	Date	Hour	Summary of Events and Information	Remarks and references to Appendices
LOCON (S.)	10.1.18	15.00	Billets have clay floors & straw drawn from forward Dumps, 4 Motor ambulances loaned to 2/2 E.L. Field Ambulance, also two civilian ambulances owing to a serious kind of casualties.	MPL Appendices 1+3.
		18.00	Lieutenant LONG proceeds to temporary gradual change 241 Bde R.F.A. (Field Ambulance late 2/29) Heavy thaw may in afts on a fortnight's frost.	
	11.1.18		Road very wet & muddy. C.O. inspected all billets & transport lines, men appear to have spent comfortable nights in spite of poor accommodation. Each of three sections & ASC are a fourth, in separate farms, and finding their own cost horses & funds ground.	MPL
		10.00	NCO inspection A. Section billets	
		14.00	NCO inspection C. Section billets seven wagons G.S. employed on divisional duties during the day, motor cars in use daily.	
	12.1.18	10.00	Met inspection B section billets	
		14.00	NCO inspection A.S.C. section	
		14.00	Spent chief a considerable time at remounts of R.A.M.C. Captain HASKINS proceeds to Divisional Hqrs as temporary D.T.D.M.S. vice Captain DALZELL on leave. One N.C.O. & S.C. (H.T.) proceeds to nearby Gas School. Two enfants & one Private qualified as ready Divisional N.C.O.s school. Lieutenant T.B.H. TABUTEAU (T.C.) attached arrive taken on strength of Unit. Lieutenant TABUTEAU proceeds to temporary medical charge 84th Army Bde R.F.A.	MPL
	13.1.18		NCO inspection of Unit completed Church parade. Latrines provided at each Billets now, though shelter not yet completed. Two men detailed bearing Sanitary section in making shelter trenches & cart filled. Three S.D. majors details for R.E. work. Unit class off taking in any cash.	MPL

WAR DIARY
INTELLIGENCE SUMMARY
(Erase heading not required.)

Army Form C. 2118

Place	Date	Hour	Summary of Events and Information	Remarks and references to Appendices
LOCON South	14.1.18	1700	Frost & heavy fall of snow during night. C.O. inspected all billets & horse lines. Recreational training of Bearers continued.	
		1300	Baths: arrangements of whole unit.	
		0800	A detail of 1 N.C.O. & 14 men proceeded to GORRE for duty with 2th. R.E. & to be attached to R.E. until further orders.	
	15.1.18	1400	Raining hard all day, no drill possible. Cross country running commenced. Roads very muddy, wet.	
		1430	O.C. #2 D[ivn] Train inspected Horse Transport.	
	16.1.18		Still raining hard, men's billets fairly dry, less roads & fields under water. 3.G.S. wagon to R.E. for day.	
	17.1.18		Still raining hard. 3 G.S. wagons to R.E. for day owing to the unsuitable state of the ground a great deal of ammunition being taken. Reported O.C. 42 Div[n]. Train embodied in Field Ambulance routine orders.	Appendix 44
	18.1.18		Roads still under water. 3 G.S. wagons to R.E. for day. Reparational Training tour. Farrier on farms as far as possible. Captain HENRY returned from leave.	
	19.1.18		Ground still very wet although rain ceased. 3 G.S. wagons to R.E. 1 limber G.S. & Sanitary Section. Programme of Lectures & N.C.O. to every week issued in Field Ambulance Routine orders. Captain DELAFIELD proceeded on leave to U.K.	Appendix 45

Army Form C. 2118

WAR DIARY
INTELLIGENCE SUMMARY
(Erase heading not required.)

Instructions regarding War Diaries and Intelligence Summaries are contained in F.S. Regs., Part II. and the Staff Manual respectively. Title Pages will be prepared in manuscript.

Place	Date	Hour	Summary of Events and Information	Remarks and references to Appendices
LOCON	20.1.18		3 S.S. wagons to R.E. The following Lectures & N.C.Os. were embodied in Field Troop & have today proceeded to be embodied in Field Troop, Mounterians Service Medal & Staff Sergeant ASHTON. Lieutenant ANDERTON.	
	21.1.18		3 S.S. wagons to R.E. 1st Lieutenant LONG returned from Temporary duty with 311th Bde. RFA. Snowing during afternoon. All billets now fitted up with Kleuten benches.	
	22.1.18	1000	3 S.S. wagons to R.E. Captain HENRY proceeded to Temporary duty with 1/4 East Lancs Regt. (Field Amb. Index 2.30) Lieutenant TABUTEAU returned from Temporary duty with 84th Bde Army Field Artillery. Staff of muster, meeting, lecture at the men of teams. County burying held on a farm to observe preparing of the Unit and Field Ambulance & Divisional Hqrs.	
	23.1.18		3 S.S. wagons to R.E. C.O. inspects each of the St. Neots clair. Bn. played Retreat at Divisional Hqrs. LOCON.	
	24.1.18		4 S.S. wagons to R.E. Tables, chairs being constructed for each billet Owing to mud & wet state of the ground, the men have again continued attention return the tents & billets retaining along site lanes today.	
	25.1.18		6 S.S. wagons to R.E. Band played Retreat at Divisional Hqrs LOCON. Enemy aircraft very active in evening, several bombs dropped in neighbourhood.	

WAR DIARY
INTELLIGENCE SUMMARY
(Erase heading not required.)

Army Form C. 2118

Place	Date	Hour	Summary of Events and Information	Remarks and references to Appendices
LOCON South	26.1.18		work on mens huts & latr. for billet continued. materials obtained for erection of drying room & incinerator.	MW
"	27.1.18		G/Surgeons Major Roberts promoted temporary Sergeant Major for the period of the war extract from London Gazette of January 4th :— INFANTRY. Brig. Genl Fusiliers Lieutenant (temp Lt Colonel RAMC.T.F.) H.H.B. CUNNINGHAM to be Captain (August 4. 1916) Notice received of Captain HENRY transferred away from the Unit, embodied in Field Ambulance Orders below No. 31.	Appendix Appendix 48
"	28.1.18	14.00	3 G.S. wagon to RE. C.O. visited 1st Army School of Instruction @ 22 C.C.S. Notice of Lieutenant G TABUTEAU to proceed temporary on detached duty embodied in Field Ambulance Orders No. 32	Appendix Appendix
"	29.1.18		15 O.R. still employed on detached duty with RE. 34 O.R. employed under "Q". 2 O.R. employed under Town Major. 3 G.S. wagon to R.E. Construction of tables, forms, boards for picquet & examination relieving room proceeding. 'C' Section billets completed with table, forms & bunks. 'B' Section completed with tables & forms. Class of instruction of junior officers graduates N.COs held daily under Sergeant Major.	Appendix
"	30.1.18	09.15 16.10	3 G.S. wagon to R.E. C.O. proceed with ADMS to 1st Army school of Instruction 22 C.C.S. Instruction of Lieut LONG to proceed on temporary detached duty embodied in Field Ambulance Orders No. 33	Appendix 50

WAR DIARY
INTELLIGENCE SUMMARY
(Erase heading not required.)

Army Form C. 2118

Place	Date	Hour	Summary of Events and Information	Remarks and references to Appendices
LOTON Sud	31.1.19		A Section billets fitted with tables & benches. B Section billets fitted with bunks & mira green. New incinerator under construction. New drying room partially built. 3.S.S wagons employed with R.E. whole day. Work on new mud walk protection for stables commenced. 15 O.R. still employed in detail duties with R.E. 94 O.R. still employed under Q. 2 O.R. still employed under Town Major & O.T.O.M.	

M.M.Cunningham
Lt.R.E.

SECRET   Copy No. ...3...

1/3rd East Lancashire Field Ambulance.

Order No. 27.

Reference Map BETHUNE Combined Sheet
A.D.M.S. 42nd Division.

January 8th, 1918.

1. Captain F.W.Craig R.A.M.C. (T.C.) is detailed for temporary medical charge of 1/8th Bn. Lancashire Fusiliers from 9th to 19th January inclusive during the absence of 1st Lieut. DICKINSON on course of instruction.

2. He will report to the Officer Commanding 1/8th Bn. Lancashire Fusiliers by 11-0 a.m. 9th instant.

3. Necessary transport will be provided.

                                            Lieut.-Colonel,
                              Commanding 1/3rd East Lancs. Field Ambulance.

Issued at 16.50

Distribution :-

Copy No. 1. Capt. F.W.Craig.
  "   " 2. O.C. 1/8th Lancs. Fus.
  "   " 3. War Diary.
  "   " 4. War Diary.
  "   " 5. File.

SECRET.   Copy No. ...7......

1/3rd East Lancashire Field Ambulance.

Order No. 28.

Reference Map 1/10,000 Sheet 36A S.E.4. 36 S.W.3.
" 36B N.E.2. 36C N.W.1.
1/40,000 BETHUNE Combined Sheet
42nd Division R.A.M.C. Order No. 33.

January 8th, 1918.

1. The 1/2nd E.Lancs. Field Ambulance will relieve the 1/3rd E.Lancs. Field Ambulance in the line on the 9th instant.

2. Captain PURVES and senior N.C.Os. of the 1/2nd E.Lancs. Field Ambulance will visit the various advanced posts in the line in the morning of the 9th instant. Os.C. A.D.Ss. will arrange for this party to be conducted round the posts, including R.A.Ps., in their respective areas.
   On the afternoon of the same day, the 1/2nd E.Lancs. Field Ambulance will take over these posts and duties; the details of the 1/3rd E.Lancs. Field Ambulance on relief will proceed by march route via MESPLAUX FARM to billets vacated by the 1/2nd E.Lancs. Field Ambulance at LOCON (South) Area.

3. The Field Ambulance equipment at the A.D.Ss. will be sent in to M.D.S. on the motor ambulance stationed at the A.D.Ss. immediately after the posts have been relieved by the 1/2nd E.Lancs. Field Ambulance.

4. All Field Ambulance equipment will be loaded on wagons on the 9th instant. The A.S.C. will be responsible that the wagons are properly loaded and sheeted.

5. A tent sub-division from the 1/2nd E.Lancs. Field Ambulance will take over the Hospital duties at MESPLAUX FARM on the afternoon of the 9th instant.

6. The Field Ambulance will parade at 10 a.m. dress marching order, and proceed by march route to billets vacated by the 1/2nd E.Lancs. Field Ambulance in LOCON (South) Area.

7. 1st Lieut. F.B.LONG and 25 Other Ranks will proceed by march route to No.18 Casualty Clearing Station LAPUGNOY on the 10th instant in relief of a detachment of the 1/2nd E.Lancs. Field Ambulance. Parade marching order 9 a.m. Transport will be provided for Officer's baggage and men's blankets.

8. All stores and equipment surplus to Mobilization Equipment will be handed over and receipts obtained.

Lieut. Colonel,
Issued at 19.20.. Commanding 1/3rd East Lancs. Field Ambulance.

Distribution :-
Copy No. 1. O.C., A.D.S., Tuning Fork.
"   "   2. O.C., A.D.S., Lone Farm.
"   "   3. 1st Lieut.F.B.Long.
"   "   4. Quartermaster.
"   "   5. O.C.,1/2nd E.L.F.Amb.
"   "   6. N.C.O. i/c A.S.C.(H.T.).
"   "   7. War Diary.
"   "   8. War Diary.
"   "   9. File.

SECRET.

Appendix 42.

Copy No. 1.......

1/3rd East Lancashire Field Ambulance.

Amendment No.1. to Order No.28.

January 9th, 1918.

Paragraph 7 is cancelled and the following substituted :-

7. The detachment of 1 Officer and 25 Other Ranks at No.18 Casualty Clearing Station, at present found by 1/2nd East Lancashire Field Ambulance will be relieved by a detachment of a Field Ambulance of another Division on 10th instant.

[signature]
Lieut.-Colonel,
Commanding 1/3rd East Lancs. Field Ambulance.

Issued at 1905.

Distribution :-

Copy No.1. O.C.,A.D.S.,Turning Fork.
 "   " 2. O.C.,A.D.S.,Lone Farm.
 "   " 3. 1st Lieut.F.B.Comp.
 "   " 4. Quartermaster.
 "   " 5. O.C.,1/2nd E.T.F.Amb.
 "   " 6. N.C.O. i/c A.S.C.(H.T.).
 "   " 7. War Diary.
 "   " 8. War Diary.
 "   " 9. File.

SECRET.
Copy No......3

I/3rd East Lancashire Field Ambulance.

Order No. 29.

Reference Map BETHUNE Combined sheet.
A.D.M.S., 42nd Division.

January 10th '1918.

1. 1st Lieut.F.B.LONG, M.O.R.C.U.S.A., is detailed for temporary medical charge of 211th BDE.R.F.A., during the absence of Capt.WARD., on leave.

2. He will report to the Officer Commanding 211th Bde R.F.A. forthwith.

3. Necessary transport will be provided.

M.W.Kennett
Lieut.-Colonel.
Commanding I/3rd East Lancs.Field Ambulance.

Issued at.14.20....

Distribution:-
Copy No.1. 1st.Lieut.F.B.Long.
 " " 2.. O.C.,211th Bde R.F.A.
 " " 3.. War Diary.
 " " 4..   "
 " " 5.. File.

ROUTINE ORDERS
by
Lieut-Colonel H.H.B.Cunningham,
Commanding 1/3rd East Lancashire Field Ambulance.

Appendix 44.

Friday 18th January 1918.

Orderly Officer.   Capt.M.E.Delafield.

Orderly Sergeant. "A" Section Billet.   Cpl.J.R.Bullivant.
Orderly Sergeant. "B" Section Billet.   Sgt.E.Odling.
Orderly Sergeant. "C" Section Billet.   Cpl.A.Hill.
Orderly Sergeant. A.S.C.   Sgt.J.Howard.

R.A.M.C.	A.S.C.
	Stables. 6.45.a.m.
Feet and Boot Inspection 9.a.m.	Feet and Boot Inspection 9.a.m

The feet of every N.C.O. and man are to be rubbed with Camphor Powder.

Recreational Training.	10.a.m.	Stables.	11.a.m.
Band Practice.	10.a.m.	Stables.	3.45.p.m.
Feet Inspection.	7.p.m.	Feet Inspection.	7.p.m.

The feet of every N.C.O. and man are to be rubbed with Camphor Powder. The Senior N.C.O. for each Section will be held personally responsible that the feet parades are conducted in an efficient manner.

Daily Parade States - AMENDMENT.   Reference Routine Orders dated
                17-1-18 for "The distribution of their sections"
        read   "The distribution of their billets."

Report
Transport.   The undermentioned report from O.C.,42nd
            Divisional Train has been received from A.D.M.S.,42nd Div:

    ANIMALS.   Very good - clean - good condition with one
                exception.Tails want trimming in a few cases.

    VEHICLES.   Good.

    HARNESS.   Very good - clean - steel work good - the
                fitting of headcollars and curb chains requires
                attention.

    GENERAL.   A great improvement all round - A very good
                turn-out.

[signature]

Lieut-Colonel,
Commanding 1/3rd East Lancashire Field Ambulance.

In the Field.
17-1-18.

ROUTINE ORDERS *Appendix 45*
by,
Lieut-Colonel H.H.B. Cunningham,
Commanding 1/3rd East Lancashire Field Ambulance.

Sunday 20th January 1918.

Orderly Officer.   Capt. H. Henry.

Orderly Sergeant. "A" Section Billet.   Cpl. J. Cowan.
Orderly Sergeant. "B" Section Billet.   Cpl. W. Longworth.
Orderly Sergeant. "C" Section Billet.   Sgt. F. Karge.
Orderly Sergeant. A.S.C.   F/Cpl. W. Raybould.

R.A.M.C.		A.S.C.	
		Stables.	6.45 a.m.
Feet and Boot Inspection.	9 a.m.	Feet and Boot Inspection	9 a.m.
		Stables.	11 a.m.
Feet Inspection.	8.30 p.m.	Feet Inspection.	8.30 p.m.

Divine Services.   C. of E.

Parade Service.	9.30 a.m.	Y.M.C.A. LOCON.
Holy Communion.	10 a.m.	" "
Y.M.C.A. Service.	6.30 p.m.	" "

Wesleyans, Presbyterians and United Board.

| Parade Service. | 11 a.m. | Y.M.C.A. LOCON. |
| Holy Communion. | 11.45 a.m. | " " |

R.C.

Mass.	8 a.m.	in LOCON Church.
Parade Mass.	9.30 a.m.	"
High Mass.	10.30 a.m.	"
Vespers.	3 p.m.	"

Waste Paper.   The following Field Ambulance Order is republished for information and must be complied with:-

> "Owing to the shortage at home, all waste paper (except Secret and Confidential matter) old newspapers, cardboard and string will be collected, and despatched to England for repulping. In order to reduce space in transport, a baling press will be installed at BETHUNE to which all waste will be sent and dealt with by skilled personnel and despatched under Corps arrangements to Railhead.
> The collection of paper will be commenced at once, but will not be despatched to the press pending receipt of further instructions.
> Units will arrange for the storage of all waste paper until such a time as the press is ready for use.
> Further instructions will be issued when the press is ready to receive paper. The issue of sacks for transporting to the press has been authorized, but they will not be issued until the press is in fully working order."

The N.C.O. i/c of Sanitation will be responsible for the collection and storage of waste paper in this Unit.

Care of Civilian Property.   Sections are individually responsible for the care of civilian property in their billets.
         Claims against the unit for damage to straw etc. will have to be paid for by the section concerned.

Continued:-

ROUTINE ORDERS   Continued:-

Appendix 45.

Water Carts.   Each section will arrange for its Water Cart to be parked in the Transport lines every fourth day commencing with "A" Section on Monday the 21st inst. for overhauling by the A.S.C..

Recreational Training.   NO.354086.Cpl.A.HILL will act as instructor in Recreational Training to "B" Section for the week ending 21-1-18..

Lectures.   A series of lectures will be given as under to W.Os., and N.C.Os. of the rank of Corporal and upwards in the Sergeants' Mess at 3.30.p.m..

Date	Lecturer	Subject
21st.inst.	Sgt.-Major.E.ROBERTS.	N.C.Os' Duties.
22nd "	Q.M.Sgt. J.C.Wilson.	Quartermasters Duties.
23rd "	Sgt.P.SEDDON.	Preparing Indents & Issues of Medical Stores.
24th "	Sgt.J.H.ALSOP.	Orderly Room Duties.
25th "	Sgt.H.E.DOWLING.	Hospital Duties, Wardmasters' Duties, care of patients etc..
26th "	S.Sgt.-Major.H.G.ROLFE.	Relations of A.S.C. to R.A.M.C. in Field Ambces. Packing of Wagons and use of Horses.
27th "	S.Sgt.J.H.ASHTON.	Comradeship.

Pay.   The Unit will be paid under arrangements made by Capt.H.HENRY..

Ration - Bread- Biscuit.- Proportion of Issue..   Commencing with issues
A.R.O.2327.   from Railhead on 19-1-18 the bread ration will be made up as follows - Bread 75%, Biscuit 25%..

Strength..   The undermentioned Officer reported his arrival from leave in U.K. on 18-1-18..

   Capt.H.HENRY.

   The undermentioned were evacuated to hospital L. of C. sick on 17-1-18 and are struck off the strength accordingly.-

   No.354190.Pte.P.CHARLES.
   No.354404. "   W.JOHNSON.

Lieut-Colonel,
Commanding 1/3rd East Lancashire Field Ambulance.

In the Field.
19-1-18.

ROUTINE ORDERS
by
Lieut-Colonel H.H.B. Cunningham,
Commanding 1/3rd East Lancashire Field Ambulance.

Appendix 46.

Monday 21st January 1918.

Orderly Officer.   Capt. H. Henry.

Orderly Sergeant. "A" Section Billet.   Cpl. V. Crosby.
Orderly Sergeant. "B" Section Billet.   Sgt. J.W. Mylchreest.
Orderly Sergeant. "C" Section Billet.   Sgt. J. Birchall.
Orderly Sergeant. A.S.C.   Lcpl. H. Roberts.

R.A.M.C.		A.S.C.	
		Stables.	6.45.a.m.
Feet and Inspection.	9.a.m.	Feet and Boot Inspection.	9.a.m.
Gas Drill.	9.30.a.m.	Gas Drill.	9.30.a.m.
Recreational Training.	10.30.a.m.	Stables.	11.a.m.
Band Practice.	10.30.a.m.	Stables.	3.45.p.m.
Feet Inspection.	8.30.p.m.	Feet Inspection.	8.30.p.m.

Cross Country Running.   "A" Section - Monday and Thursday. 2.30.p.m.
                           "B" Section - Tuesday and Friday. 2.30.p.m.
                           "C" Section - Wednesday and Saturday 2.30.p.m.

SPECIAL DIVISIONAL ROUTINE ORDER OF THE DAY.

HONOURS & AWARDS.

The following Officers and N.C.O.s have received Honours or Awards or have been mentioned in Sir Douglas Haigs Despatch dated 7th November 1917 for distinguished and gallant services and devotion to duty in FRANCE during the period February 26th 1917 to September 21st 1917.-

AWARDED THE MILITARY CROSS.

Hon. Lt & Qmr. J.E.H. ANDERTON.

AWARDED THE MERITORIOUS SERVICE MEDAL.

No. 354180. Sgt. J.H. ASHTON.

MENTIONED IN DESPATCHES.

Capt. H. HENRY. Attd. East Lancs. Regt.

"1914" Star.   Supplis of the riband for 1914 Star are now
G.R.O.3179.   commencing to arrive and indents in accordance with the instructions in G.R.O.3109 may be submitted.

Substitution of the Drab Pea jacket for the Officers' Greatcoat.
during the continuance of the War.-
G.R.O.3181.   During the continuance of the war the drab pea jacket (commonly known as "coat, British Warm") will take the place of the Officers' greatcoat. In all lists of kit and outfit wherever the Greatcoat is shown it will be understood to mean the "Drab pea jacket"(coat, British warm). Officers now in possession of greatcoats are allowed to continue them in wear.

                                                                     Continued:-

Appendix 46

ROUTINE ORDERS Continued:-

Rations for Personnel Proceeding by Re-inforcement, Leave and Unit Trains
G.R.O.3189.
1. All men leaving bases, etc., whether re-inforcements or on leave, will be supplied by the base with the unexpired portion of the days ration, to include hot tea, which will be carried in the men's waterbottles.
2. Haltes repas will be established by Armies or L.of C. at the following stations.-
    TINCQUES.   First Army Area.
3. At the above haltes repas, hot water, latrines and ablution benches, where possible should be prepared.
4. The E.F.C. will provide a suitable buffet, where suitable cigarettes, biscuits, hot tea or coffee, or soup may be obtained on payment, and the necessary hut should be erected by the Army or L.of C. concerned.
5. Rations will be taken on the train as follows, in addition to the unexpired portion carried by the men:-
Leave Train:-
    BOULOGNE. - First Army. Train C. One train ration & one reserve ration

Re-inforcement Train.
    HAVRE & ROUEN.   ditto.
    ETAPLES.   One reserve ration
    HAVRE via ETAPLES.   (One train ration &
    ROUEN " "   (one reserve ration
    HAVRE via ROUEN & ETAPLES.   Two train rations & one reserve ration

Personnel Trains.
    CALAIS H BOULOGNE.   One train ration & one reserve ration

6. In addition to the above, the Officer Commanding the mens' Depot will be responsible that each re-inforcement is issued with an Iron Ration before entrainment, and that the men are collectively warned that if they eat or lose their iron rations they will be severely dealt with.
9. On arrival of re-inforcements and details at Railheads, all complete rations will be handed over to the R.S.O.s or R.T.O.s at supply railheads. If handed over to R.T.O.s they should subsequently be delivered to Supply Officers of the Formations to which the reinforcements belong.

Turpentine.
G.R.O.3198.
Turpentine is now very expensive and difficult to obtain. Its use is therefore restricted to the Painting of Motor Cars and special work by the R.E.Special Works Park and the purpose for which it is demanded must be stated on the indent. For all other work White Spirit must be used.

Steel Helmets for Drafts.
G.R.O.3199.
After the 19th February 1918 all infantry drafts arriving in this country will be equipped with Steel Helmets before leaving England, except drafts furnished to Garrison Battalions. Drafts for all other Units will proceed without Steel Helmets as heretofore.

Strength.
    The undermentioned Officer proceeded on furlough to the U.K. on 19-1-18.-

    Capt. M.E.Delafield.

    The undermentioned man reported his arrival from furlough in the U.K. on 20-1-18.-

    No.M2/156170. Pte. A.S.Gibson.

In the Field.
20-1-18.

                                       Lieut-Colonel,
          Commanding 1/3rd East Lancashire Field Ambulance.

SECRET.
Copy No. 3   Appendix 47.

1/3rd East Lancashire Field Ambulance.

Order No. 30.

Reference Map BETHUNE Combined Sheet.
A.D.M.S., 42nd Division.

January 22nd 1918.

1. Captain H.HENRY R.A.M.C.(T.F.) is detailed for temorary Medical charge of 1/4th East Lancashire Regiment during the absence of Captain H.WILSON, sick.

2. He will report to the Officer Commanding 1/4th East Lancashire Regiment forthwith.

3. Necessary transport will be provided.

W.M.Kenney
Lieut-Colonel,
Commanding 1/3rd East Lancashire Field Ambulance.

Issued at 8.50 a.m.

Distribution:-
Copy No.1. Capt.H.Henry.
" No.2. O.C.,1/4th East Lancashire ~~EAST LANCASHIRE~~ Regt.
" " " War Diary.
" " " File.

SECRET.   *Appendix 48*   Copy No. 2

1/3rd East Lancashire Field Ambulance.

Order No. 31.

Reference Map BETHUNE Combined Sheet.
A.D.M.S., 42nd Division. M 14/176

January 27th 1918.

1. Under instructions from 42nd Divisional Headquarters Certified True Copy attached Capt. H. HENRY R.A.M.C.(T.F.) will proceed to LABUISSIERE (near BRUAY) and report to D.D.M.S., 1 Corps at 10. a.m. 28th inst.

2. Necessary transport will be provided.

3. All maps and documents the property of the Unit will be handed over before departure.

                                   Lieut-Colonel,
           Commanding 1/3rd East Lancashire Field Ambulance.

Issued at 9.50 a.m.

Distribution:-
Copy No. 1.   Capt. H. Henry.
Copy No. 2.   War Diary.
Copy No. 3.   War Diary.
Copy No. 4.   File.

Appendix 48.

A.D.M.S., 42nd Division. M14/176.

O.C.,
1/3rd East Lancashire Field Ambulance.

      Please detail Captain H.HENRY R.A.M.C.(T.F.) to report to D.D.M.S.,1 Corps at LABUISSIERE (near BRUAY) at 10.a.m. to-morrow 28th instant, with full kit.

      Captain H.HENRY, will be permanently attached to the 9th Reserve Park (NOEUX LES MINES) and will be struck off your strength accordingly.

27-1-18.
B.

                                                   N.H.H.HASKINS, Capt,
                                                         for Colonel
                                    A.D.M.S., 42nd Division.

CERTIFIED TRUE COPY.

                        Lieut-Colonel,
Commanding 1/3rd East Lancashire Field Ambulance.

SECRET.   *Appendix A9.*   Copy No. 3.

1/3rd East Lancashire Field Ambulance.

Order No. 32.

Reference Map BETHUNE Combined Sheet.
A.D.M.S., 42nd Division. M14/177.

January 28th 1918.

1. Lieut. T.B.H. TABUTEAU. (R.A.M.C., T.C.) is detailed for temporary medical charge of 1/7th Bn. Manchester Regt. in place of Captain. C.H.G. PHILP, (R.A.M.C., T.C.) proceeding to ENGLAND on expiration of contract.

2. He will report to Officer Commanding 1/7th Bn. Manchester Regt. at 9.a.m. on the morning of the 29th inst. and will be relieved in a couple of days by 1st Lieut. E.A. MILLER. MORC/USA.

3. Necessary transport will be provided.

[signature]

Lieut-Colonel,
Commanding 1/3rd East Lancashire Field Ambulance.

Issued at 1800.
Distribution:-
Copy No.1. Lieut. T.B.H. Tabuteau.
Copy No.2. O.C., 1/7th Bn. Manchester Regt.
Copy. nO, 3 & 4. War Diary.
Copy. Nº 5. File.

SECRET.   Copy No. 3.

1/3rd East Lancashire Field Ambulance.

Order No. 33.

Appendix 50.

Reference Map BETHUNE Combined Sheet.
A.D.M.S., 42nd Division. M14/178.

January 30th 1918.

1. 1st Lieut. F.B. LONG (M.O.R.C., U.S.A.) is detailed for temporary medical charge of the 42nd Divisional Ammunition Column in place of Lieut. C.H. HARVEY, proceeding on short leave to PARIS.

2. He will report to the Officer Commanding the 42nd Divisional Ammunition Column at 5 p.m. on the 30th instant. (at W.29.a.8.8.)

3. Necessary transport will be provided.

                                            Lieut-Colonel,
                  Commanding 1/3rd East Lancashire Field Ambulance.

Issued at 1610.

Distribution:-
Copy No. 1. 1st Lieut. F.B. Long.
Copy No. 2. O.C., 42nd Divisional Ammunition Column.
Copy No. 3. War Diary.
Copy No. 4. War Diary.
Copy No. 5. File.

WAR DIARY

OF

1/3rd EAST LANCASHIRE FIELD AMBULANCE.

FROM :- February 1st, 1918   TO :- February 28th, 1918.

(VOLUME 2)

Army Form C. 2118.

WAR DIARY
or
INTELLIGENCE SUMMARY.
(Erase heading not required.)

Instructions regarding War Diaries and Intelligence Summaries are contained in F. S. Regs., Part II. and the Staff Manual respectively. Title pages will be prepared in manuscript.

Place	Date	Hour	Summary of Events and Information	Remarks and references to Appendices
LOCON South	1.2.18		3. G.S. wagons employed all day with R.E. Construction of stables, from site to be found proceeding. Construction of incinerator & drying room proceeding. Captain HASKINS returned from duty as temporary D.D.M.S Division	WWF
	2.2.18		3 G.S wagons to R.E. Frost & rain all day every day, roads extremely muddy. Some aerial activity of Bosche in evening, also during night	WWF
	3.2.18	0900	3 G.S wagons to R.E. Church Parade of Unit, with Band in attendance	WWF
	4.2.18		Lieutenant TABUTEAU returned from temporary duty with 1/1 Mondalete Reg[?]. Captain DELATTFIELD returned from leave to U.K. Lieutenant TABUTEAU proceeded on temporary duty Field Ambulance Cables 21.34. 3 G.S wagons to R.E. A.C.Os. Class of instruction under Sergeant Major being continued. Work on mine huts to stables continued, also work on incinerator & drying room	Appendix 51. WWF
	5.2.18		3 G.S wagons to R.E. Both parades for whole unit. Captain HASKINS proceeded on leave to U.K.	WWF
	6.2.18		3 G.S wagons to R.E. Wristlands & Lance[?] Corporal[?] of 16. O.R. awarded 1914 Star. Captain PRESTWICH proceeded to 1st Army School of Instruction	WWF

Army Form C. 2118.

WAR DIARY
or
INTELLIGENCE SUMMARY.
(Erase heading not required.)

Instructions regarding War Diaries and Intelligence Summaries are contained in F. S. Regs., Part II. and the Staff Manual respectively. Title pages will be prepared in manuscript.

Place	Date	Hour	Summary of Events and Information	Remarks and references to Appendices
LOCON South	7.2.18		Fwd dice held at work Lilles, had on Dryingroom o incinerator containing	
"	8.2.18		Very damp day. Short inspection of whole Unit. Route march for men not employed. 3 G S wagon to R.E.	
"	9.2.18		3 GS wagon to R.E. Captain DELAFIELD attended a lecture on Sanitation at 1st Army Hqrs. Drying room + incinerator completed, also tables + forms for all billets, and in mens huts, constructed owing to shortage of material. Sergeant Major E ROBERTS / This Unit awarded the Belgian Croix de Guerre	
"	10.2.18	0900	Church Parade. Band in attendance. 3 G S wagons to R.E. 2 N.C.O.s qualified with recruits 1st Infr. Gas School	
"	11.2.18	1430	C.O. visited C.R.S. at LABEUVRIERE, + 124 Bde Hqrs @ VERDIN les BETHUNE Captain DELAFIELD + 4 O.R. marched out for LABEUVRIERE in accordance with Field Ambulance orders No. 3.5.	Posts BETHUNE Combinalion App 32
"	12.2.18		Reinforcement of 1 O.R. joined Unit. Lieutenant TABUTEAU rejoins Unit from temporary duty at 1/1.S.L Field Ambulance. 3 S S Wagons to R.E. Medical equipment taken on wagons. Incinerator a new dry in room monthly very satisfactory. Improvements going on with tent + establishing latrines. 1 O.R. returned from duty with R.E. whilst they have been for past month	

A5834 Wt.W4973/M687 750,000 8/16 D. D. & L. Ltd. Forms/C.2118/13

Army Form C. 2118.

WAR DIARY
or
INTELLIGENCE SUMMARY.
(Erase heading not required.)

Instructions regarding War Diaries and Intelligence Summaries are contained in F. S. Regs., Part II. and the Staff Manual respectively. Title pages will be prepared in manuscript.

Place	Date	Hour	Summary of Events and Information	Remarks and references to Appendices
LABEUVRIÈRE	13.2.18	11.30	C.O. assumed command of "A" Section 1. Corps Rest Station, same being found by 1/1 Field Ambulance which provided only billets in ROCOU South at 0880. Fair extensive premises comprising accommodation for 452 patients, & more accommodation in the form of huts being erected by Corps. Personnel of Field Ambulance aggregate to billets & C.R.S. in the Town. 29 patients admitted.	JMW
	14.2.18		Owing to the several moves & changes in the staff of the C.R.S. & extent which entered a certain amount of contents & want of recessive the arran- -gement of routine of the C.R.S. 44 patients admitted to C.R.S.	JMW
	15.2.18		All patients in Hospital being checked with A.D. book, many being seen a great effort to our stop arrangement of patients, much being made, the only system the any system in force standardisation to battn.s being drawn up; no system of organisation being apparent. 32 patients admitted	JMW
	16.2.18		First fairly day cleaning up of grounds of C.R.S. continued, construction went on latrines & ablution benches continued. huts & out of huts unlikely Field Ambulance contingents in several R.A.M.C school standing taken to C.R.S. drawn up & arranged outside PRESTWIC 45 Patient admitted	JMW Kundin 53
	17.2.18		Patients certain uncertain now repaired, 31 stretchers found in an attic, 25 gathered at known better, further amount no ayain, place anywhere, 2 subs. ammunition & quantity ordnance stores handed in to Salvage. Floors & wards being scrubbed 480 prs. blue & 23 yellow & linen gowns & returns to supplies in Town. 40 patients admitted	JMW
	18.2.18		40 Cases admitted DDMS 1 Corps visited C.R.S. & inspected whole station. Have fairly clean his sorting out of the place patients not great completion. 40 patients admitted 55th Division Trest performing in patients recreation room.	JMW

Army Form C. 2118.

WAR DIARY
or
INTELLIGENCE SUMMARY.
(Erase heading not required.)

Instructions regarding War Diaries and Intelligence Summaries are contained in F. S. Regs., Part II. and the Staff Manual respectively. Title pages will be prepared in manuscript.

Place	Date	Hour	Summary of Events and Information	Remarks and references to Appendices
LABEUVRIERE	19.2.18		Large barn re-arranged, mobilisation stores, on carts, are stood together, gas-war tackle assembled, transports, painters dabs all in working order. Bolsheviks average 30 hours sentence a day. Casualty of ablution after an inevitable proceeding. Pte. Sergt. Dr DOUGLAS MORUS & 4 reports of arrival & posts to this Unit. 46 cases admitted to CRS	MWL
	20.2.18		35 Cases admitted to CRS. MO & the constructional repair work & a stocktaking of lack of materials. 100 patients entertained pre S 55th Divn. troop each night.	MWL
	21.2.18	1500	32 Cases admitted Station. Pervin from Units of 24 Bde reports for course of instruction. Captain HASKINS reported from leave to U.K. Special order of the day (Field Ambulance) issued giving details of war chevrons & men entitled to wear them	MWL Afton/Log Sgt.
	22.2.18		Course of instruction continued for all reinforcements & Field Ambulance & regimental Stretcher bearers carried on daily, Captain PRESTWICH being instructor & in charge. 26 Cases admitted.	MWL
	23.2.18		Course of instruction proceeding Captain DELAFIELD lectures M. G. Battalion on funeral ceremonies, a/c the whole Battalion had been ordered to Station. 46 Cases admitted	MWL
	24.2.18	0915	Church parade & Class of Instruction. Hospital orderlies came in to march 24 Cases admitted	MWL

Army Form C. 2118.

WAR DIARY
or
INTELLIGENCE SUMMARY.
(Erase heading not required.)

Place	Date	Hour	Summary of Events and Information	Remarks and references to Appendices
LABEUVRIERE	25.2.18	1900	Course of Instruction & Hospital duties proceeding in usual way. 3.3 Cases admitted. School of Training 1st Class, for 26th an instructor to A.D.M.S. attached A.D.M.S. 42nd Division visits C.R.S. complete review read	
"	26.2.18		School. Field Engineer from 1st Corps visits C.R.S. with a view of materials required for work on land A.T. & Q.M.G. 42nd Division visits C.R.S. Returned in bed being extended. A quantity of haulage being returned. 24 Cases admitted	
"	27.2.18	1000	Practical demonstration to Class of officers from Division in "Evening Cookery" by N.C.O instructor from 1st Army School of Cookery.	
		16 15	D.D.M.S. 1st Corps visited C.R.S. 44 patients admitted	
"	28.2.18		Class being conducts as usual, including a demonstration on first aid, & one on chiropody. Captain H. HENRY, R.A.M.C.T.F. reports his arrival on being posted to this Unit. 34 patients admitted	

W.M. Cunningham

SECRET. Appendix 5. Copy....3....

1/3rd. East Lancashire Field Ambulance.

Order No. 3 4.

Reference Map BETHUNE Combined Sheet.

Febuary 3rd. 1918.

1. Lieut. T.B.H. Tabuteau R.A.M.C. (T.C.) is detailed for temporary duty at the 1/1st East Lancashire Field Ambulance.

2. He will report to the Officer Commanding 1/1st E. Lancs. Field Ambulance on 4-2-1918 at 10-a.m.

3. Necessary transport will be provided.

[signature]
Lieut-Colonel.
Comdg. 1/3rd. East Lancs. Field Ambce.

Issued at. 1655.
Distribution.-
Copy No. 1. Lieut. T.B.H. Tabuteau.
 "   " 2. O.C. 1/1st E. Lancs. Fld. Ambce.
 "   " 3 & 4 War Diary.
 "   " 5. File.

SECRET.   Copy No...10:........

1/3rd East Lancashire Field Ambulance.

Order No.35.

Appendix 52

Reference Map 1/40,000 Sheet 36 A. BETHUNE Combined Sheet.
42nd Division R.A.M.C. Order No.35.

February 11th 1918.

1. The 42nd Division is being relieved in the line by the 55th Division commencing 12th February.

2. On relief the 42nd Division moves into the BUSNES - BURBURE - FOUQUIERES Training Areas, when they come into G.H.Q. reserve at 6.p.m. 14th February.

3. The 1/3rd East Lancashire Field Ambulance will proceed on the 13th inst to LABEUVRIERE and relieve the 2/1st West Lancs. Fld Ambce. of the 55th Division, taking over "A" Section Corps Rest Station.   Relief to be completed by 12 noon.

4. An advance party of 40 Other Ranks under the command of Captain M.E. DELAFIELD will proceed on the 11th inst. to LABEUVIERE and to commence taking over the Corps Rest Stn.
This party will take with them "C" Section equipment and Transport.

5. A rear party of 9 O.Rs in charge of Sgt.J.BIRCHALL will remain behind and hand over the present billets to the 1/3rd West Lancs. Field Ambulance.

6. Route HINGES - CHOCQUES - LABEUVIERE 100 yards distance will be maintained between the R.A.M.C. and Transport of the Unit.

7. All trench and Area Stores, maps and Medical arrangements will be handed over and receipts given and obtained, duplicate receipts being sent to the A.D.M.S., 42nd Division.

8. List of all area stores in present site to be handed to Town Major LOCON who will be requested to furnish a certificate of cleanliness of each billet by the N.C.O. i/c rear party.

9. The sub-Area Commandant CHOCQUES will be notified by the Officer i/c Advance party that the billets at present occupied by the 2/1st West Lancashire Field Ambulance, will be taken over by the 1/3rd East Lancashire Field Ambulance and he will be requested to furnish a Football Field for use by the unit.

10. The Mechanical Transport will proceed independently ic Sergt. A. DOBSON A.S.C. M.T..

11. A Motor Lorry will be available for conveyance of surplus baggage.

12. In the new area the sick of the 127 Bde. will be collected by this Unit commencing 12th inst;

Issued at. 1830......
                                           Lieut-Colonel,
Distribution;-   Commanding 1/3rd East Lancashire Field Ambulance.
Copy No.1. Headquarters 127 Bde.
  " No.2. Officer i/c Advance Party.
  " No.3. O.C.,2/1st West Lancs.Field Ambulance.
  " No.4. O.C.,1/3rd West Lancashire Field Ambce.
  " No.5. Town Major. Locon.
  " No.6. Sub-Area Commandant Chocques.
  " No.7. N.C.O.i/c Rear Party.
  " No.8. N.C.O. i/c H.T.Transport.
  " No.9. N.C.O.i/c M.T. Transport.
  " No.10 & 11. War Diary.
  " No.12 File.

"A" Sec. First Corps Rest Station.

STANDING ORDERS.

Appendix 53.

1. Reveille. 6 a.m.   Tattoo. First Post. 8-30 p.m.
   Retreat. 5 p.m.   Last Post. 9.0 "
                                   Lights Out. 9.15 "

2. Orderly Room. 8-30 a.m.

3. Distribution of Patients.   "A" Block — Medical.
                               "B"   "   — Surgical, including light Duty.
                               "C"   "   — Medical, including diarrhoea
                                           and light Duty.

4. Hospital Duties —
   Officer i/c "A" Block.   Lieut. C.D.H. Tabuteau.
      Do   "B"   "   Capt. H.C. Delafield.
      Do   "C"   "   Capt. W.F. Beavistch.

   Wardmaster "A" Block.   Sergt. E. Allen.
              "B"   "   Cpl. J.R. Mulbrant.
              "C"   "   Cpl. A. Hailes.
   Night Wardmaster.   S/sgt. F.W. Richie.
   i/c Cooks.   Sergt. J. Birchall.
   i/c Dining Halls.   S/sgt. G. Osling.
   i/c Baths & Linen Store. Cpl. J. Cowan.
   i/c Sanitation.   L/Cpl. G.C. Prescott.

   The Orderly Officer will admit all patients to the C.R.S. and will be available in case of emergency in the wards. Accompanied by the Orderly Sergeant he will visit the patients and personnels dinners, and such other meals as directed. He will inspect the day duties at 8.30 a.m. daily.

   The day staff will come on duty at seven a.m., and the night staff at eleven p.m.

   The Orderly Officer will collect reports from staff parade each night at "Last Post" and then make the night rounds of the wards.

   The Orderly Sergeant will visit the Dining Halls at Breakfast and both lunch times.

   The undermentioned N.C.O.s are placed in charge of their respective billets.
        Hospital Billet   Sergt. H.C. Dowling
        School   "   A. Dobson.
        R.E. Hut   "   J. Howard.
        Other   "   Cpl. W. Longworth.

   They or a N.C.O. detailed by them will be present each night at staff parade and inform the Sergt-Major whether all are present or not.

5. Patients — Admission. Patients arriving at the C.R.S will be sent to the Inspection Room in the first instance, where they will be seen by the Orderly Officer who will order them to their wards, thereupon the orderly in waiting will take them to the Packstore where the whole of their equipment with the exception of haversack, small kit and cap comforter will be handed in, then after being bathed they will be taken to their allotted wards.

   Wardmasters are responsible that none but duly admitted patients are received into their respective wards.

   Evacuation & Discharges. Wardmasters will send to the Orderly Room by 8 a.m. daily the number of patients marked for discharge and evacuation for the following day.
                                Men for discharge deficient of clothing or equipment will parade at the Q.M. Stores at 2 p.m. on the day prior to discharge. On day of discharge they will draw up clothing and equipment and days ration from the packstore at 8 a.m.
                                They will parade in front of "A" Block at 9.30 a.m. daily for inspection by the Orderly Officer.
   Patients for transfer to C.C.S are evacuated in ..... cars from "A" Block at 2 p.m. daily.

   Discipline. All patients will be washed and shaved by 9.30 a.m.
   Patients must be in their wards by 8 p.m.

CONTINUED

STANDING ORDERS — CONTINUED.

Appendix 53

5. **Discipline.** Smoking will not be permitted in the wards, nor will patients be allowed to leave the wards [illegible] in no case before [illegible].

Patients marked light duty [illegible] fatigues under instructions from the Sgt. Major.

Coal fatigues will parade under instructions from the Quartermaster daily.

Wardmasters will be responsible for the cleanliness and discipline of their block.

6. **Ward Books.** These will be taken into use in the wards and all necessary notes as to temperature, motions, diets, treatment and clinical notes will be entered up daily.

When a patient is transferred to C.C.S. or other hospital an abstract of these notes will be entered up daily on the [illegible] Medical card.

7. **Diets.** Wardmasters are responsible for handing in their list of diets for the following day to the Quartermaster's Office at 6 p.m. daily.

8. **Change of Diagnosis.** In the event of any diagnosis being changed after a patient has been received into the C.R.S., the Orderly Room should be notified forthwith by the Wardmasters.

9. **Meals.**

	Patients	Personnel
Breakfast	7.0 a.m.	7.30 a.m.
Lunch	12.0 noon	12.30 p.m.
Dinner	4.30 p.m.	5.0 "
Supper	7.30 "	8.0 "

The patients from "A" & "C" Blocks will have their meals in [illegible] dining hall and the patients from "B" block in "D" dining hall.

Patients will fall in before their respective blocks and will be marched to the Dining Hall by a N.C.O. detailed by the wardmaster.

The personnel will have their meals in "D" dining hall.

10. **Parade for Orders.** On the bugle sounding "Orders", wardmasters and billet N.C.O.'s or others detailed by them, will parade outside the Orderly Room and report to the Sgt-Major.

11. **Fire Piquet.** The "Band" will constitute the standing fire piquet. Cpl. J.S. Harvey is responsible for the fire appliances being maintained in working order.

12. **Pay.** A weekly payment of Frcs 5 will be made on the following day to each patient in hospital on Sunday night.

Wardmasters are responsible for preparing Acquittance Rolls.

13. **Return.** Officers i/c wards will render a return by Orderly Room hour on Monday in each week of all patients who have been in hospital for seven days.

H.P. Cunningham
Lieut-Colonel R.A.M.C.
Comdg "A" Section 1st Corps Rest Station.

16-2-1918

SPECIAL ORDER OF THE DAY.
by,
Lieut-Colonel.H.H.B.Cunningham,
Commanding 1/3rd East Lancashire Field Ambulance.

Appendix 54.

Thursday 21st February 1918.

The undermentioned are entitled to wear the number and type of Overseas chevrons as shown against their names severally.
Pending receipt of these chevrons from Ordnance, permission is granted for them to be purchased by the individual.

			Chevrons.	
Regtl.No.	Rank.	Name.	Red.	Blue.
354020.	S.M.	Roberts.E.	1.	3
354032.	Q.M.S.	Wilson J.C.	1.	3
354100	Sgt.	Dowling H.E.	1	3
354295	"	Alsop J.H.		3
354287	Cpl.	Crosby V.		3
354168	Pte.	Allen.J.R.		3
354123	"	Bland.H.	1	3
354218	"	Bradbury A.		3
354418	"	Crossfield H.		2
354010	"	Cassels H.	1	3
354433	"	Chalmers J.M.		2
354278	"	Darbyshire J.		3
354365	"	Ellis P.		3
354105.	"	Findley G.W.	1	3
354181	"	Gray R.A.	1	3
354213	"	Greening J.B.		3
354465	"	Gregory R.		2
354095	"	Harvey G.W.	1	2
354455	"	Hever E.J.		2
354434	"	Jackson.J.		2
354128	"	Johnstone A.M.	1	3
354440	"	Jones W.C.		2
354016	"	Lawton F.H.	1	3
354137	"	Lawton H.I.	1	3
354345	"	Moore H.		3
354097	L.cpl.	McVennon.J.	1	2
354390	Pte.	Orchard C.A.		2
354199	"	Power A.		3
354456	"	Robinson H.		2
354125	"	Ryder R.	1	3
354442	"	Shaw J.		3
354023	"	Simcock G.	1	3
354399	"	Slavin J.		2
354022	"	Snowden G.	1	3
354228	"	Stapleton J.R.		3
354046	"	Swift J.	1	3
354171	"	Tingey W.	1	3
354024	"	Trueman P.		3
354026	"	Watson S.	1	3
354459	"	Matthewson L.O.J.		2
354375	"	Weaver C.		3
354031.	S/Sgt.	Ritchie F.W.	1	3
354034	Sgt.	Coan T.	1	3
354018	Sgt.	Odling E.	1	3
354002.	"	Cowan J.C.	1	3
354116	Cpl.	Longworth W.	1	3
354179	"	J.W.Herbert M.M.	1	3
354177	L.cpl.	Burrows R.	1	3
354169	"	Prescott.G.C.	1	3
354354	Pte.	Antley C.		2
354112	"	Bennett W.A.	1	3
354355	"	Brigg W.C.		2
354352	"	Bulger T.W.		2
354190	"	Burns W.H.		3

Continued:-

SPECIAL ORDER OF THE DAY Continued:-

			Chevrons.	
Regtl.No.	Rank.	Name	Red	Blue.
352268	Pte.	McGuire E.		2
350556	"	Standring S.		1
350559	"	Widdowson A.		1
354205	"	Whipp T.		3
320202	"	Ferguson G.		3
10268	"	Armstrong L.L.	1	3
46906	"	Ager R.H.	1	3
105628	"	Jones W.		2
44180	"	Taylor P.		3
52925	"	Taylor G.A.		3
46981	"	Thywates R.		3
52647	"	Findlay W.		3
35883	"	Fentum A.G.		3
5601	"	Kemp H.T.S.	1	3
103288	"	Littler S.		2
4316	"	Priestman J.	1	3
39470	"	Roper J.		4
7404	"	Wallineer J.	1	3
32921	"	Cook T.W.		3
92481	"	Dalgety W.H.		1
18851	"	Davis T.E.	1	3
105623	"	H.Radcliffe M.M.		2
5536	"	Rowley H.A.		3
5050	"	Sherlock T.		2
98958	"	Snape E.		1
95214	"	Wilson P.K.		1
63355	"	Bonner F.		3

A.S.C. (H.T.)

T4/247942	Sgt.	Oldfield B.	1	3
T/ 22457	"	Howard J.		3
T3/030729	E/Cpl.	Raybould W.T.		3
T4/247967	Dvr.	Anderson S.	1	3
T4/247966	"	Bailey J.H.	1	3
T4/247938	"	McCormick J.	1	3
T4/247934	"	Smith T.	1	3
T4/247933	"	Humphreys D.		3
T/ 36218	"	Boxall J.		3
T/ 061989	"	Brown A.		3
T3/023508	"	Connolly P.		3
T4/037330	"	Clayton J.		3
T/ 35123	"	Carpenter G.		3
T4/246693	"	Campbell S.C.		3
T4/062148	"	Davidson W.		3
T4/071808	"	Farr A.		3
T4/061721	"	Hunter T.		3
T4/242949	"	Horne G.F.		3
T4/237580	"	Parker F.J.		3
T4/237557	"	Rogers A.W.		3
T/ 36031	"	Wright E.W.		3
T1/ 827	"	Ward T.S.		3
T2/14282	"	Grant I.		3
T/ 35138	"	Preston A.		3
T2/ 12622	"	Pitts W.		3
TS/ 8301	S.S.	Ord. R.		3
T4/247937	Dvr.	Prior C.	1	3

P.B. PERSONNEL.

43419	Pte.	Gleadle W.E.		1
87506	"	Hughes W.		1
86812	"	Beagles J.		1
87423	"	Taylor A.		1

Continued,-

SPECIAL ORDER OF THE DAY Continued;-

Regtl.No.	Rank.	Name.	Chevrons Red.	Blue.
354035	Pte.	Couzens F.	1	3
354224	"	Fidler W.		3
354172	"	Gandy H.A.	1	3
354366	"	Gee L.		2
354451	"	Goodall J.		2
354048	"	Griffiths G.	1	3
354279	"	Humphries W.		3
354165	"	Jones W.V.	1	3
354371	"	Knott W.		2
354166	"	Leach C.	1	3
354118	"	McGovern J.	1	3
354057	"	O'Rourke A.	1	3
352320	"	Nicholson R.J.		2
354370	"	Patterson H.		2
354454	"	Pether E.		2
354331	"	Royle N.		3
354167	"	Smith J.	1	3
354436	"	Spalding J.		2
354380	"	Taylor E.		2
354234	"	Tickle W.A.		3
354411	"	Tunstall F.		2
354333	"	Wells J.		2
354174	"	Williams F.E.	1	3
354276	"	Winterbottom H.		3
354180	S/Sgt.	J.H.Ashton M.M.	1	3
354084	Sgt.	Seddon P.	1	3
354075	"	Allen E.	1	3
354064	"	Birchall J.	1	3
357099	"	Karge F.		1
354140	Cpl.	Evans J.	1	3
354086	"	Hill A.	1	3
354468	"	Thatcher A.		2
354213	L.cpl.	Ridge F.W.		3
354053	"	Upton F.E.	1	3
354458	"	Harvey J.L.		2
354173	Pte.	Allington F.E.	1	3
354136	"	Ashworth H.	1	3
354311	"	Barrett C.		3
354470	"	Beswick F.		2
350359	"	Burton W.		2
354420	"	Bradshaw J.		2
350065	"	Campbell J.		2
354291	"	Chadwick J.E.		3
354379	"	Hardman J.		2
354070	"	Horrocks A.W.	1	3
354133	"	Horrocks T.		3
354108	"	Haworth N.	1	3
354350	"	Jardine A.D.		2
354251	"	King G.		3
341093	"	Lyon J.H.		3
354176	"	Lees W.H.	1	3
354072	"	Magnall F.		3
354459	"	Maclean L.C.		2
354374	"	Sullivan H.		2
354258	"	Shute J.A.		3
354080	"	Smith E.	1	3
354413	"	Stevens J.W.		2
354257	"	Taylor R.		3
354464	"	Taylor T.		2
354381	"	Thompson C.		2
354193	"	Tucker A.		3
354188	"	Tierney J.	1	3
354189	"	Unsworth H.	1	3
354336	"	Watson A.E.		3
354325	"	White L.G.S.		3
354115	Pte.	Black W.A.	1	3
352239	"	Anderton J.		2
354222	"	Collins A.		3
352241	"	Foster J.E.		2

Continued

SPECIAL ORDER OF THE DAY Continued:-

Regtl.No.	Rank.	Name.	Chevrons. Red.	Blue.
		A.S.C.(M.T.)		
M2/121973	Sgt.	Dobson.A.		2
M2/080510	Cpl.	Clements W.T.		3
M2/265271	Pte.	Froud A.V.		1
M/ 282948	"	Harvey G.		1
M2/178141	"	Holden L.C.		1
D.M2/180180	"	Ingham O.		1
M2/156170	"	Gibson A.S.		1
M/ 282862	"	Mansell J.W.		1
M2/227489	"	Pott G.J.		1
M2/270137	"	Smee A.J.		1
M1/ 6844	"	Dormer J,	I	3
M2/120364	"	Palmer J.R.		3

21-2-18

[signature]

Lieut-Colonel
Commanding 1'3rd East Lancashire Field Amb.

A.D.M.S.,
    42nd Division.

Appendix 55.

Reference Scheme of training for Tuesday 26/2/18.

Recreational Training.	8.30.a.m. to 9.30.a.m.
Lecture " Arrest of Bleeding" by Capt.F.G.PRESTWICH.	9.45.a.m. to 10.15a.m.
Bandaging First Field Dressing Thomas Splint.	10.30.a.m. to 12 noon.
Squad Drill.	2.p.m. to 3 p.m.
Demonstration of Preparation of Meals.	3 p.m. to 4 p.m.

25-2-18.

Lieut-Colonel,
Commanding 1/3rd East Lancashire Field Amboe.

WAR DIARY

OF

1/3rd East Lancashire FIELD AMBULANCE, R.A.M.C.(T.F.)

FROM :- March 1st, 1918 TO :- March 31st, 1918.

(VOLUME 111)

Army Form C. 2118.

WAR DIARY
or
INTELLIGENCE SUMMARY.

(Erase heading not required.)

Instructions regarding War Diaries and Intelligence Summaries are contained in F. S. Regs., Part II. and the Staff Manual respectively. Title pages will be prepared in manuscript.

Place	Date	Hour	Summary of Events and Information	Remarks and references to Appendices
LABEUVRIERE	1-3-18		Course of instruction being continued. Lectures today includes Selection of R.A.P's, A.D.S, sites & Evacuation arrangement of same from thereto to O.C.S. Driving Corps Schools Station Lorry full. Cases are now retained at this C.R.S.	
	2-3-18	21.00	29 Cases admitted	
"			Relief of 1/Lieutenant E DOUGLAS to proceed & Instruct an Battalion bearers in Field Ambulance Orders No. 35.	
		15.30	Band at back of Officers mess, Afternoon released up. Party of Agricultural Reinforcements ready to BETHUNE 9 others.	
		18.00	Instr. 9 Lieutenant TABUTEAU to proceed on Temporary duty as a section of Field Ambulance Orders No 39.	
			26 Cases admitted	
"	3-3-18		Inter-sectional Football competition arranged. A.S.C. counting as a section of the purpose. Distribution of potatoes & jam issued for previous week attached.	
			54 cases admitted	
"	4-3-18	10.00	C.O. attended conference of Officer of A.D.M.S. Course of instruction to Regt. Stretcher Bearers being continued	
			54 cases admitted	
	5-3-18		14 Cases admitted	
	6-3-18		43 Cases admitted	
			Course of instruction continuing	
	7-3-18		39 Cases admitted	
		15.30	A party of 29 senior officers of the Units to be taken. Medical Service visits C.R.S trench style constructing off this place, then they were shown an section or section of equipment, tents	

Army Form C. 2118.

WAR DIARY
— or —
INTELLIGENCE SUMMARY.
(Erase heading not required.)

Instructions regarding War Diaries and Intelligence Summaries are contained in F. S. Regs., Part II. and the Staff Manual respectively. Title pages will be prepared in manuscript.

Place	Date	Hour	Summary of Events and Information	Remarks and references to Appendices
LABEUVRIERE	7.3.18		Ambulances open. Weather heavy cloud. Handed Transport of Captain PRESTWICH	
"	8.3.18		34 cases admitted. 2nd day of course of instruction	
"	9.3.18	1000	Stretcher transport made offsite to arrange their units. This service officer granted acting rank of Major under new army order by Captain H. HENRY & N.H.H. HASKINS. Instructional further competition in full swing. 38 cases admitted	
"	10.2.18	1500	15 cases admitted. C.O. attended conference at office of ADMS.	Afternoon S.9. Detached to previous week state.
"	11.3.18		Fine weather. Combatants D C.R.S being instructed in Rescuetorial Training & remaining in skill order 2 mi. Meeting also issuing to the progress of this combatants. Lieut. TABUTEAU reported this from Transport dept. next 1/4 Mounted to Regt. 13 cases admitted	
"	12.3.18		Fine weather. Batt House being reconstructed & S Stationary Section.	
"	13.3.18		Weather still fine. Attended wagon of Transport yourself being undertaken wagons being limited. Unit Mark 2 in an intermediate completion to finish G.S. wagons. 14 cases admitted	
"	14.3.18		Wet day. Work on new bath house continued, also repair work on round hutlings	

Army Form C. 2118.

WAR DIARY
or
INTELLIGENCE SUMMARY.
(Erase heading not required.)

Instructions regarding War Diaries and Intelligence Summaries are contained in F. S. Regs., Part II. and the Staff Manual respectively. Title pages will be prepared in manuscript.

Place	Date	Hour	Summary of Events and Information	Remarks and references to Appendices
LABEUVRIERE	14.3.18	16.00	Construction of Bomb-box Latrine completed and proceeding on wash stands. C.O. attended conference at Office of A.D.M.S. 46 Cases admitted	
"	15.3.18	17.00	O.C. instrs 127 Bde Sigs re entrainment in Training Farm in St Venant. Fine day. Construction work continues. 18 Cases admitted	
"	16.3.18		Reconstruction of Bath-house proceeding. Repairs to Cook No 369 + fitting of new shower. 18 Cases admitted	
"	17.3.18		1st Lt. Clancy of instruction in bn. stretcher assembly in C.R. Stn. 40 Divisional Class of instructions in bn. stretcher assembly in C.R.S. today. C.O. attended conference at Office of A.D.M.S. 25 Cases admitted	
"	18.3.18	11.15	Some heavy shelling. Landed abut 1/4 mile from C.R.S. 7 Evacuees. Hostile Raid. Demolished rest of Cooks support line. Heavy damage in gas dump. Pales work on buildings totally abandoned. Lieut. E.A. MILLER M.O.R.C. U.S.A. posted to this Unit + takes up his post. 3-6 Cases admitted	
"	19.3.18	08.45	Wed day. Lieut. MILLER proceeds on 18 Eng Regt on temporary duty. (Field Ambulance Return No 38) New Bath house almost completed. 1st Capt. Clancy instruction terminates & men rejoin their units today. 1st Inspn Q.C. Clancy instructs in note duties assemble today. D.D.M.S. & A.D.M.S. visited C.R.S.	
"	20.3.18		26 Cases admitted	

Army Form C. 2118.

WAR DIARY
or
INTELLIGENCE SUMMARY
(Erase heading not required.)

Instructions regarding War Diaries and Intelligence Summaries are contained in F. S. Regs., Part II. and the Staff Manual respectively. Title pages will be prepared in manuscript.

Place	Date	Hour	Summary of Events and Information	Remarks and references to Appendices
LABEUVRIERE	20.3.18	18.00	Accounts of Personnel balanced up their being granted pay day. One 2800 franc have paid out. Return work being continued. Entertainment given by Field Ambulance to patients in Recreation Room. 36 Cases admitted	
	21.3.18	21.00	Work for system. Return work continued. 18 cases admitted. Considerable little air raid activity in neighbourhood. Considerable amount of bombs appear on	
	22.3.18	08.30	Fire party of A.S.C. M.T., M.T. attacked today. Wind hands & reinforced to 7th field amb. Trains in the attack being unsuccessful a convoy arrived. Wet weather hinder movements of troops enabled. Vegetables ordered by letter by postal in all possible lieu of the group. D.D.M.S. + Corps blessed C.R.S. ... 38	
		15.30	2nd Long dress parade of the day of Field Ambulance orders no 38	
		16.30		
		19.00	Company present this being any sent for advance	
	23.3.18	03.30	Orders received from OC No. 4 Sec S Army D. S. for moving of XVth Div. to BASSEUX	
			... returned to Division of supplies ... captain DEASSFIELD	
		08.00		
		09.00	fire party of hand luggage to leave no 31 Stationary – 11.00, 2nd advance sec / 2nd CRS	
			Personnel & equipment left HESBIGNY en route to 13.20. Arrived HENRICOURT 9.22.30	
	24.3.18	17.30	Fine weather. W.D. transport in road when ordered to unload off this unit accured. an S.B.W. ambulance No. 38 cancelled. Orders received on movement was cancelled. Regimental ordered by authority from ... K.E.F. BULFORD the M.T. Lorries Field Ambulance will return at once by ... of Colonel CAMPR, No. 3 orders over. Orders also On Unit to proceed to trains tomorrow with pt Pr. S.Y. BURQUETT en Comdr. ... Col AHLIST, Lt. BETTI, Major NICOL, W.O. 136 Field Ambulance ... Capt ... ... Co for LABEUVRIERE. Asst. HEMRK proceeds by Motor car to be there to meet unit on return	

Army Form C. 2118.

WAR DIARY
or
INTELLIGENCE SUMMARY.
(Erase heading not required.)

Instructions regarding War Diaries and Intelligence Summaries are contained in F. S. Regs., Part II. and the Staff Manual respectively. Title pages will be prepared in manuscript.

Place	Date	Hour	Summary of Events and Information	Remarks and references to Appendices
BUCQUOY	25.3.18	1030	Advanced to hotsoil road to BIENVILLERS	
		0800	Left HQ in war to meet with CO 15/3 S. Lanc	
		1030	Unit moved to BIENVILLERS and arrived at destination	
		1945	Interviewed an officer i/c of 1/5 S. Lanc Field Ambulance Captain DOLAMEAD provide accomodation	
		2000	The 3 horse ambulance wagon which the Divn S and O of BUCQUOY SR return later after changing & repairing having taken the return wounded cases on way to 139 FA a billet for night	
		2110	Unit received orders to proceed at once to MONCHY nr 275 a to be sent to MDS 7pm	
		2330	Unit arrived MONCHY and billets 136 F Amb de billets.	
MONCHY	26.3.18		Ourstrength 13 officers & 148 wounded forced through lines. Have twenty officers details which proceed until they being hung off from BIENVILLERS Transport continued joint road between LARBRET, present S of SAULTY and taken to OSSon	
			26.3.18 Routes uncompleted to take 2A (14/8.) 19th 40th 141st GR 59th 62nd 43rd details and Regimental 31st 34th 19th 40th 41st R. 59th 62nd R. to be taken R. returned under orders awaiting instructions from unit orders Rest formed a line beyond the [?] with orders to hold any form under auto cover of MOST [?] hence with field [?] Rest of two day and down to 418 nothing noteworthy happened during day and up to [?] HQ CCS a withdrew to BAILLEUMONT 4 that CCS [?] Courtable at No 3 Coy HQ to DOUELEUS. A heavy [?] ammunition [?] hit and exploded S. [?] near [?] [?] after [?] [?] small arms ammunition fire.	

WAR DIARY

Army Form C. 2118.

Instructions regarding War Diaries and Intelligence Summaries are contained in F.S. Regs., Part II. and the Staff Manual respectively. Title pages will be prepared in manuscript.

INTELLIGENCE SUMMARY.
(Erase heading not required.)

Place	Date	Hour	Summary of Events and Information	Remarks and references to Appendices
MONCHY	2/3/18		Over 300 cases pass through during previous 24 hrs. Capt MYBURGH & Capt LAWRENCE PRESTWICH leaving on leave also under 1/2 & Field Ambulance. Captain DELAFIELD reported sick & to 1/2 E.L. Field Amb. Sgt LONG who came with Party at LABRET. 30th MAC in vicinity. MDS at MAC Alain running smoothly. Lorry lines being used in moving sitting cases. Cars now being evacuated to St POL of FREVENT. Salvage continuing collection of material to details. Right LEE B of attached MDS being a field Officer. Lay tendered & was being too still examined by officer. Cases seemed warm & was also happy but a warm air stove alongside & he was kept comfortable & was on warm. Point kept in light to boil dix H.T. water to serve army, tea, malted milk, Bovril & horlicks whenever required by any sort of the wounded waiting to gain full doses of the night. A/C used to clear all sitting cases on night.	M.H.
			... 3 OR with CO with all the horses 3 OR with the Decauville Lorry 3 OR with the Decauville Lorry 3 OR stealing from Decauville 9 OR for all other duties. After seeing the C Bearers off in morning Lt. Col. N.W. JONES Joined class held by the A.D.M.S. 2/ Army at 9/30am. until 4:15 pm Tried 12 MT AID HOSPITAL & EN Captain Deaf with more ADS to MONCHY	M.H.

A5834 Wt. W4973/M687 750,000 8/16 D.D. & L. Ltd. Forms/C.2118/13

WAR DIARY
INTELLIGENCE SUMMARY
(Erase heading not required.)

Army Form C. 2118.

Place	Date	Hour	Summary of Events and Information	Remarks and references to Appendices
HOMBL EUX		23.30	[illegible handwritten entries]	
	29.3.18		[illegible handwritten entries]	
	30.3.18		[illegible handwritten entries mentioning PRESTWICH, DEANFIELD, RIEMILLERS, SOUASTRE, BAYENCOURT, BELLEVUE etc.]	

Army Form C. 2118.

WAR DIARY
INTELLIGENCE SUMMARY.
(Erase heading not required.)

Instructions regarding War Diaries and Intelligence Summaries are contained in F. S. Regs., Part II. and the Staff Manual respectively. Title pages will be prepared in manuscript.

Place	Date	Hour	Summary of Events and Information	Remarks and references to Appendices
BAYENCOURT	31.3.34		Advanced with 150th Infantry Bde to Sus. Lieut. LONG still i/c forward of HQ HENU. He detailed 72 O.R.s to 1/4th Green Howards for routine employment. The remaining 28 O.R.s temporarily attached to Field Ambulance Coy. at HENU. Lieut. MILLER reports from temporary HQ at Field Ambulance HQs. STREVECOURT.	
		14.30	CO attended conference of C/officers. ADMS Division. Lieut. MILLER and other officers of HQ attended THESTRUCH DETAILED, And four men - each left at places of HQ on 31 st 1/HQ. O.R.'s details. KILLED OR II WOUNDED OR 8.	
				[signature]

A3834 Wt. W4973/M687 750,000 8/16 D. D. & L. Ltd. Forms/C.2118/13

Appendix 56. Copy No. 3

1/3rd East Lancashire Field Ambulance.

Order No. 36.

Reference Map BETHUNE Combined Sheet
A.D.M.S. 42nd Division M14/188.

1st March, 1918.

1. 1st Lieutenant R.A. DOUGLASS, M.O.R.C., U.S.A., is detailed for duty as Officer in Medical Charge of 42nd Division Machine Gun Battalion.

2. He will report to Officer Commanding 42nd Division Machine Gun Battalion on 2-3-1918.

3. Necessary transport will be provided.

H.W. Cunningham
Lieut.-Colonel,
Commanding 1/3rd East Lancs. Field Ambulance.

Issued at 2100

Distribution :-

Copy No. 1 1st Lieut. R.A. Douglass.
 "   " 2. O.C. 42nd Division Machine Gun Battalion.
 "   " 3. War Diary.
 "   " 4. War Diary.
 "   " 5. File.

SECRET.

Copy No... 3

1/3rd East Lancashire Field Ambulance.

Order No. 37.

Reference Map BETHUNE Combined Sheet.
A.D.M.S., 42nd Division. M14/289.

2nd March 1918.

1. Lieut. T.B.H. TABUTEAU R.A.M.C.(T.C.), is detailed for duty as Officer in temporary medical charge of 1/7th Batt. Manchester Regt. during the absence of Lieut. MILLER on leave.

2. He will report to Officer Commanding 1/7th Batt. Manchester Regt. by 9.a.m. 3/3/18.

3. Necessary transport will be provided.

Lieut-Colonel
Commanding 1/3rd East Lancashire Field Ambulance.

Issued at ....

Distribution:-

Copy No.1. Lieut. T.B.H. Tabuteau.
Copy No.2. O.C., 1/7th Manchester Regt.
Copy No.3. War Diary
Copy No.4. War Diary
Copy No.5. File.

"A" Section 2 Coys Est Mess Appendix 58

Diets out Beef for men & Indians March 5th 1915

	Sunday	Monday	Tuesday	Wednesday	Thursday	Friday	Saturday
Breakfast 7:0 am	Tea, Rolled Oats, Fried Bacon, Bread	Tea, Rolled Oats, Fried Bacon, Bread	Tea, Rolled Oats, Fried Bacon, Bread	Tea, Rolled Oats, Fried Bacon, Bread	Tea, Rolled Oats, Boiled Jam, Bread	Tea, Rolled Oats, Boiled Jam Roll, Bread	Tea, Rolled Oats, Fried noodles, Jam, Bread
Dinner 12:0	A.B. Irish stew, Boiled potatoes, Tapioca pudding	A.B. Roast Beef, Boiled potatoes, Beans, Rice pudding	A.B. Irish stew, Boiled potatoes, Orange Custard, Fried noodles, Boiled potatoes, Beans, Jam pudding	A.B. Roast Beef, Rolled potatoes, Gravy, Jam pudding, Greens, Custard	A.B. College Pie, Rice pudding, Boiled potatoes, Boiled noodles, Jam, Tapioca pudding	York Stew, Boiled Beans, Rice pudding, Boiled potatoes, Nutty Crust, Beans, Boiled potatoes, Rice pudding	
Tea 4:30 pm	Tea, Bread & Butter, Minced meat, Jugged Tongue, Jam	Tea, Bread & Butter, Toasted Cheese, Stewed dates	Tea, Bread & Butter, Toasted Cheese, Boiled Beef, Pickles, Jam	Tea, Bread & Butter, Minced meat, Jam	Tea, Bread & Butter, Minced meat, Cakes	Tea, Bread & Butter, Toasted Bacon, Jam, Custard	
Supper 7:30 pm	Cocoa, Biscuits	Cocoa, Biscuits	Cocoa, Fancy Biscuits	Cocoa, Biscuits	Cocoa, Biscuits	Cocoa, Biscuits	Cocoa, Fancy Biscuits, Jam

1/3rd East Lancashire Field Ambulance. Appendix 58

Personal Diet Sheet for week ending March 3rd 1915

	Sunday	Monday	Tuesday	Wednesday	Thursday	Friday	Saturday
Breakfast 7.30 AM	Tea, Bread, Fried Bacon	Tea, Porridge, Bread, Boiled Ham	Tea, Bread, Fried Rissoles, Jam	Tea, Porridge, Boiled Ham, Bread	Tea, Bread, Fried Bacon	Tea, Porridge, Boiled Ham, Fried Bacon, Bread	Tea, Bread, Fried Bacon
Lunch 12.30 pm	Tea, Bread Butter, Toasted Cheese, Jam	Tea, Bread Butter, Boiled Meat, Stewed Dates	Tea, Bread Butter, Mock Crab, Jam	Tea, Bread Butter, Fried Rissoles, Jam	Tea, Bread Butter, Toasted Cheese, Dates	Tea, Bread Butter, Mince meat, Jam	Tea, Bread Butter, Cheese, Jam
Dinner 5.0 pm	A.B. Irish stew, Rice pudding	A.B. Boiled Beef, Boiled potatoes, Lent pudding	A.B. Roast Beef, Boiled potatoes, Beans, Rice pudding, Oranges	A.B. Stewed Steak, Onions, Boiled potatoes, Boiled batter	A.B. Roast Beef, Beans, Boiled potatoes, Rainbow pudding	A.B. Roast Beef, Mash. potatoes, Boiled batter, Rice pudding	A.B. Roast Mutton, Beans, Boiled potatoes, Bread pudding
Supper 8.0 pm	Tea, Biscuits	Tea, Biscuits	Tea, Biscuits, Cheese cakes	Tea, Biscuits, Cheese cakes	Tea, Biscuits	Tea, Biscuits	Tea, Biscuits

1/3 East Lancs Field Ambulance   Appendix
                                                   "A" 5a.

Personnel Diet Sheet for week ending March 9th 1918

	Sunday	Monday	Tuesday	Wednesday	Thursday	Friday	Saturday
Breakfast 7.30 am	Tea Porridge Fried Bacon Bread	Tea Fried Bacon Bread Jam	Tea Porridge Boiled Ham Bread Jam	Tea Fried Bacon Bread Jam	Tea Porridge Fried Bacon Bread Jam	Tea Porridge Boiled Ham Bread Jam	Tea Porridge Fried Bacon Bread
Lunch 12.30 pm	Tea Bread Butter Fried Rissoles Jam	Tea Bread Butter Toasted Cheese Jam	Tea Bread Butter Corned Beef Pickles Jam	Tea Bread Butter Dripping toast Jam	Tea Bread Butter Minced meat on toast Jam	Tea Bread Butter Cheese Jam	Tea Bread Butter Fried Rissoles Jam
Dinner 5.0 pm	A. Baked M't & brown Beans B. Stewed Meat + Onions Boiled potatoes Beans	A.B Boiled Beef Beans Boiled potatoes Rice pudding	A.B Irish stew Boiled potatoes Rice pudding	A.B Stewed Meat + Onions Beans Boiled onions Baked pudding	A.B Roast Beef Boiled onions Rice pudding	A.B Boiled Ham Boiled onions Boiled potatoes	A.B Irish stew Rantern pudding
Supper 8.0 pm	Tea Biscuits	Tea Biscuits	Tea Biscuits	Tea Biscuits	Tea Biscuits	Tea Biscuits	Tea Biscuits

13th East Lancs Field Ambulance — March 9, 1918.

Morlix

Patients Diet Sheet for week ending March 9th 1918.

	Sunday	Monday	Tuesday	Wednesday	Thursday	Friday	Saturday
Breakfast 7.0 am	Coffee, Rolled Oats, Toasted Cheese, Bread	Tea, Rolled Oats, Boiled ham, Bread	Coffee, Rolled Oats, Fried Bacon, Bread	Tea, Rolled Oats, Fried Bacon, Bread	Coffee, Rolled Oats, Toasted Cheese, Bread	Tea, Rolled Oats, Fried Bacon, Bread	Coffee, Rolled Oats, Fried Bacon, Bread
Dinner 12.0 noon	A-B. Roast Beef, Beans, Boiled potatoes, Sago pudding	A. Baked Mt salmon, Tapioca pudding B. Stewed Meat + onions, Rice pudding, Boiled potatoes	A-B. Roast Beef, Irish stew, Sago pudding, Boiled potatoes B.	A. Baked Mt salmon, Sago pudding B. Boiled potatoes, Irish stew, Tapioca pudding + white sauce	A. Boiled Beef, Cottage pie, Plum pudding + white sauce B. Baked potatoes	A-B. Boiled Beef, Baked potatoes, Rice pudding + white sauce	
Tea 4.30 pm	Tea, Bread Butter, Fruit, Tongue, Jam, Stewed pears	Tea, Bread Butter, Fruit, Toasted cheese, Jam	Tea, Bread Butter, Sardines, Jam, Bananas & Apple	Tea, Bread Butter, Cheese, Jam	Tea, Bread Butter, Minced meat, Cheese, Jam	Tea, Bread Butter, Toasted cheese, Jelly, Custard	
Supper 7.30 pm	Cocoa, Ham Sandwiches	Cocoa, Jam Biscuits	Cocoa, Bread, Biscuits	Cocoa, Bread, Jam	Cocoa, Bread, Biscuits	Cocoa, Bread, Jam	Cocoa, Bread, Jam

1/3rd East Lancashire Field Ambulance.   Copy No. 3

Order No. 38.

19th March, 1918.

Reference Map BETHUNE Combined Sheet.
A.D.M.S., 42nd Division M14/195.

1. 1st Lieut. E.A.MILLER, M.O.R.C., U.S.A., is detailed for duty as Officer in temporary medical charge of 1/8th Bn. Lancashire Fusiliers during the absence of Captain F.S.BYDALE on leave.

2. He will report to Officer Commanding 1/8th Bn. Lancashire Fusiliers by 9 a.m. 19th instant.

3. Necessary transport will be provided.

[signature]
Lieut.-Colonel,
Commanding 1/3rd East Lancs. Field Ambulance.

Issued at 1230

Distribution:-

Copy No. 1. 1/Lieut.E.A.Miller.
"   "   2. O.C.,1/8th Lancs. Fusiliers.
"   "   3. War Diary.
"   "   4. War Diary.
"   "   5. File.

Copy No. 3

1/3rd East Lancashire Field Ambulance.

Order No. 39.

Reference Map BETHUNE Combined Sheet
A.D.M.S. 42nd Division 67.

22nd March, 1918.

1. 1st Lieut. F. B. LONG, M.O.R.C., U.S.A., is detailed for duty as Officer in temporary medical charge of 1/6th Bn. Manchester Regiment during the absence of Captain H. WILSON on leave.

2. He will report to Officer Commanding 1/6th Bn. Manchester Regiment on morning of 24th inst.

3. Necessary transport will be provided.

Lieut.-Colonel,
Commanding 1/3rd East Lancs. Field Ambulance.

Issued at 1630

Distribution:-

Copy No. 1. 1st Lieut. F. B. Long.
 "   " 2. O.C., 1/6th Manchester Rgt.
 "   " 3. War Diary.
 "   " 4. War Diary.
 "   " 5. File.

WAR DIARY

OF

1/3RD EAST LANCASHIRE FIELD AMBULANCE

FROM :- April 1st, 1918 TO :- April 30th, 1918.

(VULUME IV)

WAR DIARY
or
INTELLIGENCE SUMMARY

Army Form C. 2118.

Place	Date	Hour	Summary of Events and Information	Remarks and references to Appendices
BAIENCOURT	1.4.18	10.45	[illegible handwritten entry]	Appendix 63
		10.00	C.O. visited Divisional HQ + Professional Museum. When the stores 29 Regimental duty Field Ambulance Order 22/10 received by today meeting the men on Gen. Davis's own the stores [illegible] afternoon No. 10 Lorry of SD Section and A and B [illegible] MONT messed at A Table Sym at ESSARS arr 11 p.m. 13th [illegible] Field Ambulance [illegible]	
		14.00	[illegible] 134 th Field Ambulance men [illegible] BIENVILLERS at 11 am [illegible] all ADS to [illegible] on 2h. 4. 18 [illegible] arr 9.30. [illegible] HUSKINS reported from BELLE ALLIANCE Captain DETACHFIELD ? LENS	
BIENVILLERS	2.4.18		For day [illegible] ADMS [illegible] visit Divisional ADS.	
		10.00	ADMS. visited ADS	
		11.15	CO followed, arrived accompanied by our [illegible] advised DRS [illegible] PERRIERS & SSCo 19 [illegible]	Appendix 64
			Pte Taylor & Pte FORD A & F 20, 4, 69 a Music Hall Stop DISCRIPTING FRIDAY Situation satisfactory.	
			Major HENRY and Captain PRESTWICH at ADS	
			Major WEBSTER acted as GIBSON [illegible] Field Ambulance until 19th for [illegible] enquiring in the morning [illegible] Field [illegible]	
	3.4.18	8.00	In the evening found visibly of Medical number of stores came and 12 days supply.	
			From WEBSTER and Captain GIBSON also Captain DELFIELD & Capt LONG	
			Owing to Army order [illegible] ADS [illegible] [illegible] HENRY taking [illegible] MASN is [illegible] [illegible] typing [illegible]	
		19.00	Major M.A. LEACH HORS. USA. [illegible]	
		19.30	[illegible] Lieut PARRIS Lieut LORIE [illegible] reported to the [illegible] Field Ambulance also at M.I.	Appendix 65

Army Form C. 2118.

WAR DIARY
or
INTELLIGENCE SUMMARY.
(Erase heading not required.)

Instructions regarding War Diaries and Intelligence Summaries are contained in F. S. Regs., Part II. and the Staff Manual respectively. Title pages will be prepared in manuscript.

Place	Date	Hour	Summary of Events and Information	Remarks and references to Appendices
BENVILLERS	4.4.18		[illegible handwritten entries]	

Army Form C. 2118.

WAR DIARY
or
INTELLIGENCE SUMMARY.
(Erase heading not required.)

Instructions regarding War Diaries and Intelligence Summaries are contained in F. S. Regs., Part II. and the Staff Manual respectively. Title pages will be prepared in manuscript.

Place	Date	Hour	Summary of Events and Information	Remarks and references to Appendices
BIENVILLERS	1.4.16		[illegible handwritten entry]	
		10.10	[illegible handwritten entry]	
		1.30	[illegible handwritten entry]	
		13.10	[illegible handwritten entry]	
		16.30	[illegible handwritten entry]	
HÉBUTERNE	2.4.16	9.40	Lieut. J Lord Wounded [illegible] in HEAD	
			Casualties 5th & 4th Coys. Killed O.R. 2. Wounded O.R. 31, Wounded grave O.R. 12 N/D N.Q.	
		14.00	[illegible]	

Army Form C. 2118.

WAR DIARY
or
~~INTELLIGENCE SUMMARY~~

(Erase heading not required.)

Instructions regarding War Diaries and Intelligence Summaries are contained in F. S. Regs., Part II. and the Staff Manual respectively. Title pages will be prepared in manuscript.

Place	Date	Hour	Summary of Events and Information	Remarks and references to Appendices
HENU	9.4.18	0900	Lieut. SB TABUTEAU proceeded to Boulogne to sit Field Ambulances & Embus. 2 & 3.	
		1800	C.O. obtained Cookhouse & Office of A.D.M.S.	
			seen if everything has got for the Engineers to start work on tomorrow	
			slow whitewashing & area for tents	
			Taking of Strength of Unit as listed:	
			Bearers as usual	
			Section officers carrying out list exchange of Personal and checking of kits & arms	
			Equipment	
			Used tents. Tormor Lock after permanent sheds	
			Veterinary Officer inspects Horses & reported satisfactory.	
10.4.18			C.O. visits A.D.M.S, 126 Bde Hqrs, & 4th Ambulance Hqrs.	
			11 Sick admitted	
			See transfer of wagons being issued & new features got after	
			Personnel being refitted with clothing as much good for attention	
			Band practice necessary.	
			No rain today but refuse was deep in mud	
			Polled A.B.C wing at	
			Lieut. T. FAUSTINE (T.C.) M.S.D. reported, came on tour on duty after examinations	
11.4.18			All Motor Ambulances & Lorries being repaired	
			18 cases admitted	
			C.O. visits UI XIII Corps appointment apart confirmed	
			Pts. LEACH, BLAND, CONNER & HUMPHRIES award Military Medals for gallant service in action	
12.4.18			Band practice Military Band gave Selections of music outside Y.M.C.A. huts	
			mostly songs, hymns led.	
			11 cases admitted. Satisfactory Reports.	
		1620	C.O. attended a Lecture & Hon. of D.M.S.	
			14 cases admitted	

Army Form C. 2118.

WAR DIARY
or
INTELLIGENCE SUMMARY
(Erase heading not required.)

Place	Date	Hour	Summary of Events and Information	Remarks and references to Appendices
HENU	13.4.18		Equipment of MDS checked overhauled & needed Total taken on in future embodied in letter to ADMS.	Appendix 38. App.
		1400	C.O. went to ambulance dumps.	
			C.O. visits ambulance to see upon state of ambulance car. Pruning 14 cases admitted	
	14.4.18		11 cases admitted during the past. Orders received from ADMS to move Division	App.
	15.4.18	1500	15 Horses sent to the three Battalions of 126th Bde Field Ambulance takes over 20.44 lines & many of the MSP. Major HENRY visits new site reconnaissance supplies.	Appendix 69.
	16.4.18	11.20	C.O. visited new site @ SOUASTRE, & found accommodation very limited Orders received from Lt. LEACH to proceed in my motor car. (Field Ambulance taking 20.45)	App 70. App.
		11.30	Reinforcement of 1 12.0 to Rank admitted in.	
		11.30	Major HENRY with advance party moved out.	
	17.4.18	0900	MDS at SOUASTRE Taken over by Major HENRY & advance party. Unit proceeded by march route to SOUASTRE meeting up 49th Field Ambulance @ MDS.	App.
		1000	DDMS visits MDS & informs considerable increase of extra accommodation in shape of Field Ambulance of the 63rd Division.	
		1130	Accommodation comprises M.I. room & waiting room, quite distinct from receiving room, dressing room evacuating ward of stretcher cases, walking wounded, also gas ward, duty Room, QM Stores, dispensary, cook house, billets for personnel, canteen. Staff of horse lines left at MDS. 9 wounded, 33 sick = 2 detained cases admitted.	

Army Form C. 2118.

WAR DIARY
or
INTELLIGENCE SUMMARY

(Erase heading not required.)

Instructions regarding War Diaries and Intelligence Summaries are contained in F. S. Regs., Part II. and the Staff Manual respectively. Title pages will be prepared in manuscript.

Place	Date	Hour	Summary of Events and Information	Remarks and references to Appendices
SOUASTRE	18.4.18	1000	C.O. visited ADMS Office ARM, DADOS & Salvage Coy on matters connected with the Unit. ADMS visited the MDS. O.C. 31 MAC (supplying cars & evacuation) visited the MDS. Working of MDS (receiving arrangements, an office being detailed to M.I. room to sort wounded, two officers to dressing room to receive cases by day & three by night. Day duty finishing morning at 8 am, night duties at 8 pm. Full complement of NCOs accompanying their duties. 20 wounded & 35 sick admitted	WWWJ
	19.4.18	1000	Attended conference at Office of ADMS. Snowing all morning. Both in forenoon & afternoon many attending of visited of MDS, ten men were being killed in former. Hot cocoa provided every day for patients of visited of MDS. 51 sick & 20 wounded admitted	WWJ
	20.4.18		Frost during night, first day without daylight air raids. 44 sick & 18 wounded admitted	WWJ
	21.4.18		O.C. 2 MAC visited MDS on service of the coy. During day MDS was held & cases on the line established. 61 sick & 24 wounded admitted	WWJ
	22.4.18		Fine day very quiet. ADMS visited MDS group. 72 sick & 12 wounded admitted	WWJ

WAR DIARY
or
INTELLIGENCE SUMMARY.

(Erase heading not required.)

Army Form C. 2118.

Place	Date	Hour	Summary of Events and Information	Remarks and references to Appendices
SOUASTRE	24.4.18		Today Billets changed, all officers shifting to new billets. Fine day, bright sunshine. 101 Sick & 19 wounded admitted. Village shelled during the day.	MM
	25.4.18		D.A.D.M.S. LNCC & 9 Mag refts them arrived. A.D.M.S. visited M.D.S. Thunderstorm today: 41 Sick & 12 wounded admitted	MM
	26.4.18		Strain medication of unit. A.D.M.S. visited M.D.S. The Corps Officer visited M.D.S. with regard to supply stores, gas diet. £12.3 admitted. 8 unit of transmitted to R.A.M.C. Corps & Memory War Fund. 35 Sick & 8 wounded admitted	MM
	27.4.18		A quiet day. Major HENRY awarded the Military Honors 51 sick & 11 wounded admitted	MM
	28.4.18		D.D.M.S. visited M.D.S. & forward installations. & anything was made of Captain FAIRSTONE to Canal or headquarters established (field ambulance taken as 146) consisted around of ability in neighbourhood during night 66 sick & 14 wounded admitted. Draft of 10 O.R. refts them arrived	MM

WAR DIARY
or
~~INTELLIGENCE~~ SUMMARY.

(Erase heading not required.)

Army Form C. 2118.

Instructions regarding War Diaries and Intelligence Summaries are contained in F. S. Regs., Part II. and the Staff Manual respectively. Title pages will be prepared in manuscript.

Place	Date	Hour	Summary of Events and Information	Remarks and references to Appendices
SOUASTRE	29.4.18		First day. Some settling around MDS in village. ADMS visited MDS. Band practice now carried on daily, improvement everything this late show. 72 sick + 12 wounded admitted.	A/MS
	30.4.18	11.05	New arrangements made by which 1/1 2/1 Field Ambulance further not though than A.T.D. took instead of this being done 3 MDS. ADMS HQ of 59 minute MDS. 57" Division as expect tomorrow. A.D. O.C. 2/2 wessex F Ambulance visited MDS on that unit teacher details total men the MDS. Was day had quiet, no shelling. 29 sick + 14 wounds admitted.	A/MS

M.M. Cunningham Lt Col

Copy No. 3

1/3rd East Lancashire Field Ambulance
Order No 40

Appendix 62

Reference Map LENS 11
A.D.M.S. 42nd Division

1st April 1918.

1. 1st LIEUT. E.A. MILLER, M.O.R.C. U.S.A, is detailed for duty as Officer in ~~temporary~~ medical charge of 1/10th Battn. Manchester Regiment.

2. He will report to Officer Commanding 1/10th Battalion Manchester Regiment

3. Necessary transport will be provided.

W. Murray
Lieut Colonel
Comdg. 1/3rd East Lancs Fld. Ambce.

Issued at 10.45
Distribution :-
Copy No. 1. 1st Lieut E.A. Miller
 "   " 2. OC 1/10 Bn Manchester Regt.
 "   " 3. War Diary
 "   " 4. War Diary
 "   " 5. File

A.D.M.S.
42nd Division.

Situation report.

1. There is a continuous stream of sick parading at the M.D.S., BIENVILLERS, coming from a variety of Units and Formations, detail of units forms the subject of a separate communication.
One officer on duty by day, and one by night is necessary for the work of the A.D.S. alone.

2. On visiting the forward area today, the collecting post at ESSARS was found to be in an unprotected iron hut, out of which they were actually shelled in my presence, there being no protection for either patients or bearers.
A cellar was obtained, some details of another Division (37½), who were out of their area, being moved out to make way for the R.A.M.C., and instructions were given as to the erection of a shelter for stretcher cases, whilst being dressed.
Arrangements were also made for the maintenance of hot cocoa for patients and bearers at this post, both by day and by night.
The car stand (2 Ambulance cars) was moved about 50 yards west of its original place, owing to its being too near a battery, and shelter for the drivers arranged for.
The G.O'sC. the three infantry brigades were visited and expressed their satisfaction of the arrangements made for the evacuation of casualties.
The forward bearer officer is stationed in the 125 Bde. Headquarters.
The Relay Post at F.20.b.1.9. requires some work in the provision of shelter for personnel and patients, the existing shelter being quite inadequate, instructions as to this procedure being given to the N.C.O. in charge.
Arrangements were made here for the provision of hot cocoa for patients and bearers, both by day and by night.
The bearer post at DIEVILLE FARM was found satisfactory.
Communication has been established, and is being satisfactorily maintained between all the R.A.P. and the bearer posts in connection with them.
A detachment of the Salvage Company, attached to the Field Ambulance, is working satisfactorily.
The detachment of the Burial Company has reported its arrival and commenced work.

A.D.S., BIENVILLERS,
2-4-1918.

Lieut Colonel
Comdg. 1/3rd East Lancs Field Ambulance

Copy No. 3.

1/3rd East Lancashire Field Ambulance
Order No. 1.

Reference map. Sheet 57 D 1/40,000 J.6.b.
57ms & 2nd Division

3rd April, 1918.

1. 1st Lieut. F.B. LONG, M.O.R.C., U.S.A. is detailed for duty as Officer in medical charge 93rd Army Field Artillery Brigade.

2. He will report to O.C. 93rd Army Field Artillery Brigade at CHATEAU-DE-LA-HAIE, J.6.b. Sheet 57a, 1/40,000, on 4-4-1918.

3. Necessary transport will be provided.

4. All maps and documents to be handed in to the Orderly Room prior to departure.

V. McCumming
Lieut.Colonel
Comdg. 1/3rd East Lancs Field Ambulance

Issued at 1930

Distribution:-
Copy No. 1. 1st Lieut. F.B. Long
. 2. O.C. 93rd A.F.A. Bde
. 3. War Diary
. 4. War Diary
. 5. File.

1/3rd East Lancashire Field Ambulance

Copy No. 3

Order No 47.

Reference map 1/40,000 Sheet 57D.
ADMS 4th Div. 31/3/18

1st April 1918

1. Lieut. BREWER, M.O.R.C. U.S.A, attached 1/3 East Lancashire Field Ambulance, is detailed for duty as officer in temporary medical charge 1/5 Bn. Manchester Regiment.

2. He will report to O.C. 1/5 Bn Manchester Regt. forthwith.

3. Necessary transport will be provided.

M W Cumming
Lieut Colonel
Comdg 1/3 E. Lancs. Field Ambulance

Issued at 21/5
Distribution :-
Copy no 1. Lieut. Brewer
       2. O.C. 1/5 Manchester Rgs.
       3. War Diary
       4. War Diary
       5. File

A.D.M.S.
42nd Division.

SITUATION REPORT.

Owing to the heavy shelling, the BUCQUOY Road East of HANNESCAMPS is quite impossible for ambulance car traffic, therefore a car post (1 N.C.O. and 4 men) has been established at E.10.c.1.7, and a new relay post (12 bearers) on the road between HANNESCAMPS and ESSARTS.

The Collecting Post at ESSARTS, and the relay posts at F.20.b.1.9 and F.27.b.2.9 remain as in last report.

A new relay post (4 bearers) has been established at F.21.d.5.8.

The Forward Bearer Officer (Major HENRY) reports that he has personally reconnoitred the only other road of evacuation, viz. that from Relay Post F.20.b.1.9 to MONCHY-au-BOIS, and found it to be impassable for ambulance car traffic.

The position of the R.A.P's appears to have undergone some alteration, but as soon as their map references can be ascertained they will be forwarded.

Hot cocoa is provided night and day at the A.D.S. BIENVILLERS Collecting Post ESSARTS, and Relay Post F.20.b.1.9.

Stretcher cases have been and are being satisfactorily collected and sent on to the M.D.S in the Field Ambulance Motor Ambulances.

A considerable number of walking wounded, on arrival at the A.D.S, are rested, dressed, and after being given food, are being despatched to the M.D.S. in the Horse Ambulance wagons of the Division.

A considerable number of gassed cases on arrival at the A.D.S. on G.S. Wagons are similarly being dealt with.

Between 8 a.m. and present hour, 319 casualties have passed through the A.D.S, including 1 of 1st Field Ambulance, 1 of 2nd Field Ambulance, and 11 of 3rd Field Ambulance

A.D.S.
BIENVILLERS
5-4-1918.
18.45.

W. M. Cunningham
Lieut Colonel
Comdg. 1/3 East Lancs. Field Ambulance

Copy No. 3.

1/3ᵈ East Lancashire Field Ambulance
Order No 43

Reference Map Sheet 57D.
A.D.M.S. 42ⁿᵈ Division. M14/196

8th April 1918

1. Lieut. T.B.H. TABUTEAU, R.A.M.C.(T.C) is detailed to proceed to 1/4th Bn. Manchester Regiment, for duty as Officer in Medical Charge.

2. He will report to O.C. 1/4 Bn. Manchester Regiment forthwith.

3. Necessary transport will be provided.

M. _____
Lieut Colonel
Comdg. 1/3ᵈ East Lancs. Field Ambulance.

Distribution:-
Copy No 1. Lieut. T.B.H. Tabuteau
"   " 2. O.C. 1/4 Bn. Manchester Rgt.
"   " 3. War Diary.
"   " 4. War Diary.
"   " 5. File.

A.D.M.S.
42nd Division

The experience of recent warfare in France having shown that the equipment and transport laid down in A.F.G 1098 for a Field Ambulance would bear some alterations, that shown below has been adopted by the 1/3º East Lancashire Field Ambulance.

Sectional Transport

A, B & C each
1 Horse Ambulance
1 Limber G.S.
1 Wagon G.S.
1 Water Cart

Headquarters

1 Limber G.S.
3 Wagons G.S.
1 Maltese Cart

Each Ambulance Wagon (H and M T) carries 2 Thomas Splints in addition to stretchers and blankets.

The Horse Ambulance Wagons also carry a small box of dressings and a small box of Medical Comforts, so that at a roadside halt each Ambulance Wagon could form a miniature A.D.S.

The contents of the section limbers have been found by experience sufficient to construct an A.D.S., and are shown in detail on attached sheet. In the case of an advance, one can push forward to open a new A.D.S., whilst the open one is packing up.

The Section G.S. Wagons carry such articles as are required to supplement those on the limbers, and in addition such as tents, stretchers, blankets, ground sheets, personnel blankets, etc.

The Headquarters Limber takes the Orderly Room Stationery in one half, and the Cooks' Utensils in the other half.

The Headquarters G.S. Wagons carry blankets authorized under G.R.O., Quartermaster's Stores, Drugs, Dressings, Medical Comforts, Repair Pannier for transport, Reserve Stationery boxes, and also reserve Medical Pannier etc.

The Maltese Cart carries the Farrier's implements, and forge etc.

Lieut Colonel
Comdg 1/3º E Lancs Field Ambulance

13-4-18

Contents of Section Limbers

"A" Pannier

Basins enamel 7½ × 5¾	3
Clippers hair	no 1
Flags pendant	4
Forks	10
Knives table	10
Spoons	10
Scissors hair	prs 1
Towels hand	10
" operating	3
Basins enamel 6"	6
Covers, tin 6¼"	6
Faders enamel	4
Plates dinner	10
Pannikins	12
Jug enamel	1
Forks flesh	1
Hammers claw, 20 oz	1
Ladles cooks	1
Bowl dressing	1
Gowns operating	2
Aprons "	2
Box, tin (9 candles)	1
Bandages many tailed belt	1
Hook, belt	1
Line, clothes, hemp 40 yds	1
Pincers	prs 1
Axe hammer headed	1
Urinals zinc	2
Warmers stomach	6
Funnel enamel	1
Pyjama suits	6
Instruments, surgeons case	1

Articles carried loose

Medical companion	1
Haversacks surgical	2
Water bottles surgical	6
Lamps acetylene	2
Soap case	1
Carbide	lbs 8
Box, dressing (compd. dressings)	1
Stools close	2
Blankets	30
Oilsheets	10

"B" Pannier

Lamp hurricane	1
Cans, oil (paraffin) 5½ pt	3
Cans, meth. 5½ pt	1
Brush whitewash	1
Brushes, scrubbing hand	1
" washing	2
Pans, bed	1
Saw hand	1
Trowels	1
Stove primus	1
Brackets for acet. lamps	2
Openers tin	2
Tow, carbolized	lbs 5
Buckets canvas	4
Bowls enamel 14"	2
Zinc bowls 11"	1
Nails and screws assd.	lbs 7
Cotton waste	lbs 5
Flag, union	1
Tape measuring 100'	1

F.S.P. I. (intact)

F.S.P. 2.
Do away with contents of lower tins except—
 1 pkt. jaconet
 1 tin for bandages assorted
 1 " " wool
 1 " " cut gauze & boric lint

Transfer from "B" basket to "A":—
Nail brushes, tourniquets and tin opener. Do away with meat extract and replace with Eusol, and Samways tourniquets and 1 razor (from F.S.P.2)

Poles flag, directing	4
Axe felling	1
Spades G.S.	2
Case butchers	1
Kettles camp oval	4
Tents bell with pegs & poles	2
Splints Thomas with necessary attachments	4
Box medical comforts containing Tea, sugar, milk, cocoa, brandy (bott 2) biscuits, arrowroot & oxo	
Stools camp	2

Secret.   Copy No. 5.
                                                                Appendix 69

1/3rd East Lancashire Field Ambulance
Order No. 4.

Reference map 1/40,000 Sheet 57 D.
42nd Division R.A.M.C. Order No. 42.

15th April 1918.

1. The 1/3rd East Lancashire Field Ambulance will relieve the 49th Field Ambulance at SOUASTRE on the 17th inst., taking over the M.D.S. as from 9 a.m. Parade, marching order 10 a.m.

2. 15 Other Ranks, constituting one bearer squad, and 1 runner each will be attached to the Battalions of the 126 Bde. on the 15th inst., and so attached to the 1/2nd East Lancashire Field Ambulance whilst in charge of the Forward Evacuating Area. They will be rationed up to and including the 17th inst.

3. An advance party, consisting of one Officer to be detailed by O.C. "B" Section, with that section Tent Sub-division and limber will proceed to the M.D.S. SOUASTRE on 16-4-1918.

4. Present billets will be handed over to 49th Field Ambulance. Rear parties to be left in each billet for the purpose, if necessary.

5. The Horse Transport will proceed to a site to be notified later, the Mechanical Transport, less that required by the 1/2 East Lancashire Field Ambulance, proceeding to the M.D.S.

                                            N. M. Mummich
                                            Lieut. Colonel
                                    Comdg. 1/3rd East Lancs Field Ambulance.

Issued at 1740
Distribution :-

Copy No. 1. O.C. 'A' Section
  "   " 2. O.C. 'B' Section
  "   " 3. O.C. 'C' Section
  "   " 4. Quartermaster
  "   " 5/6. War Diary
  "   " 7. File.

Copy no. 3
Appendix 70

1/3° East Lancashire Field Ambulance
Order No 45

Reference Map 1/40,000 Sheet 57D
A.D.M.S. 42nd Division

16th April 1918

1. Lieut. M. A. Leach, M.O.R.C., U.S.A. is detailed for duty as Officer in Medical Charge 210th Bde, R.F.A. in relief of Capt. HOWARD, M.O.R.C., U.S.A.

2. He will report to OC 210 Bde, R.F.A. forthwith.

3. Necessary transport will be provided.

M.M Cunningh
Lieut Colonel
Comdg 1/3 E Lancs Field Ambulance

Issued at 1730
Distribution:-
Copy no. 1. Lieut. M. A. Leach
     "   2. OC 210 Bde R.F.A
     "   3. War Diary
     "   4. War Diary
     "   5. File

Copy No. 3

1/3rd. East Lancashire Field Ambce.

ORDER No. 46.

Reference Map. 1/40,000 Sheet 57 D.
A.D.M.S., 42nd Division.

Appendix 71.

28th April 1918.

1. Captain J.FANSTONE R.A.M.C. T.C. is detailed for duty as Officer in Temporary Medical Charge 1/8th Manchester Regt.

2. He will report to O.C.1/8th Manchester Regt. forthwith.

3. Necessary transport will be provided.

Lieut-Colonel,
Comdg.1/3rd. East Lancs. Field Ambce.

Issued at 1130

Distribution.-
Copy No.1. Capt. J. Fanstone.
  "   " 2. O.C.1/8th Man. Regt.
  "   " 3. War Diary.
  "   " 4. War Diary.
  "   " 5. File.

WAR DIARY

OF

1/3rd EAST LANCASHIRE FIELD AMBULANCE.

FROM :- May 1st, 1918. TO :- May 31st, 1918.

(VOLUME V)

Army Form C. 2118.

WAR DIARY
or
INTELLIGENCE SUMMARY.
(Erase heading not required.)

Instructions regarding War Diaries and Intelligence Summaries are contained in F. S. Regs., Part II. and the Staff Manual respectively. Title pages will be prepared in manuscript.

Place	Date	Hour	Summary of Events and Information	Remarks and references to Appendices
SOUASTRE	1.5.18	1230	Wet dull day. Very quiet, no shelling. D.M.S. 3rd Army, DDMS IV Corps, ADMS 42 Division inspected MDS. DMS expressed his satisfaction refering with Capt Harris. Lecture in the theatre music hall given from 7th Band. Gas practice of cellars & underground shelters of MDS commenced. 21 wounded & 31 sick admitted. Quarterly Meeting of officers was held.	WMF
	2.5.18	0730	Two G.S. wagons detailed for duty with Divisions. Fine warm spring day. Lecture & talking pictures. CO visited Art Sanitaire & 1/2 transe Field Ambulance. 30 sick, 14 wounded admitted.	WMF
	3.5.18		Fine day, warmer.	WMF
		1000	C.O. attended conference at Office of ADMS.	
		10.15	25 sick & 11 wounded admitted.	
			Men were of relief of Divisions in the line.	
	4.5.18		Fine day. C.O. visited 1/2 transe Field Ambulance. ADMS visited MDS. Gas practice of dugouts & underground shelters almost completed. 21st MAC Bearers detailed party of 4 carry 4 splints & a complete case. 21 Sick - 10 wounded admitted	WMF

WAR DIARY or INTELLIGENCE SUMMARY

Army Form C. 2118.

Place	Date	Hour	Summary of Events and Information	Remarks and references to Appendices
SOUASTRE	5.5.18		Many harassments of ROCHE lines during evening. 14 SCR + attack of our brigade. Instructions made to evacuate fortunate only 7 casualties came through.	Appendix 72
		0945	Field Ambulance below 20 hy to relief means 29 Sant + 13 wounded admitted	
	6.5.18	1000	Field Ambulance proceeded out of PAS a bivouaced in wood E of PAS @ C.18.C.93.	Appx F37/8
		1200	A.D.S troops closed SOUASTRE M.D.S. Fine afternoon grows + drying up after heavy rain during previous night. 4 + wat + 12 wounded admitted Lieutenant LEACH + details returned from duty as Divisional Rest Camp at MARIEUX	WWJ
P.A.S.	7.5.18		Wet day raised all night, opened any work recently 11 Sick admitted	WWJ
	8.5.18	0930	Fine day, ambulance hut & grounds wet + deep in mud in places	WWJ
		1000	Captains PRESTWICH + 60 OR proceeded to MARIEUX to work under direction of D.D.M.S.	
		1500	CO attended conference 98 Field Amb D.M.S CO visited camps of Units in Brigade Area 22 patients admitted	
	9.5.18	0710	Reconnaissance of tents location a hostile reconnaissance. Major HASKINS Captain Dotefield will 2 horse ambulance proceeded to COCIN a district in neighbourhood. Major HENRY to PAS headed estate of M.D.S.	WWJ
	10.5.18	1000	CO + Major HASKINS attended conference at office of A.D.M.S to discuss tactics of preceding day	WWJ

WAR DIARY
or
INTELLIGENCE SUMMARY.

(Erase heading not required.)

Army Form C. 2118.

Place	Date	Hour	Summary of Events and Information	Remarks and references to Appendices
PAS	11.5.18	10.00	Fine, dry day. Capt DELAFIELD proceeded to 210 Bde SQUAITRE, to give evidence on a R.E. C.M, who had been arraigned.	APPX I
		12.30	Half funeral parade for BATHS at PAS.	
			11 patients admitted.	
	12.5.18	14.00	Received Prel. Arrangements for reconnaissance - r.e. DOESNOG SCHEME	APPX II
		07.00	Fine day, sunshine.	
		08.00	Parade for Church Service at PAS, Sunderland	
		12.30	Other half of Bn. paraded & marched for BATHS, PAS	
			Patients admitted - Sick 16 Wounded 1.	
	13.5.18	04.00	Very rainy day -	APPX III
			Routine	APPX IV
			Patients admitted - Sick 11	
	14.5.18	09.00	Fine day.	
			Arranged ground at PAS for arrival of an American Field Ambulance - Major Henry drew 20 tents, built latrines and cookhouses - and billeting Office of the Ambulance.	APPX V
			MONDICOURT STATION	
		17.00	Capt Delafield proceeded to BERTRANCOURT with motor amb. and two horsed ambulance wagons - to meet Americans in 2 parties, arriving, and carry into - meet these trains 7 p.m 11 p.m and 3 a.m (15/5/18) about 40 patients carried, with one Caseload, at little - Self admitted during day - 7	
	15.5.18	03.00	Capt Delafield as above put American 7 U.S. A.F. into billets - guided to carrying ground after R.A.M. was ready Monday April 3rd 365.	APPX VI
		10.00	Quartermaster Sgt. Sergeants and NS SGTS Sergeants attended lectures today by Commandant 8th Army School of Cookery -	
		12.00	Relief of 46 D.R. reported to Capt Penland at CORPS REST STATION, MARIEUX.	
		15.00	Major Hoskins, on behalf of C.O. visited Capt Penland, work proceeding well in his (Capt Penland's) upper parade D.O.M.S. instructions	

Army Form C. 2118.

WAR DIARY
or
INTELLIGENCE SUMMARY.
(Erase heading not required.)

Instructions regarding War Diaries and Intelligence Summaries are contained in F. S. Regs., Part II. and the Staff Manual respectively. Title pages will be prepared in manuscript.

Place	Date	Hour	Summary of Events and Information	Remarks and references to Appendices
PAS	15.5.18	19.30	Party relieved (450 O.R.) from MARIEUX reported back.	MARTHA
		19.30	D.R.O. Nº 42. Dis received. 2 Military Medals presented to Pte ANER and Pte SMYES. A.S.C. attd. nopitals. Also 1 M.M. to PtR DURHAM Expedy A.S.	MARTHA
	16.5.18	08.30	Very fine sunshiny day — wrote Capt FANSTONE	
		09.50	Half the available personnel paraded to Div GAS OFFICER at PAS. Respirators re-fitted and retested, what necessary - found throat protector	
		10.00	the remainder under full kick, practised as above.	
		10.00	Arrival message from Sgt HUARD A.S.C., conveying the D.A.D.V.S. at Div employment stating the horses having been inspected by him	
			are in a very satisfactory condition.	
			6 Patients (sick) admitted	
	17.5.18		Fine warm day	M.M.
			18 Patients admitted	
	18.5.18		Thunderstorm Today.	M.M.
			The unit Sing Song Concert was held on Wgt in Town hypon Kitchen PAS.	
			10 Patients admitted	
	19.5.18		Church Parade. Unit marched to PAS Bosch attached	
			16.S wagon employed today hypod with 4 O.R. of J.D.H.Q.	M.M.
			6 patients admitted	
	20.5.18		Today quite full of Supplies 60 O.R. still on the ground. PDM.S. Corps @ MARIEUX.	W.H.T.
			Unit paid today	
			Squad drill & Pulmotor is practised being carried on daily, during past period gas mask are worn.	
			Major HARKINS proceeded to MARIEUX on relief of Captain PRESTWICH	

WAR DIARY or INTELLIGENCE SUMMARY

Army Form C. 2118.

Place	Date	Hour	Summary of Events and Information	Remarks and references to Appendices
PAB	21.5.18		Weather very hot. ADMS visited camp. All ofrs on full working order eg Tanks, showers, bakers, grave, hairc[utter], chiropodist & canteen. 10 patients admitted. Captain DELAFIELD proceeded to Divisional H.Q. as Temporary D.A.D.M.S.	MM
	22.5.18	1030	Closed instruction to junior officers & selected N.C.O.'s commenced. Fatigue party at MARIEUX returned today. Capt. PRESTWICH returned to Bn. 12 patients admitted.	MM
	23.5.18	2000	Gas mask worn by all ranks for one hour.	
		2100	Capt. Delafield returned from Divisional H.Qrs. 13 patients admitted.	MH.
	24.5.18	2000	Field Day. Capt. Prestwich & Capt. Delafield conducted reclassification of 229 Employment Coy. Gas mask worn by all ranks for one hour. 8 patients admitted.	MH.
	25.5.18	2000	Fine day. Capt. Prestwich & Capt. Delafield continued reclassification of 229 Empt. Coy. Gas mask worn by all ranks for one hour. 5 patients admitted.	MH.
	26.5.18	0815	Unit paraded in drill order & proceeded to ground provided by G.O.C. 42nd Divn. The following were inspected by Lieut-Colonel Hutcheson & presented awards in the name by Major Henry M.C. Sgt Maj E.Cobden Belgian Croix de Guerre Btt Lt/Col Hetch M.M. S.S. 377.	
		0930	Sgt T.Evans M.M. Pte W Humphreys M.M. Pte 6. Lead M.M. – also Pte F Mullen 235 Div Bn. "M.M." awarded for service while attached Capt Prestwich & Capt Delafield continued reclassification of 229 Empt. Coy.	MH.
		0600	Gas mask worn by all ranks for one hour. 5 patients admitted.	

Army Form C. 2118.

WAR DIARY
or
INTELLIGENCE SUMMARY.
(Erase heading not required.)

Instructions regarding War Diaries and Intelligence Summaries are contained in F. S. Regs., Part II. and the Staff Manual respectively. Title pages will be prepared in manuscript.

Place	Date	Hour	Summary of Events and Information	Remarks and references to Appendices
P+S	27.5.18		Staff Serjeant DOBSON admitted to hospital. Class of instruction for officers commenced. 6 cases admitted. D.D.M.S. 3rd Army visited this transport.	
	28.5.18		Serjeant DOBSON (M.T.) transferred to hospital. Firing butts & firearms drug and L & L9 as a protection against bombs. 6 cases admitted.	M/1
	29.5.18		10 cases admitted. Both of the trumpeters of A turn was found in P.A.3. Captain DELATIER 1/c shops watch a detail of other ranks to carrying out this statement.	M/1
	30.5.18		Warmer day. Until dark no such case occurred. 1/2 turn exercised in all work after dusk in small lines respirators. 4 cases admitted.	M/1
	31.5.18	1015	Eight bunglers & two drummers proceeded to G.H.Q. B.E.F. to sound General Salute for departing D.G. (M.S.) at ceremony being held on that parade.	M/1
		1100	All available Officers attended lecture in P.A.3 by Consulting Surgeon 3rd Army. 1/2 turn exercised in all work in small box respirators after church. Class of instruction for officers proceeding. 22 cases admitted.	

M.M. Summers Lt Col.

SECRET   Copy No. .....8....

                  1/3rd East Lancashire Field Ambulance.
                              Order No. 47.

Reference Map Sheet b 57D.
           42nd Division R.A.M.C. Order No. 44.

                                                    5th May, 1918.

1. The 42nd Division (less Artillery) is being relieved by the
   57th Division (less Artillery) in the Centre Sector IV Corps
   Area.

2. On relief the 42nd Division move into Army Reserve.

3. While in Army Reserve the Division is at the disposal of the
   IV Corps in case of attack. All field units of the Division
   are to be in readiness to move at an hour's notice from 9 p.m.
   to 9 a.m. and at 2 hours notice from 9 a.m. to 9 p.m.

4. The Field Ambulance will be relieved by the 2/2nd Wessex Fie[ld]
   Ambulance at the Main Dressing Station, and on relief will ta[ke]
   over the ambulance site near PAS at present occupied by the
   2/2nd Wessex Field Ambulance. Relief to be complete by 12
   noon 6th inst.

5. The Quartermaster with Advance Party will proceed to the new
   area and take over site from outgoing Field Ambulance at 8
   a.m. on the 6th inst.
   The Rear Party, under command of Captain M.E. DELAFIELD, will
   remain at M.D.S. up till 12 noon of the 6th inst. and the
   A.& D. Books of this Unit will be closed, and party marched
   off to rejoin Unit.

6. The unit will parade at 10 a.m. 6th inst. Band will attend.

7. The transport will remain in existing wagon lines, but 2
   Water Carts filled will join the Advance Party at HENU.

8. The Headquarters Limber will proceed with the Advance Party.
   "B" Section special limber will proceed with the rear party.
   "C" Section water cart will proceed with Rear party as far as
   the wagon lines.

9. Mechanical transport will proceed to the new area independent[ly]

10. All tents, trench shelter, tarpaulins and trench maps, (exclu[d]-
    ing mobilization equipment) will be handed over and taken ove[r]
    in situ, receipts being taken or given in each case.

11. Supplies. The 1/3rd East Lancashire Field Ambulance will swit[ch]
    from the Divisional Troops Company on the night of 5th inst.
    to Company fo the 126th Inf. Bde. at C.23.d.8.1.

                                                    Continued

(2)

12. D.A.D.O.S. moves to PAS on 5th inst.

13. Medical Arrangements. Sick and wounded will be collected from

    126th Inf. Bde.   PAS WOODS
    S.A.A.   PAS
    One Field Company R.E.   PAS
    One Company A.S.C.   PAS
    D.H.Q.   PAS

Issued at 0245...

Lieut.-Colonel,
Commanding 1/3rd East Lancs. Field Ambulance.

Distribution :-

Copy No. 1. O.C., "A" Section.
  "   " 2. O.C., "B" Section.
  "   " 3. O.C., "C" Section.
  "   " 4. Capt. M.E.Delafield.
  "   " 5. Quartermaster.
  "   " 6. O.C., 2/2nd Wessex Field Ambulance.
  "   " 7. File.
  "   " 8. War Diary.
  "   " 9. War Diary.

WAR DIARY

OF

1/3rd EAST LANCASHIRE FIELD AMBULANCE.

FROM :- JUNE 1st, 1918   TO :- JUNE 30th, 1918.

(VOLUME VI)

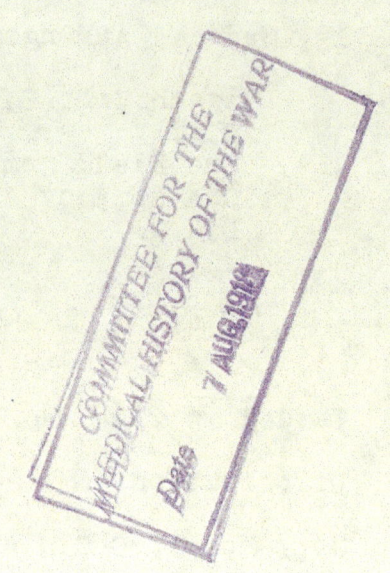

WAR DIARY
or
INTELLIGENCE SUMMARY.

Army Form C. 2118.

Place	Date	Hour	Summary of Events and Information	Remarks and references to Appendices
PAS	1.6.18		Fine day. Classes/Instruction to junior officers continued. Band played A.S.C during PAS hour. 10 patients admitted	MM
	2.6.18		Fine day. Church parade CMP moved to HQ PAS Band in attendance. 10 patients admitted	MM
	3.6.18	1645 1730 2000	Officers classes continued. Major HASKINS & 6 OR returned from Coy work at MARIEUX. Divisional Band played in Field Ambulance at Orders received for Division to move the line again. 11 patients admitted.	MM
	4.6.18	1100	Officers class continued. CO visits 3° NZ Field Ambulance with view to taking over their site at LOUVENCOURT 9 patients admitted	MM
	5.6.18	1100	Officers class continued. Batman parade for kit. View for man named F.C.Q Amblykine adv. P. 48. Major HASKINS awarded Military Cross. Birthday Honours 15 patients admitted	Appendix 73

WAR DIARY
or
INTELLIGENCE SUMMARY.
(Erase heading not required.)

Place	Date	Hour	Summary of Events and Information	Remarks and references to Appendices
PAB	6.6.18	14.00 / 15.00	Flying Day continued. Officers & men wounded. PRESTWICH & men wounded party proceeded to LOUVENCOURT. Officer FAIRSTONE to details proceeded to Divn Reception Camp MARIEUX 1 Field ambulance of 2/2 Field Ambulance	MM / Prof Form S.D. MM
	7.6.18	08.00	Unit paraded in marching order & proceeded on marchout via AUTIME — VAUCHELLES to LOUVENCOURT arriving at destination at 11.00 & immediately relieved 3rd New Zealand Field Ambulance at the D.R.S. 134 sick & wounded handed on to this Unit. D.R.S. reopened 1.35. C & 8. The section & officers billeted newings onto block of huts & all adjacent to Fd. A.M. 39 OR & 2 other officers of 2 Fd Ambulance.	
LOUVENCOURT	8.6.18		Block arrangements Scabies & others Surgical Medical	
			Dining room established, ante room taken, billiard table, chiropodists shop also, Salvage dump arranged. Receiving room (Surgical arranged) Bath, Clothing store, other than dressing, taken over from Major a Staffords Units for ablutions & treatments of patients. Arrangement made to disinfect Band & Hq in Chateau grounds twice a week. Racked celling job taken over a Staffs also train to everything nick covered spares grand & wounded admitted. Major HENRY evacuated to C.C.S sick	MM
		20.45	Instructions issued by Lt A LEACH to proceed on temporary duty to Field Ambulance when 20.49 C.O. attended conference by officer of ADMS ADMS visited D.R.S. Inspection only would said	Appointed MH

Army Form C. 2118.

WAR DIARY
or
INTELLIGENCE SUMMARY.
(Erase heading not required.)

Place	Date	Hour	Summary of Events and Information	Remarks and references to Appendices
LOUVENCOURT	9.6.18	1000	ADMS field work & mine unfit for duty in the line	
		1800	Work in wards & adjts continued. Convoy held for patients	
			31 cases admitted	
	10.6.18		White washing & cleaning of wards continued. Sorting out of kits in Pack store continued. Reconstruction of work force continued. Divisional Band played to patients in grounds.	
			21 patients admitted	
	11.6.18		Fine day. Reconstruction of tent lines & sanitary arrangements continued. Arrangements to make of winter palliasses at Raithes Collecting Post. Repairs necessitated by additional wards in grounds commenced. Field Ambulance had flaps in scabies compound in annex. 21 cases admitted & 6 dental case found.	
	12.6.18		Fine day. Potatoes & continuous work heavily. 20 cases admitted & 6 dental case found. Diet sheet of first three days eg 8th 9th & 10th attached	officers 75
	13.6.18	1930	Butchers shop in [tent] work commenced on Latrine staff. Divisional Commander visited DRS & inspected all wards & grounds, except Railhead Collecting Post. Proposed Tents erected in Chateau grounds, so that if neyed cases can be transferred from school buildings in the Town.	

A.5834. Wt.W4973/M687. 750,000. 8/16. D.D.&L.Ltd. Forms/C.2118/13

WAR DIARY
or
INTELLIGENCE SUMMARY

Army Form C. 2118.

(Erase heading not required.)

Place	Date	Hour	Summary of Events and Information	Remarks and references to Appendices
LOUVENCOURT	14.6.18		All surgical cases now found in Chateau ground. Details of officers duties changed.	WMZ
		1030	DDMS Lt Colp visits DRS. & inspects every detail. Conference re-arising compilation work commenced at Railhead Collecting Post in erecting shelters to assist wounded. A fatigue party of 12 O.R. from 1st N.Z. Field Ambulance hired to work at the D.R.S. 14 Potents admitted — 14 elective cases forwarded.	
	15.6.18	0930	C.O. proceeds to Corps Hqrs to proceed with DDMS to visit a site for a new C.R.S.	WMZ LENS
		1900	C.O. visits A.D.M.S. at DHQ.	
		2330	Re active transport proposed round route to Mt RENAULT for new HEUZECOURT the site of the new 1Nth Corps Rest Station.	
	16.6.18		C.O. details of Commandant of new C.R.S. at Mt RENAULT for proceed privately forwards	WMZ
		0930	Party in command temporarily of Lieut & Major HARKINS. M.C. Captain PRESTWICH & party are stores ambulances proceeded in connection with new C.R.S. & duty there	
	17.6.18	0930	Details of duties of O.R. changed to accord with removal of party on 16/6/18	DMSR
		1700	Lieut Sergeant PRICE reported from 1/2 Scot hospital for short hours for transport duty	
			28 patients admitted — 11 Dental cases forwarded	
	18.6.18	0930	A.D.M.S. visits & inspects the D.R.S.	ADMSR
			35 patients admitted — 9 Dental cases forwarded.	

Army Form C. 2118.

WAR DIARY
or
INTELLIGENCE SUMMARY.
(Erase heading not required.)

Instructions regarding War Diaries and Intelligence Summaries are contained in F.S. Regs., Part II. and the Staff Manual respectively. Title pages will be prepared in manuscript.

Place	Date	Hour	Summary of Events and Information	Remarks and references to Appendices
Boulogne	November 19/16	14.00	Routine. Inspected 10 beds at 2nd Convalescent Camp. 10 S.B. Div. Bath supplies. From A.D.M.S. D.D.O.M.S. A.D.M.S. & officer i/c Base laundries reported for duty in connection with Bath 13 N. H. H S. M.R.C. B.E.F. reported for duty in connection with Baths.	
"	20/16	14.00 4.15	Admitted 26 patients. 11 clients were furnished. Organized certain arrangements. O.C. 3rd Canadian Stationary Hospital came over & inspected hospital for Baths. Working personnel were provided for Baths. Admitted 40 patients. 13 Sanitorium feeders.	
"	21/16	10.30	A.D.M.S. visited Base Station – O.C. 3rd Canadian Field Dressing St. arrived. Part Station – no of beds promised 60 of personnel	
"		16.00	E.F.C. Cinema gave performance in Camp. No. of patients present. Admitted 35 patients & sent discharged 20 to Convalescent Camp.	
"	22/16 10.00a	16.00	It. C.O. visited Base Camp M. HALLEY & the O.C. 3rd Canadian Stationary Hospital. Arranged about beds for his unit. Admitted 40 patients – 20 discharged to Convalescent Camp.	
"		8.00	E.F.C. cinema again performed	
"	23/16	10.00	A.D.M.S. field visited & Board made up Capt Gillespie & Lieut Gillespie	
"		14.00	Cinema performed – (Jim Bowie School) 43 patients admitted.	

Army Form C. 2118.

WAR DIARY
or
INTELLIGENCE SUMMARY.

(Erase heading not required.)

Instructions regarding War Diaries and Intelligence Summaries are contained in F. S. Regs., Part II. and the Staff Manual respectively. Title pages will be prepared in manuscript.

Place	Date	Hour	Summary of Events and Information	Remarks and references to Appendices
Duisans T.1.O.E.N.COURT	24/4/18		Routine. Patients admitted 21	Appx
"	25/4/18	09.30	Lieut Gillespie proceeded to 41st Reception Camp to take over duties as duty Capt. Prior to S.L. Ibbeson	Appx
		11.00	Patients admitted 47	
"	26/4/18		Routine Patients admitted 62	Appx
		11.00	Major HASKINS joined A.D.M.S. 14.00 Major HASKINS joined 1/1 C.R.S.	
"	27/4/18	10.30	Major HASKINS attended M.O.M.S. conference at 13 U.S.	Appx
		18.30	Lieut GILLESPIE posted to 1/1st Field Amb Trs in relief of Capt. JOHNSON	
			Patients admitted 68	
"	28/4/18	16.30	Routine Capt. A.M. TOMPSON reported at 56 M.D.S. & Instructions as Senior Commander. Patients admitted 6B	Appx
"	29/4/18		Routine Patients admitted 100	
"	30/4/18	10.00	A.D.M.S. III Corps Army - A.D.M.S. and Major HARRISON 62 Reception Camp Hall. Reception Camp Hall - B amalgamated	Appx
		13.00		

Army Form C. 2118.

WAR DIARY
or
INTELLIGENCE SUMMARY.
(*Erase heading not required.*)

Instructions regarding War Diaries and Intelligence Summaries are contained in F. S. Regs., Part II. and the Staff Manual respectively. Title pages will be prepared in manuscript.

Place	Date	Hour	Summary of Events and Information	Remarks and references to Appendices
FOUENCOURT	30/10/16	19:00	Promising det. demands for Cpt JOHNSON to new regiment – from N.O.M.S. Relict minutes 100	VIIIB?

M M Robertson Major

A5834 Wt. W4973/M687 750,000 8/16 D. D. & L. Ltd. Forms/C.2118/13

SECRET.   Copy No. 6.

1/3rd East Lancashire Field Ambulance.

Order No. 48.

Reference Map Sheet 57D 1/40,000.
          42nd Division R.A.M.C. Order No.45.

5th June, 1918.

1. The 42nd Division (less Artillery) is relieving the New Zealand Division (less Artillery) in Right Sector of IV Corps Front on 6/7 & 7/8th inst.

2. The 1/3rd East Lancashire Field Ambulance will take over the Divisional Rest Station, LOUVENCOURT, from the 3rd New Zealand Field Ambulance. Relief to be completed by 12 noon, 7th inst.
   The 1/3rd East Lancashire Field Ambulance will hand over the present site to 48th Field Ambulance, 37th Division. Relief to be completed by 12 noon, 7th inst.

3. All defence schemes, trench maps, programmes of work, trench stores, etc., will be taken over from the 3rd New Zealand Field Ambulance.
   All defence schemes, etc. of present area will be handed over to the 48th Field Ambulance.

4. Captain J.FANSTONE with 2 Other Ranks will proceed to HALLOY for duty with the Battle Surplus of this Division on the 6th inst. to arrive there by 5 p.m.
   Two days' rations to be taken.

5. An advance party of 12 Other Ranks with "C" Section Limber under Captain F.G.PRESTWICH, will proceed to LOUVENCOURT on the 6th inst. to arrive there by 3 p.m.
   One day's rations to be taken.

6. The Field Ambulance with Band will parade in marching order, steel helmets to be worn, at 8 a.m. on the 7th inst., and proceed by march route to LOUVENCOURT.
   Horse Transport to arrive at present site from HENU at 7-45 a.m. Feeds will be carried on horses.
   Mechanical Transport will proceed to destination independently.

7. An advance party of the 48th Field Ambulance will arrive on the 6th inst.

8. 15 Bearers will proceed to the 126th Infantry Brigade to arrive at Battalions in time to proceed with them on the morning of the 7th inst. Two days' rations to be carried.
   Dress Battle Order.

                                                    Lieut.-Colonel,
                              Commanding 1/3rd East Lancashire Field Ambulance.

Issued at 1100.

Distribution :-

Copy No. 1.   O.C. "A" Section.
  "   " 2.   O.C. "B" Section.
  "   " 3.   O.C. "C" Section.
  "   " 4.   Quartermaster.
  "   " 5.   O.C. 3rd New Zealand Field Ambulance.
  "   " 6.   War Diary.
  "   " 7.   War Diary.
  "   " 8.   File.

Copy No. ...3...

1/3rd East Lancashire Field Ambulance.

Order No. 49.

Reference Map Sheet 57D.
A.D.M.S., 42nd Division. M 14/207

8th June, 1918.

1. Lieut. M.A. LEACH, M.O.R.C., U.S.A., is detailed for temporary duty as Officer in Medical Charge 210th Brigade, R.F.A.

2. He will report to Officer Commanding 210th Brigade R.F.A. by 12 noon 9th instant.

3. Necessary transport will be provided.

[signature]
Lieut.-Colonel,
Commanding 1/3rd East Lancs, Field Ambulance.

Issued at 2045.

Distribution :-

Copy No. 1. Lieut. M.A. Leach
" " 2. O.C. 210th Bde R.F.A.
" " 3. War Diary.
" " 4. War Diary.
" " 5. File.

Appendix 75.

Diet Sheet for the period ending 10ᵗʰ June. 1918.

	Saturday 8ᵗʰ June		Sunday 9ᵗʰ June		Monday 10ᵗʰ June	
	Patients School Chateau	Personnel Chateau A.S.C.	Patients School Chateau	Personnel Chateau A.S.C.	Patients School Chateau	Personnel Chateau A.S.C.
BREAKFAST	Tea Bread Minced meat Bacon	Tea Bread Toasted Cheese	Tea Bread Minced meat Bacon	Tea Bread Liver Bacon	Tea Bread Rolled oat Baked Tom	Tea Bread Bacon Rolled oats Baked Tom M & V Ration
LUNCH	Tea Bread Butter Toasted Cheese Jam	Tea Bread Butter Toasted Cheese/M&V Ration Jam	Tea Bread Butter Cold meat Jam	Tea Bread Butter Toasted Cheese Jam	Tea Bread Butter Cheese Jam	Tea Bread Butter Toasted Cheese Jam
DINNER	Roast Beef Boiled Beef Potatoes Gravy Rice Baked Beans pudding	Boiled Beef Potatoes Gravy Rice pudding	Roast meat and Potatoes Sago pudding Tea	Roast Beef Salad potatoes Onions Custard pudding Tea	Roast Beef Boiled potatoes Custard pudding Tea	Roast Beef and Stew Boiled potatoes Boiled pudding Jam Tea
SUPPER	Cocoa Tea Biscuits	Cocoa Tea Biscuits	Cocoa Tea Biscuit Doughnuts Cheese	Cocoa Tea Biscuit Doughnuts Cheese	Cocoa Tea Biscuit Beef sandwiches	Cocoa Tea Lemon Biscuits

WAR DIARY.

OF

1/3rd EAST LANCASHIRE FIELD AMBULANCE.

FROM :- July 1st, 1918.   TO :- July 31st, 1918.

(VOLUME VII)

Army Form C. 2118.

WAR DIARY
INTELLIGENCE SUMMARY
(Erase heading not required.)

Instructions regarding War Diaries and Intelligence Summaries are contained in F. S. Regs., Part II. and the Staff Manual respectively. Title pages will be prepared in manuscript.

Place	Date	Hour	Summary of Events and Information	Remarks and references to Appendices
GOUVENCOURT	1/7/18	19.30	Routine. Body reported from ETAPLES to C.R.S. - C.O. and 2.O.R. 1 Ranking. 115 Patients admitted.	1/7/18
	2.7.18	12:00	C.O. Asked O.C. C.R.S. & O.C. ½ (no.159) Field Ambulance returned to Unit Hqrs. Plan of C.R.S. as laid out starts along site 18 of various buildings. The Rows huts when repaired + turned into tents, The bath house (being repaired), Q.M. stores also the kitchen are new buildings also are the C.O's office, dispensary, Blanket store etc. The ground to have irrigation, a building erected (acting as) section of hospital tents also proved on the site. The whole C.R.S. is capable of accommodating 600 patients.	Appendix 46
	3.7.18	13:15	Field Ambulance has been working under difficulties owing to depletion of personnel + epidemic of influenza. Lieutenant WHITE R.M.C. O.R. directed to proceed on detached duty. (Field Ambulance orders Par 50) 53 Cases admitted.	Appendix 47
	4.7.18		Still fine dry warm weather. Evident that epidemic is on the wane. refurnished and one of the transmissions was cancelled with no materials returned. 90 patients admitted.	

A 5834 Wt. W4973/M687 750,000 8/16 D. D. & L. Ltd. Forms/C.2118/13

Army Form C. 2118.

WAR DIARY
or
INTELLIGENCE SUMMARY.
(Erase heading not required.)

Instructions regarding War Diaries and Intelligence Summaries are contained in F. S. Regs., Part II. and the Staff Manual respectively. Title pages will be prepared in manuscript.

Place	Date	Hour	Summary of Events and Information	Remarks and references to Appendices
LOUVENCOURT	5.7.18	12.15	First day. Admission from Influenza decreasing. ADMS 3rd Army, DADMS 4th Corps, ADMS 42 Division visited DRS & inspected. It was agreed various Officers expecting off work afternoon, situation officers men.	MM/
		14.45	Band of Division played to patients for two hours. 93 patients admitted	
	6.7.18		Warm day. Only 2 Officers available teaching in station tents (CO, Sergeant Major, & Mrs Sergeant) today Room Sergeant, & several others down with Influenza. Work carried on under difficulties. Bennett's Pay to Unit today.	MM/
	7.7.18	11.0.0	[struck through line] ADMS Fds weekly Record	MM/
			104 patients admitted	
	8.7.18		C.O. down with Influenza. Major Haskins assumed duties	MM/
		17.45	Band of Division played to patients for one hour. 106 patients admitted	
	9.7.18		Stormy day - light at intake	MM/
		15.00	ADMS called - ADMS Hope moving to BOURTON	
		18.00	[illegible] DDG, AS, add 42nd M.G. Battn adopted for [illegible] July 80 patients admitted	

Army Form C. 2118.

WAR DIARY

INTELLIGENCE SUMMARY

(Erase heading not required.)

Instructions regarding War Diaries and Intelligence Summaries are contained in F. S. Regs., Part II. and the Staff Manual respectively. Title pages will be prepared in manuscript.

Place	Date	Hour	Summary of Events and Information	Remarks and references to Appendices
GOUVENCOURT	10.9.18	1500	Stormy day, bright at intervals. Unit met S.B. Refresher for one hour. 59 patients admitted	
"	11.9.18	1200	ADMS visits D.R.S.	
		1700	Heavy thunderstorm passed over. 63 patients admitted. Unit wearing S.D. respirators for an hour during duties	
"	12.9.18		Rain today. Unit wearing S.B. respirators for one hour during duties. New rack in Pack Store being erected. 68 patients admitted	
"	13.9.18		55 patients admitted	
"	14.9.18	1000	Lime also being carted at trestran road in D.R.S. grounds. ADMS dotting weekly round @ DRS. 61 patients admitted	

Army Form C. 2118.

WAR DIARY

INTELLIGENCE SUMMARY.

(Erase heading not required.)

Instructions regarding War Diaries and Intelligence
Summaries are contained in F. S. Regs., Part II.
and the Staff Manual respectively. Title pages
will be prepared in manuscript.

Place	Date	Hour	Summary of Events and Information	Remarks and references to Appendices
LOUVENCOURT	15.7.18		Repair of roading in DRS ground continued. Building of public in Pack Store continued. Patients in D.R.S. paid.	
	16.7.18	06.00	Day warm, warm first ground start. Air 300 patients in DRS. 93 patients admitted. Plans of 10° CRS. as laydown of Unit grounds through visual element to War Museum.	
			Heavy Thunderstorm accompanied by very heavy rain. Repair work in DRS ground continuous. 340 patients in DRS. 99 patients admitted	
	17.7.18		Very fine day DRS. ADMS visits DRS. 350 patients in DRS. 61 patients admitted	
	18.7.18		357. patients in D.R.S. Quartermaster of this Captain T.E. JONES R.AM.C.T.F. reports his arrival for duty from England. Repair work continues. 61 patients admitted.	
	19.7.18		55 patients admitted 359 patients in D.R.S.	

WAR DIARY
INTELLIGENCE SUMMARY

Army Form C. 2118.

Place	Date	Hour	Summary of Events and Information	Remarks and references to Appendices
LOUVENCOURT	20.7.18	0800	386 patients in D.R.S.	
		1000	DDMS Corps visits ADMS Division visits DRS & inspects whole of the station. 52 Cases admitted	
"	21.7.18		355 cases in D.R.S. 49 Cases admitted. ADMS held usual monthly medical board. Bennetts pay of personnel carried out. Captain FANSTONE rejoins unit from leave.	
"	22.7.18		Construction of pack store continued. 361 patients in D.R.S. 30 patients admitted. New Prince Divining table brought in to use, as is distinct from patients dining hall. All patients in D.R.S. had games &c. (weekly pay)	
"	23.7.18		Wet day, very heavy showers. 396 patients in D.R.S. Divisional Band played for patients. 30 cases admitted.	
		19.15		
"	24.7.18		316 patients in D.R.S. Considerable amount of ordering room work afterwards. Taking up a deputation of the day. ADMS 21" Divisional visits unit & makes arrangements about casualties on the railway. Extra latrine accommodation in addition decide erected. 48 Cases admitted.	

Army Form C. 2118.

WAR DIARY
INTELLIGENCE SUMMARY
(Erase heading not required.)

Instructions regarding War Diaries and Intelligence Summaries are contained in F. S. Regs., Part II. and the Staff Manual respectively. Title pages will be prepared in manuscript.

Place	Date	Hour	Summary of Events and Information	Remarks and references to Appendices
LOUVENCOURT	25/9/16	105-1020	326 Cases in DRS. ADMS arrived DDMS Corps arrived & inspected DRS with a view to its being converted into a forward operating centre	MW
		1130	OC 2/2 Weaver Field Ambulance arrived & arrangd over the DRS having been warned that his Unit would be taking over the DRS on the 59th relieving the 40 Division. Wrote Band sounds "retreat" & plays various marches drawn in the ground. 34 patients admitted	MW
"	26.9.16		Heavy showers during day. Erection of huts in fact store continues. 323 Cases in DRS. 42 cases admitted	MW
"	27.9.16		304 Cases in DRS. very heavy showers during the day. AA & QMG 59 Division visited DRS today. 54 Cases admitted	MW
"	28.9.16		368 Cases in DRS. ADMS held his usual weekly Parade. 34 Cases admitted	MW

WAR DIARY

INTELLIGENCE SUMMARY

Army Form C. 2118.

Place	Date	Hour	Summary of Events and Information	Remarks and references to Appendices
LOUVENCOURT	29.7.18		24 Cases in D.R.S. ADMS, DDMS Corps, Consultant Army, visited DRS with a view of starting centre. Captain DELAFIELD returns from leave to U.K. 41 Cases admitted.	Appendix
	30.7.18		24 2 Cases in DRS. Fine warm day. Divisional Band played for benefit of patients during afternoon. 54 Cases admitted.	Appendix
	31.7.18	1415	Fine warm day. Latrines & roads in DRS continued. 26 6 Cases in DRS.	
		1230	Instructions received, also news of an officer (Captain FANSTONE) (proceed on temporary detached duty) Field Ambulance Orders No.51. 32 Cases admitted. Field Ambulance had novelty street choir with subsequent march	Appendix 78

M. Mummery D.S.O

Copy No. ...3......

1/3rd East Lancashire Field Ambulance.

Order No. 50.

Appendix 77

Reference Map Sheet 57D.
     A.D.M.S., 42nd Division M28/76.

3rd July, 1918.

1. 1st Lieut. H.R. WHITE, M.O.R.C./U.S.A., and 14 Other Ranks are detailed to proceed for duty to No. 3 Canadian Stationary Hospital.

2. They will report to O.C. No. 3 Canadian Stationary Hospital today.

3. Necessary transport will be provided, leaving Field Ambulance Headquarters at 2 p.m.

                                              Lieut.-Colonel,
                Commanding 1/3rd East Lancs. Field Ambulance.

Issued at 1315.

Distribution :-

Copy No. 1.   1st Lieut. H.R. White.
  "   " 2.   O.C. 3rd Canadian Stationary Hospital.
  "   " 3.   War Diary.
  "   " 4.   War Diary.
  "   " 5.   File.

Appendix I

Detached and filed with Plans.
"Rest Stations"

Copy No. 3

1/3rd. East Lancashire Field Ambulance.

Order. No. 51.

Appendix 78.

Reference Map Sheet 57D.
A.D.M.S. 42nd Division M14/230.   31 July 1918.

1. Capt. J. FANSTONE R.A.M.C. T.C. is detailed for duty as Officer in Temporary Medical Charge 1/7th Northumberland Fusiliers during the absence of Capt F.J. LIDDERDALE on leave.

2. He will report to O.C. 1/7th Northumberland Fusiliers forthwith.

3. Necessary transport will be provided.

[signature]
Lieut-Colonel.
Comdg. 1/3rd. E. Lancashire Fld. Ambce.

Issued at 1220

Distribution.-
Copy No. 1. Capt J. Fanstone.   Copy No. ~~xxxxx~~ 3/4. War Diary.
"   No. 2. O.C. 1/7th N. Fus.   "   No. 5. File.

WAR DIARY

OF

1/3rd EAST LANCASHIRE FIELD AMBULANCE.

From 1st August 1918 to 31st August 1918.

VOLUME VIII.

Army Form C. 2118.

WAR DIARY
or
INTELLIGENCE SUMMARY.
(Erase heading not required.)

Instructions regarding War Diaries and Intelligence Summaries are contained in F. S. Regs., Part II. and the Staff Manual respectively. Title pages will be prepared in manuscript.

Place	Date	Hour	Summary of Events and Information	Remarks and references to Appendices
LOUVENCOURT	1.8.18		240 Cases in D.R.S. Repairs work on Pack Store & Rentbed Collecting Post continued; also repairs to reading in D.R.S. ground. Warm day.	WWC
			Unrestricted battle air activity during previous night	
		0925	Indents received of Captain DELAFIELD = 13 O.R. to proceed on temporary detached duty as a Stationary Hospital	Appendix 49.
		1530	Lieut. WHITE & details reported taken over on relief from the Stationary Hospital. 48 Cases admitted	WWC
	2.8.18		292 Cases in D.R.S. Wet day. Fairly heavy continuous rain. 28 Cases admitted	WWC
	3.8.18		285 Cases in D.R.S. Wet day. Work on Pack store continued. 44 Cases admitted	WWC
	4.8.18		255 Cases in D.R.S. Fine day. Bad roads. Returns with altered effect in view of the date. 32 Cases admitted	WWC

Army Form C. 2118.

WAR DIARY
or
INTELLIGENCE SUMMARY.
(Erase heading not required.)

Instructions regarding War Diaries and Intelligence Summaries are contained in F. S. Regs., Part II. and the Staff Manual respectively. Title pages will be prepared in manuscript.

Place	Date	Hour	Summary of Events and Information	Remarks and references to Appendices
LOUVENCOURT	5.8.18		255 patients in D.R.S. Round all day. C.O. visits B.R.C.S. Hqrs to obtain some atlas for the D.R.S. 36 cases admitted	MW/
	6.8.18		262 patients in D.R.S. Still wet. Roads in foul state – constructor of 260 pits. Q/Mr Sergeant WILSON hunts Tinton Sergeant Pryor (RAMC at duty). 36 cases admitted. Regt. Band held to chapel three nights – value reinforcements Divisional Band plays to wounded in D.R.S. grounds.	MW/
	7.8.18	1730	Funday. 267 patients in D.R.S.	MW/
		1030	C.O. visits A.D.M.S.	
		1200	A.D.M.S. inspects scabies section @ D.R.S. Work in isolation to scabies patients commenced. 30 cases admitted.	
	8.8.18	1030	260 cases in D.R.S. C.O. visits A.D.M.S. New stretcher & blanket store opened. New joinery shop inaugurated. 36 cases admitted.	MW/
	9.8.18	1330	257 cases in D.R.S. Inauguration of Lieut. WHITE to proceed in detached duty Field Ambulance below Tr. 53.	Appendix 20. MW/
		1500	Q/Mr Sergeant attended a lecture by S.S.O. 32 cases admitted.	

Army Form C. 2118.

WAR DIARY
or
INTELLIGENCE SUMMARY.
(Erase heading not required.)

Place	Date	Hour	Summary of Events and Information	Remarks and references to Appendices
LOUVENCOURT	10.8.18		250 Cases in D.R.S. Five thirty the Bugle Band soundly retired a playing afternoon clay in DRS ground Field Ambulance Bugle Band 31 patients admitted	M/M
	11.8.18	1000	256 Cases in DRS. ADMS held weekly medical Board in DRS	M/M
		1105	Captain DELAFIELD returned from detached duty. 55 cases admitted	
	12.8.18		Fine day 249 Cases in DRS	M/M
		1530	O.C. Divisional Train inspects Horse Transport of Unit, accompanied by ADMS 37 cases admitted	
	13.8.18	1210	273 Cases in DRS. DDMS visits DRS	M/M
		14.30	Divisional Band play to patients 1st Lieutenant R.L. VINEYARD N.R.R. U.S.A posted to Unit & taken on strength today 42 cases admitted	
	14.8.18	1530	284 Cases in DRS. ADMS visits DRS 35 cases admitted	M/M

Army Form C. 2118.

WAR DIARY
or
INTELLIGENCE SUMMARY.
(Erase heading not required.)

Instructions regarding War Diaries and Intelligence Summaries are contained in F.S. Regs., Part II. and the Staff Manual respectively. Title pages will be prepared in manuscript.

Place	Date	Hour	Summary of Events and Information	Remarks and references to Appendices
HOUVENCOURT	15.8.18	0430	234 patients in D.R.S. 2/Lt GR HB Cunningham departed on 14 days Gen Leave. Major Hoskins Stay as in command. 29 patients admitted.	Appx XXIII
	16.8.18	1500	275 patients in D.R.S. Capt TANSTONE detached from temp duty with 1/4 Northumberland Fusiliers 30 patients admitted.	Appx XXIV
	17.8.18	1410	235 patients in D.R.S. S/M DUTSON A.S.C. attchd of Suff Regt attchd — Temply attached pending — 1 N.C.O and 13 O.R. attchd for temp duty with D.S. on duty instruct to report immediately 37 patients admitted.	Appx XXV
	18.8.18	10.00	236 patients in D.R.S. A.D.M.S field weekly Board Capt PRESTWICH proceeded to 1/4 Hampshire Batln for temp duty in place of Lieut TASITEAU on leave O.K. Patients admitted 31	Appx XXVI
	19.8.18	10.00	231 patients in D.R.S. 1st Lieut WHITE MARC.USA. reported back for temp. duty with 1/4 Army Amm. (Horse) Coy.	
		1400	C.O. visited A.D.M.S. at B.03	
		1700	Major JOHNSON M.C. and 1st Lieut WHITE with 19 O.R. proceeded to IV CR.S. MT RENAULT FARM Patients admitted 63	Appx XXVII

Army Form C. 2118.

WAR DIARY
or
INTELLIGENCE SUMMARY.
(Erase heading not required.)

Instructions regarding War Diaries and Intelligence Summaries are contained in F. S. Regs., Part II. and the Staff Manual respectively. Title pages will be prepared in manuscript.

Place	Date	Hour	Summary of Events and Information	Remarks and references to Appendices
LOUVENCOURT	21.8.16		Officer 2nd Lt. attack in Hospital	
		0630	Orders received from A.D.M.S. to dispatch empty Aid Station, 92 sent to 3 C.C.S. (43 by special train 29 by motor amb.)	
		11.15	D.D.S. empty arrived.	
		11.15	A.D.M.S visited D.R.S. gave instructions to prepare to receive WALKING WOUNDED and Motor in Charge new/so orders to be prepared to move at short notice, train complete for 250 patients to remain in station	N.H.H.?
		1400	12 O.R. sent to Mount RENAULT FARM, relay, transport of Brocton Bus Horse Amb. - transport to Major JOHNSON M.S.	
		1600	36 O.R. sent and attached to 1/2 East Lancs Field Amb. for duty of the Field	
		2230	R.A.M.C. 42nd Field Order No 45 received - instructions to be ready to move at short notice and other details	
do	22.8.16	0100	Telegram received from A.D.M.S. - 1 Officer and dispatchman & infantry for fatigue to 29 C.C.S. SERAIMCOURT - 1 Lieut. VINEYARD and 190-R. Only 1 motor ambulance available, - 2nd VINEYARD dispatch was complete at 00.30 27 O.R. remaining (including B rule) 3 Motor ambulances proceeded complete forward to 1/1 East Lancs Fd Amb for duty -	N.H.H.?
		1700	A.D.M.S. visited - detail verified with arrangements for WALKING WOUNDED, method of recording etc - gave instruction now to register as A.P.S	
		12.00	party held to be ready to move at 12 hrs notice - remainder to unpack.	
		1800	D.M.S. III Army & D.D.M.S. 4 Corps visited - object not apparent - questioned re arrangements -	N.H.H.?

WAR DIARY
or
INTELLIGENCE SUMMARY.
(Erase heading not required.)

Army Form C. 2118.

Place	Date	Hour	Summary of Events and Information	Remarks and references to Appendices
GOUVENCOURT	23/8/16	1100	A.D.M.S. visited unit - inspected W. WOUNDED arrangements -	
		1400	C.O. visited A.D.M.S. at 1305 with QUARTERMASTER to arrange to draw medical comforts urgently - arranged to draw special additional in morning - visited 14th & 9th to learn if Ant: to be, if supplies of dressings mobilised carts sufficient were being separate for supplying other units on demand.	
		1600	T.O.R. arrived from MT. RENAULT FARM	
		1900	S.O.R. " "	
		1800	127 Walking Wounded admitted since 1100 21/8/16	
			EVACUATIONS	
			1 officer, 92 by tram. - 2 officers, native civil TRAIN	
			adt. 14. 2. 8. - sem by motor amb. - NONE by special train.	
			63 Sick, 17 wounded patients admitted	
	24.8.16		94 patients in D.R.S.	
		1800	Major JOHNSON M.C. and 1st Lieut WHITE reported back from IV C.R.S., MOUNT RENAULT FARM, with 100 O.R.	
		2000	2 O.R. sent to 29 C.C.S. for duty as clerks.	
		2200	B' Section Personnel reported from MT. RENAULT FARM - now reported complete to A.D.M.S.	
			Patient admitted 40.	

Army Form C. 2118.

WAR DIARY
or
INTELLIGENCE SUMMARY.
(Erase heading not required.)

Instructions regarding War Diaries and Intelligence Summaries are contained in F. S. Regs., Part II. and the Staff Manual respectively. Title pages will be prepared in manuscript.

Place	Date	Hour	Summary of Events and Information	Remarks and references to Appendices
Gavrencourt	25 Aug.	1000	Patients admitted in Hospital 121	AW/99
		1600	A.D.M.S. held Weekly Board	
			CAPT DELAFIELD and LIEUT WHITE proceeded to 1/1st East Lan Field Amb for duty	W/99
	26 "		Patients admitted 56	
		1000	138 patients in D.R.S. A.D.M.S. visited unit.	
		10.30	D.D.M.S. called ref WALKING WOUNDED	
		1500	O.C. visited A.D.M.S. at BUS re opening Walking Wounded collecting Post at PUISIEUX	
		1600	12 O.R. proceeded to PUISIEUX to report to an Officer of 1/1st East Lan for duty	
			5-9 patients admitted	
	27 "		Patients in D.R.S. 149	W/99
			Showery day	
			Patients admitted 5-9	
	28 "		178 patients in D.R.S.	W/99
			26 patients admitted	

Army Form C. 2118.

WAR DIARY
or
INTELLIGENCE SUMMARY.
(Erase heading not required.)

Place	Date	Hour	Summary of Events and Information	Remarks and references to Appendices
GOUY EN ARTOIS	29/1/18		169 patients in D.R.S. Wet stormy day 31 patients admitted	MMMM
	30/1/18	08:30	172 patients in D.R.S. T/S.G. M. Wilson proceeded under orders to report 5.79 C.C.S. for duty Daily work proceeding satisfactorily, 3/5 A.R. RAMC now available for duty 49 officers — 23 patients admitted	MMMM
	31/1/18		182 patients in D.R.S. Officers present Maj the O.C. Major Johnson M.C. + Capt A. MR Jones. Patients admitted 56	MMMM

Signed [signature] Major

Copy No. ..4..

1/3rd. East Lancashire Field Ambulance.

Order No. 52.

Reference Map Sheet 57 D.
A.D.M.S. 42nd Division M.30/336.
1-8-1918.

1st August 1918.

1. Captain M.E.Delafield R.A.M.C. T.C. and 13 other ranks are detailed to proceed to 3rd. Canadian Stationary Hospital for duty in relief of Lieut. H.R. White M.O.R.C. U.S.A. and details who on relief will report to Field Ambulance Headquarters.

2. They will report to O.C. No.3. Can. Stationary Hospital, forthwith.

3. Necessary transport will be provided.

Lieut-Colonel. R.A.M.C. T.
Comdg. 1/3rd. East Lancashire Fld. Ambce.

Issued at .. 0925 ..
Distribution.-

Copy No.1. Capt. M.E. Delafield.   Copy No.2. O.C. 3rd. Can. Sty. Hosp.
  "   3.& 4. War Diary.   "   5. File.

Copy No. 5

1/3rd East Lancashire Field Ambulance.

Order No. 53.

Reference Map Sheet 57 D,
A.D.M.S. 42nd Division M.14/233. 8-8-1918.
A.A.&Q.M.G. 42nd Division A7/1512. 8-8-1918.   9th August 1918.

1. 1st Lieut H.R.White, M.O.R.C./U.S.A. is detailed to proceed to 8th Army Aux.(Horse) Coy, for temporary duty in replacement of Capt. J.Livingston, R.A.M.C. who on relief will proceed to No. 3 Canadian Stationary Hospital for temporary duty.

2. He will report to O.C. 8th Army Aux. (Horse) Coy, forthwith.

3. On arrival of Capt. J.Livingston at No. 3 Canadian Stationary Hospital, Capt. M.E.Delafield R.A.M.C. will rejoin 1/3rd East Lancs Fld Ambce for duty.

4. Necessary transport will be provided.

Issued at 1330

Lieut-Colonel, R.A.M.C.T.
Cmdg 1/3rd East Lancashire Field Ambulance.

Distribution:-
Copy No.1. 1st Lieut.H.R.White.   Copy No. 2. O.C.8th.Army Aux (Horse)
 "   No.3. O.C.3rd Can. Sty. Hospl.   Coy.
 "   No.4 & 5. War Diary.   Copy No. 6. File.

WAR DIARY

OF

1/3rd EAST LANCASHIRE FIELD AMBULANCE.

September 1st 1918 to September 30th 1918.

VOLUME IX.

Army Form C. 2118.

WAR DIARY
or
INTELLIGENCE SUMMARY.
(Erase heading not required.)

Instructions regarding War Diaries and Intelligence Summaries are contained in F. S. Regs., Part II. and the Staff Manual respectively. Title pages will be prepared in manuscript.

Place	Date	Hour	Summary of Events and Information	Remarks and references to Appendices
LOUVENCOURT	Sept. 1st 1918	1000	166 patients in the D.R.S.	
			D.D.M.S. IV Corps revisited the D.R.S. with ref: to meeting of units a C.R.S. inspected the sports to opened.	W.K.TON
			Four beds of ordinal tent sent to from C.R.S. MT REVAULT FARM and MARIEUX WOOD D.R.S.	
			A.D.M.S. arrived to held weekly travel — no patients arrived — ...	
			45 patients admitted	
	2nd Sept	1600	193 patients in the D.R.S.	MKM
			broken lorry + motor lorry of tents & blankets arrived from C.R.S.	
		1700	TRAIN 1 which finally evacuated C.C.S. patients to GEZAINCOURT at 2.18 / in charge — stopped to 5 p.m. daily	
			84 patients admitted	
	3rd Sept	1100	194 patients in Hospital	MKM
			C.O. revisited D.D.M.S. IV Corps MARIEUX ; C.C.R.S. REST STATION freshly not being enacted at LOUVENCOURT, to	
			action forming a dump at LOUVENCOURT.	
		1600	17 patients transferred from C.R.S. MT REVAULT FARM. Patients admitted 56	

Army Form C. 2118.

WAR DIARY
or
INTELLIGENCE SUMMARY
(Erase heading not required.)

Instructions regarding War Diaries and Intelligence Summaries are contained in F. S. Regs., Part II. and the Staff Manual respectively. Title pages will be prepared in manuscript.

Place	Date	Hour	Summary of Events and Information	Remarks and references to Appendices
GOUVENCOURT	4th Sept.	1400	Patients in the D.A.S. 212	MMM
		1700	6 Hussars/ 3 Drivers + 6 horses attd to 1/1 West Lancs Field Amb for duty with amb wagons (of this unit) returned — two sick, all in fair condition, rebuy had been discontinued day previous. 2 G.R. of forty attd to 1/1 West Lancs Field Amb, reported for leave — thought the absence of this Division ———— since 20/8/16 of R.A. of this unit have proceeded on leave to U.K. every 3 "blue" this is more than has been taken from this div regularly maximum num in due being asked for. Patients admitted 43 —	
	5th Sept		Patients in D.R.S. 195 — Routine Patients admitted 21	MMM
	6th Sept	12.15	Patients in D.R.S. 168 A.D.M.S. arrived at O.R.S. bringing instructions to move forthwith to IRLES and reform D.R.S. forthwith	MMM
		1400	All patients except 11 evacuated 103 to Convalescent Camp, 65 to C.C.G., 4 to duty	
		1500	Capt PRESTWICH reported back from lights duty with 1/1 Manchester Regt	
		1600	Transport horsed, fully loaded, + proceeded to IRLES	

A5834 Wt.W4973/M687 750,000 8/16 D. D. & L. Ltd. Forms/C.2118/13

WAR DIARY
or
INTELLIGENCE SUMMARY

(Erase heading not required.)

Army Form C. 2118.

Place	Date	Hour	Summary of Events and Information	Remarks and references to Appendices
GOUVENCOURT	6/9/16	16.30	Major JOHNSON & Capt. PRESTWICH and details proceeded by 2 Motor Amb. to IRLES	
		18.00	Handed over CHATEAU to specialists of AREA COMMANDANT - began advance party to be moved	
		21.00	Motor Army reported for our journey - rest of to rearguard	
		22.00	6 Motor Ambs reported for duty with 1/1 6th East Lancs Field Amb - C.O. proceeded to IRLES	
IRLES		22.00	Transport reported from HOUVENCOURT	
			Rations obtained N.S.	
	7/9/16	08.00	Evacuated 2 marquees - known sick	
			Site - a muddy family occupied by German Dressing Station, surrounded with shelter or nest of masking - most urgent in need for beds - 20 yds beyond - about 200 yds from main IRLES - GREVILLERS Road - ground much cut up by shell fire - rusty wagged - difficulties to get sites for marquees	
		10.00	C.O. & Major JOHNSON visited A.D.M.S. Office at D.H.Q. near RIENCOURT - arranged to get lorries to bring D.R.I. down at HOUVENCOURT to IRLES	
			The remainder of personnel all 1/1 6th East Lancs Field Amb replenished with exception of 5 wtd ratd to R.T.A. of 11 Division.	
			D.O.S. ready to receive patients.	
			Camp - has installed difficulties, 4 many changes necessary especially of was cook houses & hutter	

No patients admitted 9

Army Form C. 2118.

WAR DIARY
or
INTELLIGENCE SUMMARY.
(Erase heading not required.)

Instructions regarding War Diaries and Intelligence Summaries are contained in F. S. Regs., Part II. and the Staff Manual respectively. Title pages will be prepared in manuscript.

Place	Date	Hour	Summary of Events and Information	Remarks and references to Appendices
IRLES	8 Sept		F20 platoon to D.R.S. Carried on with erection of camp - building cookhouses and sleeping marquees - much salvage lotz, gathered - and much channy required - as ground in a very dirty state. 3 horse and ox wagons reported back from 1/1st East Lancs Field Amb. Patients admitted 18	MMM
	9 Sept		3 Sept platoon to D.R.S. Carried on with erecting D.R.S. and collecting salvage; great quantities of British + enemy — Patients admitted 21	MMM
	10 Sept	1100 1130 Noon	50 platoon to D.R.S. A.D.M.S. inspected D.R.S. expressed satisfaction. Capt PRESTWICH proceeded on leave to U.K. Capt SIMMONS started temp/s from 5th Army Authorized. Patients admitted 27	MMM

A.5834 Wt. W4973/M687 750,000 8/16 D. D. & L. Ltd. Forms/C.2118/13

Army Form C. 2118.

WAR DIARY
or
INTELLIGENCE SUMMARY.
(Erase heading not required.)

Instructions regarding War Diaries and Intelligence Summaries are contained in F. S. Regs., Part II. and the Staff Manual respectively. Title pages will be prepared in manuscript.

Place	Date	Hour	Summary of Events and Information	Remarks and references to Appendices
IRLES	11th Sept.	16.00	Patients in D.R.S. 59	
			Capt. Johnstone reported from temp. duty with 1/1st Essex Yeo.	
			Patients admitted 22	
	12th Sept.		Patients in D.R.S. 70	
		10.00	A.D.M.S. visited D.R.S.	
		11.30	Lieut. White 1/1st East Lancs Fd. Amb. reported for duty temp. duty	
			Selected a tent sub-ar	
			Patients admitted 24	
"	13th Sept.		Patients in D.R.S. 75	
		11.00	2 G.S. wagon full of Salvage to Div Salvage Dump - Tent out in last 3 days = 6	
		16.00	C.O. accompanied by Maj Johnson M.C. inspected sanitary arrangements of 128th Bde. - quite satisfactory	
			Unit in D.R.S. providing satisfactorily although much impeded during last 2 days by rain.	
			Patients admitted 45	

Army Form C. 2118.

WAR DIARY
or
INTELLIGENCE SUMMARY
(Erase heading not required.)

Instructions regarding War Diaries and Intelligence Summaries are contained in F. S. Regs., Part II. and the Staff Manual respectively. Title pages will be prepared in manuscript.

Place	Date	Hour	Summary of Events and Information	Remarks and references to Appendices
IRLES	14 Sept	12.00	Patients in D.R.S. 106.	
			1 Coy reported sick from D.R.S. dump TOUVENCOURT - ordered to carry on work	
		14.00	Lieut WHITE proceeded from duty to 1/10 from for instructions from A.D.M.S. through 1/4 Batt Army Field Amb. RAMC	
			Patients admitted total 41	
	15 Sept	10.00	Patients in D.R.S. 125.	
			A.D.M.S. visit newly formed	
			Work proceeded with - incinerator built - white washing during fine. ??? latrines etc - work in stables for horses commenced Baths commenced working	
		12.00	2 G.S. wagons detailed to proceed to TOUVENCOURT to remain night return with remainder of D.R.S. dump	
			2 G.S. wagon of SALVAGE to dump TOTAL 9.	
			Patients admitted 22	
	16 Sept		Patients in D.R.S. 111	
		20.30	Lieut Col. CUNNINGHAM returned from leave in U.K.	
			Patients admitted 28	

Army Form C. 2118.

WAR DIARY
or
INTELLIGENCE SUMMARY.
(Erase heading not required.)

Instructions regarding War Diaries and Intelligence Summaries are contained in F. S. Regs., Part II. and the Staff Manual respectively. Title pages will be prepared in manuscript.

Place	Date	Hour	Summary of Events and Information	Remarks and references to Appendices
IRLES	17.9.18		Heavy shelling during previous night. ADMS visited DRS. 20 patients admitted 134 cases in DRS	
	18.9.18		32 patients admitted Cookhouse & latrines completed Dressing room & surgery. Supply of water properly Chaplains & R.C. & presbyterian Major JOHNSON proceeded on leave to U.K.	
	19.9.18		Stand out, obtained from Seventh section no later to latrine completed Whilst the site was good, no all latrine arrangements of patients & personnel completed. Fatigue party being issued in cookhouse strength of patients & personnel. Arrival of Serieant was informed being admitted. 134 cases in DRS New arrival Lieut. Elmwood, who reliev – relief	
		21.45	Unexpired Captain FARNSTONE Evacuated Company detachments at LofC. RAMC Captain JONES evacuated sick to LofC.	
	20.9.18	12.00	148 Cases in DRS. ADMS visited DRS and Capt Quincy, Berry, Lambe & Mitchell. 8 O.R. returned from temporary duty with 311 Div. R.F.A.	
			Pte MATTHEWSON proceeded to Depot at 2 Lodge Camp, having been selected for Commission in Infantry.	
			36 patients admitted	
		19.00	Major HASKINS MC and 19 OR proceeded to D.E.F & wheel transportation of detachment can with 3 M.T ambulance.	
			Construction of new stables continued.	
			Captain Campbell 8th Bn Nova Scotia seconded for temporary duty.	

Army Form C. 2118.

WAR DIARY
or
INTELLIGENCE SUMMARY.
(Erase heading not required.)

Instructions regarding War Diaries and Intelligence Summaries are contained in F.S. Regs., Part II. and the Staff Manual respectively. Title pages will be prepared in manuscript.

Place	Date	Hour	Summary of Events and Information	Remarks and references to Appendices
IRLES	21.9.18		134 Cases in D.R.S. 44 patients admitted. 16 O.R. R&MC proceeded to 125 Bde. H.Q. attached to Units. Tony Sublieutenant Lieut I Officer 1 O.R. which had been attached to 29 C.C.S. returned to Unit. Captain DELAFIELD returned from IV Corps W.W. T-2-8. Three G.S. wagons out everyday bringing up salvage & material for construction of D.R.S.	
	22.9.18	1030	151 Cases in D.R.S. ADMS [?] field with medical board. No H.D. ambulance wagon condemned as refilling. This proceeded for duty with 1/2 E. Lanc Field Ambulance. Construction of stables continues. Lectured plenty to stemming men, top sergeant majors & officer commanding. 21 Patients admitted. Band arrived village returned duty. 21 O.R. R&MC proceeded to 1/2 E. Lanc Field Ambulance for duty in forward area.	
	23.9.18		160 Cases in D.R.S. Sent 3.8 wagons loads of [?] forms collected & brought in and annex to dining room confts [?]. Stables party finished & now occupied. Dental Eqpt for n-thing cases now collected & dealt with by 1/1 E. Lanc Field Ambulance, this Unit having to lift for this duty. 24 Cases admitted. O.C. Reception Camp visits D.R.S. to make mutual arrangements for discharge from D.R.S. Reception [?]	
	24.9.18	0800	114 Cases in D.R.S. 5 NCOs and 9 NCOs proceed to IV Corps New Troops before Selection Committee with a view to Commission.	

Army Form C. 2118.

WAR DIARY
or
INTELLIGENCE SUMMARY
(Erase heading not required.)

Instructions regarding War Diaries and Intelligence Summaries are contained in F. S. Regs., Part II. and the Staff Manual respectively. Title pages will be prepared in manuscript.

Place	Date	Hour	Summary of Events and Information	Remarks and references to Appendices
IRLES	24.9.18	0845	C.O. proceeded to DHQ & taken entrance at Officer of ADMS.	
		1500	To 9 Subdivision forwarded to 56 C.C.S. for transfer duty, 1st Lieut WHITE ½ doing report from 37 ccs	
			25 patients admitted to DRS	
		1530	DDMS IVth Corps visits DRS accompts to every details of the Camp.	
		1745	Field Ambulance Band Played return in Fleet (a return for first time)	
	25.9.18		162 Cases in DRS	
			Erection of Revetion Huts for patients commenced.	
			A quantity of duck board being bought in to lay pathways in DRS	
			25 patients admitted	
	26.9.18		190 Cases in DRS	
			Building of revetion Huts continued	
			Erection of Q.M. Stores commenced	
			Returns of the 8th & 1st Infantry Brigade to 7th hospl. kept commenced	
			Flour & some stables being refit.	
			Huts. Hut a (D) being laid throughout	
			Capt. J.R. BULLIVANT proceed on road for a call and having been asked for an infantry commission	
			41 Cases admitted	
	27.9.18		190 Cases in DRS	
			Capt died started to work, entry 25th attained	
			Small evaporation huts continued	
			13 patients admitted	

Army Form C. 2118.

WAR DIARY
or
INTELLIGENCE SUMMARY.
(Erase heading not required.)

Instructions regarding War Diaries and Intelligence Summaries are contained in F. S. Regs., Part II. and the Staff Manual respectively. Title pages will be prepared in manuscript.

Place	Date	Hour	Summary of Events and Information	Remarks and references to Appendices
IRLES	28.9.18		143 cases in D.R.S. Wet & cold in morning, construction work carried on during afternoon. Captain PRESTWICH returns from leave in U.K. 7 O.R. reported wounded in action. 55 patients admitted.	
	29.9.18		189 cases in D.R.S. Fine day. Construction work continued. Framework of new reception hut almost completed. Erection of framework for O.R's room commenced onto hut. Preparations for moving and transport commenced. New standard of moveable transport commenced. Instructions received for Unit to move with D.R.S. to new site. 4 patients admitted.	
	30.9.18	1750	150 cases in D.R.S. Final orders for D.R.S. move received. C.O. visited A.D.M.S. to make details arrangements involved in move.	
		1000	Orders to move issued (Field Ambulance Orders No 52.)	
		1610	Advance party under O.C. Sergeant proceeded to new site to take over ground & prepare for reception of patients in personnel, all medical equipment bar details required in D.R.S. packed on transport wagons ready for moving.	Appendix 1/A/23.

M.W. Armitstead

A5834. Wt. W4973/M687 750,000 8/16 D.D.&L.Ltd. Forms/C.2118/13

1/3rd. E.Lancashire Field Ambce.   Copy No. 3

Order No. 54.

Appendix 81

Reference Map. Sheet 57 C.
A.D.M.S. 42nd.Div.366 dated 19-9-18.   19th.September 1918.

1. Captain J.FANSTONE R.A.M.C. T.C. is detailed to proceed to 1/5th.Bn.Lancashire Fusiliers for temporary duty in relief of Captain F.G.SERGEANT.

2. He will report to O.C.1/5th.Bn.Lancashire Fusiliers forthwith.

3. Necessary transport will be provided.

Issued at 21.45.
Distribution:-

Copy No. 1. Captain J.Fanstone.
"   " 2. O.C.1/5th.Bn.Lancs.Fus.
"   " 3&4. War.Diary.
"   " 5. File.

                                                    Lieut-Colonel
                                   Comdg.1/3rd.E.Lancs.Fld.Ambce.

DIET SHEET FOR THE PERIOD ENDING 26th SEPT 1918.

	Thursday 19th Sept	Friday 20th Sept	Saturday 21st Sept	Sunday 22nd Sept	Monday 23rd Sept	Tuesday 24th Sept	Wednesday 25th Sept
BREAKFAST	Bread Brown Biscuits Tea Bread Butter Porridge Butter Ham Bacon Jam	Bread Brown Biscuits Tea Bread Butter Porridge Butter Bacon Jam	Bread Brown Biscuits Tea Bread Butter Porridge fried Bacon Jam	Bread Brown Biscuits Tea Bread Butter Porridge fried Bacon Jam	Bread Brown Biscuits Tea Bread Butter Porridge Bacon Jam	Bread Brown Biscuits Tea Bread Butter Porridge Bacon Jam	Bread Brown Biscuits Tea Bread Butter Porridge Bacon Jam
LUNCH	Tea Bread Butter Cheese Jam Pickles	Tea Bread Butter Tomato Cheese Jam	Tea Bread Butter Cheese Jam	Tea Bread Butter Cheese Jam	Tea Bread Butter Cheese Jam	Tea Bread Butter Cheese Jam	Tea Bread Butter Cheese Jam
DINNER	Roast Beef Potatoes & Peas Gravy Tapioca Pudding Tea	Boiled Mutton Potatoes & Peas Gravy Rice Pudding Tea	Stewed Mutton Potatoes & Peas Gravy Stewed fruit Tea	Roast Mutton Potatoes Peas Gravy Jelly Tea	Boiled Beef Potatoes Peas Gravy Jelly Tea	Roast Mutton Potatoes Peas Gravy Jelly Tea	Roast Beef Potatoes & Peas Gravy Jelly Tea
SUPPER	Cocoa Bread Biscuits Butter Cheese	Cocoa Bread Biscuits Butter	Cocoa Bread Biscuits Butter	Cocoa Bread Biscuits Butter	Cocoa Bread Biscuits Butter	Cocoa Bread Biscuits Butter Cheese	Cocoa Bread Biscuits Butter

1/3rd E.Lancashire Field Ambce.   Copy No. 4

Order No 55.

Reference Map. Sheet 57 C.
R.A.M.C. 42nd Divn Order No 53.   30th September 1918.

1. The 1/3rd East Lancashire Field Ambulance will vacate its present site, which will be handed over to the O.C. Reception Camp, and proceed on 1-10-18 to I29,b2.4,LEBUCQUIERE, taking the 42nd D.R.S. with it.

2. R.A.M.C. personnel, dress marching order, and patients will proceed by motor lorry under the command of Capt M.E.Delafield, first convoy to leave IRLES at 8 a.m.

3. A.S.C. personnel and Horse Transport will parade under the command of Capt F.G.Prestwich at 8 a.m. dress marching order, and proceed by march route to the new site, feeds to be taken.

4. A loading party under the command of Capt F.G.Sergeant will remain on the present site until all personnel, patients, and stores have been moved. He will detail 2 men as baggage guard to proceed with each lorry load of stores. Receipts for stores handed over to be obtained, also certificate of cleanliness of the camp.

5. The pack store will be transferred intact by lorry i/c of the Pack-Store keeper.

6. All tents will be struck and packed ready for loading by 11-30 a.m.

7. The Foden Thresher Disinfector will proceed to workshops on 1-10-18.

8. Field Ambulance Headquarters will move from IRLES to the new site at 8 a.m.

9. Capt F.G.Sergeant will take all sick parades at IRLES on 1st prox. Capt M.E.Delafield will take sick parades and admit patients to the D.R.S. at the new site on same date.

                                             Lieut-Colonel,
                    Commanding 1/3rd East Lancashire Field Ambulance.

Issued at 16 10

Distribution:-

    Copy No 1. Capt F.G.Prestwich.
       "   2. Capt M.E.Delafield.
       "   3. Capt F.G.Sergeant.
       "   4. War Diary.
       "   5. War Diary.
       "   6. File.

WAR   DIARY

OF

1/3rd EAST LANCASHIRE FIELD AMBULANCE.

October 1st 1918 to October 31st 1918.

VOLUME X.

WAR DIARY

INTELLIGENCE SUMMARY

(Erase heading not required.)

Army Form C. 2118.

Place	Date	Hour	Summary of Events and Information	Remarks and references to Appendices
IRLES	1.10.18	0010	28 patients admitted	
			Evacuation: 104 patients of 24 hours to arr. of 2th Aust. D.R.S.	
			107 patients in D.R.S.	
			54 patients discharged to duty yesterday	
		1000	C.O. visits attrs new site for D.R.S. & gave necessary instructions to ensure hasty move & arrival on site ere night.	MM
	2.10.18	0800	30 patients admitted	
		1000	Unit commenced move. Hope proceed in ambulance cars, patients & stores in 3 ton lorries, to new site.	
		1100	Advance party left. In fact last proceed two new destination ny. RUYAULCOURT hope arrive at new site just four. Site occupied by a Field Ambulance of 62nd Division, before moving. Stores of N.Z. Division & mobile unit auxiliary. Tents could be managed for the night in view of the congestion on the patients. Found in tents in field.	MM
		1530	The lorries completing this journey. Last lorries arriving at 10 pm.	
			D.D.M.S. IV Corps visits the new site, patents collected, sent & even examined in the new site.	
RUYAULCOURT	3.10.18	1000	62nd Division Field Workshop hour as exactly an inspection of site & accommodation to be estimated	MM
		1100	A.D.M.S. visits site & inspects equipment.	
		1200	Four groups of men organized including hospital marquees.	
			Hospital marquees, potato gathering hall, Structure detailed in tact. Sites: Scabies, Jack Store, Food Mental Stow, Bath House, Ablution House, Showers att. Inoculate att., Paints att., Painters att., Quarter att., Canteen, Sunday Store, Mortuary Temps. Stores, Horses Food Saddle room, Recreation Hall, Sisters, N yard cleaned & readied for use. A hole peep a latrine with tins, fell of pebble, also tons of manure. 25 patients admitted	

WAR DIARY
or
INTELLIGENCE SUMMARY

(Erase heading not required.)

Army Form C. 2118.

Instructions regarding War Diaries and Intelligence Summaries are contained in F. S. Regs., Part II. and the Staff Manual respectively. Title pages will be prepared in manuscript.

Place	Date	Hour	Summary of Events and Information	Remarks and references to Appendices
RUYAULCOURT	4.10.18		Cleaning up of site continued, repair work on all adapts & rafts in hand. Clean hover filters several tons of manure removed from sites of Field Ambulance cit, stables being filled in. Step clear horses' servery & remains buried. ADMS visits site. 23 cases admitted	
	5.10.18		165 Patients in D.R.S. General cleaning up of ground continued. Erecting of new Cook House commenced, repair work on other structures continued. Batt hand completed filter appears in working order. Divisional Commander visits ADMS visits DRS & inspects whole site all round. Div Stores Cook house during eleven half funning filter, stoves etc, adequate heracrdation of the whole organization. 28 cases admitted	
	6.10.18	1445 1450	183 Patients in DRS ADMS receives felling her walls medical board in the Field Ambulance. 6.G.S. wagons sent off to FREMICOURT to collect building material. 31 cases admitted	
	7.10.18	1000 1800 1230 2000	183 Patients in D.R.S. Cleaning up of ground continued. Laying out of small garden commenced. Recently filter nearly fit use, though flow not complete. New Cook House well in process of erection. Dining room & bath room of tiring stones a dining room in connection with bath House well in hand. 24 cases admitted Orders issued to Officer i/c roosters on temping details that Captain DELAFIELD detailed (Field order notes No 35) R.S. wagons returns with timber 16. Clean drafts to 134. Inf. Odr w/s receipt of urgent orders for attachment to Battalion a All hrs.	

WAR DIARY
INTELLIGENCE SUMMARY

Army Form C. 2118.

Place	Date	Hour	Summary of Events and Information	Remarks and references to Appendices
RUYAULCOURT	8.10.18	0600	In order to maintain record during night, 3 horse ambulance wagons with orderlies, 4 pair motor ambulances with orderlies proceed to duty with 1/2 2 Lanc Field Ambulance	
		0930	A.D.M.S. visited D.R.S. to hold a Board on an officer.	
			Repair work & construction continued.	
			New kitchen in use though not yet completed	
		1110	3. S.S. Wagons with stores arrived during day	
		1205	Telegram received giving detail of whole Division moving forward less D.R.S. remaining status	
			184 patients in D.R.S.	
			48 cases admitted	
			2 pair H.D. horse ambges take forward mobile divisional canteens	
	9.10.18	0530	Weather still fine but cold & frosty	
			36 Bearers under command of Major Johnson M.C. proceed to 1/2 2 Lancs Field Ambulance to duty in forward area	
			228 patients in D.R.S.	
			Cleaning up of grounds & repair work on building continued	
			H.D. horse hours returned with empty mobile divisional canteens. les had little stores from us today, again	
			8 cases admitted	
	10.10.18		216 patients in D.R.S.	
			Cleaning up of ground & construction of small gymkhana in fancy arena & officers canteen	
			Sectional gymkhana and hurdle & vapour field of exercise	
		1400	New wagon equipment started	
		1430	From Dfrd disinfector arrives for duty.	
			24 cases admitted	

Army Form C. 2118.

WAR DIARY
INTELLIGENCE SUMMARY.
(Erase heading not required.)

Instructions regarding War Diaries and Intelligence Summaries are contained in F.S. Regs., Part II. and the Staff Manual respectively. Title pages will be prepared in manuscript.

Place	Date	Hour	Summary of Events and Information	Remarks and references to Appendices
RUYAULCOURT	11.10.18		218 patients in Hospital. Cleaning of ground continued. Also retain work on huts.	
		1430	Below receive a futile draft of Homes of the Line. 30 cases admitted.	
"	12.10.18	0600	36 O.R. R.A.M.C. proceeded to 1/2 T Lanes Field Ambulance for duty in the line. Personel of Unit now reduced to 2 Officers & 38 O.R. R.A.M.C. with D.R.S. containing over 200 patients and necessitating the employment of 40 party men on R.A.M.C. duties.	
		1400	Competition for 7 cardboard articles continues & hands officer as judges. 224 patients in D.R.S.	
		2015	Ambulance with instructions received to evacuate walking patients in D.R.S. 32 patients discharged to Reception Camp & 46 patients evacuated to C.C.S. Intimation the newly diagnosed sun now will at at 450 pm. 32 cases admitted.	
"	13.10.18	0930	176 patients in D.R.S. O.C. together with O.C. Reception Camp proceeded to reconnoitre for new sites, in accordance instructions received 3rd Division, a suitable site found at LES RUES DES VIGNES M.4. B3.Y.2	
		1500	All available equipment left in preparation for moving. 18 patients discharged today to Reception Camp and 33 patients evacuated to C.C.S. 34 cases admitted.	
"	14.10.18		152 patients in D.R.S. Being to moving Divisional D.H.Q from D.R.S. at the last extent of the road, the divisional issue now running position from 0940 to 2359. YA and visits D.H.Q Tunis. Notes supply breakdown completely today owing tribal extra group. 39 cases admitted.	

Army Form C. 2118.

WAR DIARY
or
INTELLIGENCE SUMMARY.

(Erase heading not required.)

Instructions regarding War Diaries and Intelligence Summaries are contained in F. S. Regs., Part II. and the Staff Manual respectively. Title pages will be prepared in manuscript.

Place	Date	Hour	Summary of Events and Information	Remarks and references to Appendices
RUYAULCOURT	15.10.18	1030	168 patients in D.R.S.	
		1305	3.S.S. wagons unloaded & sent to left O.C. Reception Camp re moving stores. A.A. & Q.M.G. visited D.R.S. & gave verbal instructions along the D.R.S. army transfer site, admin along with army of twin siding.	Sheet 57B sheet M.A.D.S.
		1415	Captain PRESTWICH proceeded with advance part topher recruits at LES RUES DES VIGNES. By making several journeys, an advance party of 30 O.R. sent to new site 37 cases admitted.	
	16.10.18		166 patients in D.R.S. Section equipment again loaded on wagons. All hospital marquees plus one striped & packed ready for loading.	
		1600	Bell tents struck & ready for loading. 4 car loads of convalescents sent up to new site.	
		2010	Latrines & ablution benches with details proceeded by road route to new site. Instructions received forenoon to proceed to new site of the trem being now cancelled. 24 cases admitted.	
	17.10.18	0430	124 patients in D.R.S. Two convoys to LES RUES DES VIGNES taking back Captain PRESTWICH & above half class 2½ convalescents were dispatched on to Reception Camp wagons bring empty & all wards & stores, bell tents etc returns with then normal weekly condition. A.D.M.S. visited D.R.S. & gave hourly instructions for future.	
		1130	D.A.D.V.S. inspected teams of Units & expressed satisfaction with their condition. 35 Cases admitted.	
	18.10.18		160 patients in D.R.S. Sundry details of H. Sanmains He dumb in the neighbourhood taken in return strength. Major MASNING returned from leave to U.K. 40 Cases admitted.	

Army Form C. 2118.

WAR DIARY
INTELLIGENCE SUMMARY.
(Erase heading not required.)

Instructions regarding War Diaries and Intelligence Summaries are contained in F. S. Regs., Part II. and the Staff Manual respectively. Title pages will be prepared in manuscript.

Place	Date	Hour	Summary of Events and Information	Remarks and references to Appendices
RUYAULCOURT	19.10.18		182 patients in D.R.S. Return went of troops in hand. Refair made of ladies in hand, also to know other fittings in Reception Room. 43 cases admitted.	
	20.10.18		186 patients in D.R.S. No ward of 24 beds (stretcher) prepared as separate staff Isol. off in fever ward, in view of an outbreak of influenza alongside adjoining Reception Camp Iroeclerquoit, 13 midg cleared. Ambulance car being a lot. Raining ground very wet & muddy.	
		1900	We both have no communication of any kind received for Division; no returns sent thirty returns sent for to D.R.S. hour who staff are to rule over. 14 cases admitted.	
	21.10.18		169 patients in D.R.S. Another wet day. Army par monthly	
		0915	Lorry with 33 cwt arrived from N.Z.L. Field Ambulance, bringing some disinfectant, few comments and with D.H.Q. since 19th.	
		1210	Lorry with rations & ??? arrived, having driver since 8409 miles so it to obtain than separate packets & plain store contents of adjacent fever ward. 59 cases admitted.	
	22.10.18		Very wet day whole place a mud. Cleanse of fatal wounded. 181 patients in D.R.S. No mail received 2 king if 6 days.	

WAR DIARY
INTELLIGENCE SUMMARY.
(Erase heading not required.)

Army Form C. 2118.

Place	Date	Hour	Summary of Events and Information	Remarks and references to Appendices
RUYAULCOURT	22.10.18	18.15	Orders received to D.R.S. to move on 24.10.18 near all dressing cases, dismountable portions of C.C.S., C.C. section equipment, Hospital units in reserve. Both tents dismantled, other Installations of the same, 27 cases admitted.	
	23.10.18	0400	23 patients, stretcher lifts, evacuated by ambulance.	
		0815	Hospital completely packed and ready to depart.	
		0830	CO reconnoitres site at main hospital, arrangements for D.T.S. at TERNOIS to remove to ? location and ? locates new site & then proceeds to RUE ANDRE LANDRY.	
		1145	The 12 lorries arrived & were then loaded.	
			Advance ?? at 1640.	
			The two transport parties for the night of 3. LES RUES DES VIGNES. 1/2 hr I hr collecting ½ case admitted.	
CAUDRY	24.10.18		The 128 patients brought on lorries carried in plain stretcher with quarters A.54. hours ? ? 59. The site consists of a large ???? cafe of ???? 300 patients, one whole floor with detail ? ? for staff, god staked to know, all various sites ? ????? days ? full. During ?? attempt at ? ?, a prisoner ? was known in steering ?? occupy ?. All was attended ? ?.	
		1530	Major ? ?, ? 59 OR. reports to Hosp dev with 1/2 1 Man Field hospital	
		1700	40 3 ton ambulances & 2 mon ambulance reports on by the hour.	
		1800	C.O. ? at Main/ADMS	

Army Form C. 2113.

WAR DIARY

INTELLIGENCE SUMMARY.

(Erase heading not required.)

Instructions regarding War Diaries and Intelligence Summaries are contained in F.S. Regs., Part II. and the Staff Manual respectively. Title pages will be prepared in manuscript.

Place	Date	Hour	Summary of Events and Information	Remarks and references to Appendices
CAUDRY	25/10/18		134 patients in D.R.S. Large quantities of material brought in from Bath House Cook house & very mostly. Dinner Hall & new Resident room & another annexe. Ration 130 Rats taken up in built later. Rations 30 litres of petrol received here. Casualties. A female of Unit during patrols attack:— OR the WO1, also 1 wounded. Wounded H. NEWRI MC. attd to R.E.	
		09.05	ADMS visits DRS & made th'ough ik inspection.	
		11.12	Attn'g W.L. and Officers given two hour'ly reliefs. 29 Cases admitted.	
	26.10.18		141 patients in D.R.S. Cleaning & whitewashing of rooms of wards now proceeding. Being found it very difficult in adverse ward being frost at normal temp ... B. Force continues being ... Barracks for patients found for front line... taken as ... Men start obtaining the experience of nursing arrangements than large patients, now obtaining large amount of units electric lighting & Baths plants a central Watts cook house ... 38 cases admitted.	
	27.10.18	14.00	185 patients in D.R.S. Scavenging & repairing continued. Bath House in fullest operation of blanket turnover.	

(A.7092) Wt W12839/M1293 75,000 4/17 D.D. & L. Ltd. Forms/C.2118/14.

WAR DIARY
INTELLIGENCE SUMMARY.
(Erase heading not required.)

Army Form C. 2118.

Place	Date	Hour	Summary of Events and Information	Remarks and references to Appendices
CAUDRY	27.10.18		Cases of Influenza amongst D.R.S. personnel. Influenza seems of a virulent & malignant type in different parts of District. G.S.O.3 + D.R.D.M.S. visits D.R.S. Strong escort to D.R. officers passing X with firearms + hand stars or flares. 25 cases admitted	W/F
	28.10.14	1100	20C Patients in DRS. Cleaning up of main street and evacuation with preceding Building of Inc. to cope with command. A.D.M.S. visits D.R.S. + inspects all wards + blocks	W/F
		1500	D.D.M.S. + C.R.E. late Tech visits D.R.S. entrusts the various wards & offices, cause found out everything required by the Officer employed. 18 Case of Influenza with D.R.S. 23 Cases admitted.	W/F
	29.10.18		272 Patients in DRS. Cleaning up of amputations, wards tary squad. Shrinking of Band plays to convalescent patients. A.D.M.S. visits D.R.S.	W/F
		1430		
		1500	Return of new street park & serious privacy. 24 class admitted	
	30.10.18	1045	242 Patients in D.R.S. Lieutenant White posted to A.Sh-V "Division" (Field Ambulance Letter No. 58) Cleaning up of Institution and procuring	A/Kingh 8c. W/F

WAR DIARY
INTELLIGENCE SUMMARY
(Erase heading not required.)

Army Form C. 2118.

Place	Date	Hour	Summary of Events and Information	Remarks and references to Appendices
CAUDRY	30.10.18	12.00	D.A.M.S. D.D.M.S. & D.A.D.M.S. visits. D.R.S. accompanied C.O. able to do so. Informed that D.T.S. is not & will not expect BTs go out. Have also ordered that these influenza patients are not to be evacuated to ambulance trains until 7 days after temperature has reached normal. Strength of 2 zone buster and 4 ambulance trains. (50,000) 1.57 offers 34 Officers D.R.S. 360 O.R. Total ± 10 Officers. 50 patients admitted.	MM
	31.10.18	16.00	236 Patients in D.R.S. 44 influenza cases admitted 12.00 30th to 12.00 31st. Plans of extension of being carried on on lorryans brought but there. O.C. Omni Train x Govt transport infects Lt. C. Traveler. 2 O.M. & Lieutenant TURNER also to revisit staff visit the Unit. 40 cases admitted.	MM

1/3rd East Lancashire Field Ambulance.   Copy No. 3

Order No 56.

Reference Map Sheet 57 C
A.D.M.S. 42nd Division, 117 dated 7-10-18.   7th October 1918.

1. Capt M.E. DELAFIELD. R.A.M.C., T.C. is detailed to proceed to 1/7th Bn Manchester Regt., for temporary duty in relief of Lieut TABUTEAU, sick.

2. He will report to O.C. 1/7th Bn Manchester Regt forthwith.

3. Necessary Transport will be provided.

Issued at....1255.....
Distribution;

Copy No 1.   Capt M.E. Delafield.
Copy No 2.   O.C. 1/7th Bn Manchester
             Regiment.
Copies No 3 & 4. War Diary.
Copy No 5.   File.

                                        Lieut-Colonel,
                                  Cdg 1/3rd E. Lancs Field Ambce.

1/3rd East Lancashire Field Ambulance.   Copy No. 3

Order No. 57.

Appendix 85.

Reference Map Sheet 57B.
A.D.M.S. 42nd Division, M14/250 dated 24-10-18.

25th October 1918

1. Capt H.Henry.M.C. R.A.M.C.T.F. is detailed to proceed to 42nd Divisional Reception Camp for temporary duty.

2. He will report to O.C. 42nd Division Reception Camp forthwith.

3. Necessary transport will be provided.

Issued at 0905
Distribution:-

Copy No.1. Capt.H.Henry M.C.
Copy No.2. O.C.42nd Division Reception Camp.
Copies No.3 &4. War Diary.
Copy No. 5. File.

Lieut-Colonel,
Cmdg 1/3rd East Lancashire Fld Ambce.

Appendix 86

1/3rd East Lancashire Field Ambulance. Copy No. 2

Order No. 58.

Reference Map Sheet. 57B.
A.D.M.S. 42nd Division. M14/252 dated 29-10-18.   30th October 1918.

1. 1st Lieut H.R. White M.O.R.C./U.S.A. will proceed to 5th Division for duty.

2. He will report to A.D.M.S. 5th Division, CAUDRY, forthwith.

3. Necessary transport will be provided.

Issued at 10.45.

Distribution:-

Copy No. 1.   1st Lieut. H.R. White.
Copies Nos. 2&3 War Diary.
Copy No. 4.   File.

Lieut-Colonel,
Cmdg 1/3rd East Lancashire Field Ambulance.

W A R   D I A R Y

OF

1/3rd EAST LANCASHIRE FIELD AMBULANCE

FROM :- November 1st, 1918   TO :- November 30th, 1918.

(VOLUME XI)

WAR DIARY
INTELLIGENCE SUMMARY.
(Erase heading not required.)

Army Form C. 2118.

Place	Date	Hour	Summary of Events and Information	Remarks and references to Appendices
CAVDRY	1.11.18	1000	241 patients in D.R.S. including 6 officers. A.D.M.S. visits D.R.S. & views about wards. Bathing hand pumps inspected. Louse terminator being erected, but not in use at present from large supply. Ambulance convoys to D.M.S. & to D.R.S. Mine also orders. All N.C.O.'s of D.R.S. inspected & regularly by me and dying if mine addressed by me which reference to the much reduced scale of admissions. 93 cases admitted.	
		1430	293 patients in D.R.S. Heavy work detail on all staff of D.R.S. by the absence of patients in my hospital many cases barely heavy patients. Routine construction work in progress. 65 cases admitted	
	2.11.18			
	3.11.18	1000	327 patients in D.R.S. Unit dust man. Stuff of Division completion of gymnastic band & large asphalt land. had fallen to same extent. Huge working party on its all.	
		1200	C.O. attends interview of officers of D.M.S.	
		1530	U.S. Game Pic @ 7.15 18.N.S. the holiday.	
		1730	Captain PRESTWICH — leaves ambulance of 4 M C.R.	
		1800	S.M. Mr. M.O.'s Sany a 2 D.R.S. & patients accommodated. Large wards of M. Coy arriving of D.R.S. only the few detached to duty with Division Engineers. Duty staff now a 4 for the personnel all R.D's for ambulatory cases only. 131 Casos admitted	

Army Form C. 2118.

WAR DIARY
or
INTELLIGENCE SUMMARY.
(Erase heading not required.)

Instructions regarding War Diaries and Intelligence Summaries are contained in F.S. Regs., Part II. and the Staff Manual respectively. Title pages will be prepared in manuscript.

Place	Date	Hour	Summary of Events and Information	Remarks and references to Appendices
CA/DRS	4.11.18		431 patients in D.R.S. Infects syph & day staffs rented case of large numbers of patients only 4 officers the Quartermaster & 65 O.R. available (855 on D.R.S. Admin personnel) had the men to work. The waitings for cot cases in Dining Hall, all C.D. wards in the compound, patients on stretchers. RE commenced to say lugs in addition to Polish Blankets. Few were stretchers covered in extend over Station. All later in evening TD on +4 new Bessonneau from being laid on both lungs. Motor ambulance employed continually day in evacuating case to C.C.S. & 47 in wards. Statistical Table of sick & con revealed membr affections & pneumonia available in the ward attacks. 483 Cases admitted G.S. wagon attached to Nowhere Stationary Office	
	5.11.18	14.15	395 patients in DRS. Defects affecting taxes is clearly with large numbers of pneumonia & influenza Park horse flesh almost completed. All motor ambulance cars been on duties proceed to 8 17 3 cam field stationary hospital in forward area. The two GS wagons which have been enter hy. 21 ccs. days could not arrive they an CAS wagon attached day 0900 to 1800 with 35.7 influenzy cap. 96 cases admitted	
	6.11.18		398 patients in D.R.S. Heavy rain fell last night & all day nightfall today is very not many Bessf all test attempts being made today to clean camp of the still been much no forward	

(A7092) Wt W12859/M1293 75,000. 1/17. D.D.&L., Ltd. Forms/C.2118/24.

WAR DIARY
INTELLIGENCE SUMMARY.

(Erase heading not required.)

Army Form C. 2118.

Instructions regarding War Diaries and Intelligence Summaries are contained in F. S. Regs., Part II. and the Staff Manual respectively. Title pages will be prepared in manuscript.

Place	Date	Hour	Summary of Events and Information	Remarks and references to Appendices
CAUDRY	6/11/18		Nasty wet cold N.E.ly. day. Prisoners being taken they would with care in stretcher over the plane. Light working with great difficulty over uneven ground. Such hilt of roads as were available being used to extreme limit. Two sittings of sick made in the shining tent. 98 cases admitted.	
	7/11/18		423 patients in D.R.S. Nasty raw outside but somewhat improved. Nearly all the real time made constructing new sheds. Ambulance arranged today to go to Inchy to collect wounded still lying there. No trains from H.D. this week. Another convoy of am[bulance] cars sent another evening of pm. 103 cases admitted	
	8/11/18		489 patients in D.R.S. Very windy day. Heavy rain established at 1 D.R.S, 30 Infantry men employed on R.H.E. duties. Only the wounds R.H.E. 59 cases admitted	
	9/11/18		412 patients in D.R.S. Fine day. 100 [?] patients were sent home this am for BRETON by Amb[ulance] trains	

Army Form C. 2118.

WAR DIARY
INTELLIGENCE SUMMARY.
(Erase heading not required.)

Instructions regarding War Diaries and Intelligence Summaries are contained in F. S. Regs., Part II. and the Staff Manual respectively. Title pages will be prepared in manuscript.

Place	Date	Hour	Summary of Events and Information	Remarks and references to Appendices
CAUDRY	9.11.18		[illegible] Diary has at this point been lost between this unit + 3rd Cav. Division comp. G.S. began afresh returns from Div: units until 9 February 1919. 42 Cases admitted	
"	10.11.18		439 patients in D.R.S. Confirming print issued 4.3 Disciplinary Rec. plan being sent to D.R.S. in case no. [illegible] carriage in previous buildings + equipment. 9.S.S.M. HALSEY proceeds to Army Officers School of Education of Army. 31 Cases admitted	
"	11.11.18	08.30	446 patients in D.R.S. DD.M.S. called at D.R.S.	
		12.55	D.D.M.S. rang. A lorry of stores to be sent to D.R.S.	
		16.30	Telegram received announcing hostilities cease @ 1100. 120 O.R's to see Kin [illegible]. 18 Cases admitted	
"	12.11.18		430 patients in D.R.S. Work may now lighten, sick being cared as good as usual. Find all day motor dying up hospital admin from D.H.Q. w hostilities ceasing + movements Batteries moving going tomorrow for Ambulance instruction + instruction of H. Kelly. 1M Cases admitted	

WAR DIARY

INTELLIGENCE SUMMARY

Army Form C. 2118.

Place	Date	Hour	Summary of Events and Information	Remarks and references to Appendices
CAVDRY	13.11.18		385 patients in D.R.S. 2 patients in D.R.S. moved in about 14 of town, remainder patient in D.R.S. They were completely unhoused, & sent to town 2 & returned to their units in vagotin & R.P. All evacuation made on train lines. 9 cases admitted.	
	14.11.18	11.00 14.15	301 patients in D.R.S. RAMC visits D.R.S. to take away arrange for delivery of return. 240 patients lying in the 26 O'ROURKE arrived "The Fighting Irish" One admitted.	
	15.11.18	9.00	509 patients in D.R.S. All patients transferred to all sites, but allocations to take place. Surgeon SINGLEY RN returned from there, did not reach D.R.S. 9 cases admitted to D.R.S. today.	
	16.11.18	12.00	18 patients in D.R.S. held up prisoners. Received one of the undersigned (Foot soldiers numbers 27354) also ODU who had just given up post of papergetting. 15 cases admitted.	

WAR DIARY
INTELLIGENCE SUMMARY

Army Form C. 2118.

Place	Date	Hour	Summary of Events and Information	Remarks and references to Appendices
CAUDRY	17.11.18		25 Patients in D.R.S. Fit for evacuation [illegible]	
		0920	Transport attached R.F.[?] [illegible]	
		1200	Hqs moved by car to HAUTMONT	
HAUTMONT	18.11.18		Defined wards & Officers sleeping huts. Received into hospital [illegible]	
			Till just started. 11 East Lancs. Field Ambulance [illegible]	
		1500	[illegible] 9 Nurses on Matron's D.R.S. [illegible]	
		19.10	Sister HARVEY[?] had to work as transport was [illegible]	
		20.30	Letter [illegible]	
	19.11.18		Cleaning up & obtaining furniture. Working hospital & supplies arranged with a view of being left to 11 General Hosp. who are to take over Bath House France in site. Dining Hall & recreation room [illegible]	
	20.11.18		13 Cases in D.R.S. Have fitted out and 30 beds in [illegible] to supplement 4 [?] 750 [illegible] accomodation [illegible] arranged 45 places in any emergency case could be made available there. 39 Cases admitted.	
	21.11.18		56 Patients in D.R.S. [illegible]	

WAR DIARY
INTELLIGENCE SUMMARY.
(Erase heading not required.)

Army Form C. 2118.

Place	Date	Hour	Summary of Events and Information	Remarks and references to Appendices
HAVINCOURT	22/11/18	5:00 / 16:00	Divisibility of Cloth house ordering DRS open at about 14:00. [illegible] of men against [illegible] for full purposes. Quantity of water still had. To open [illegible] and water[illegible] in a [illegible]. Returns [illegible]. DRS's at [illegible]. EO staff [illegible]. C.O. stated fresh staff DMS. 6 cases admitted.	
	23/11/18		63 patients in DRS. Cleared up grounds containing trenches on [illegible] ground. [illegible] RESTRICTED notice on [illegible] and [illegible] [illegible]. [illegible] admitted to the DRS. 12 cases admitted.	
	23/11/18	9:00	74 patients DRS. Full Ambulance bus transport & [illegible] [illegible] of most [illegible] [illegible] [illegible] to [illegible]. Further ambulance [illegible] [illegible] in [illegible]. 20 cases admitted.	
	24/11/18	10:45	58 patients in DRS. Church service held in [illegible]. 31 cases admitted.	
	25/11/18	9:00	103 patients in DRS. Full Ambulance bus transport [illegible] patients [illegible] [illegible] [illegible] [illegible]. [illegible] case admitted.	

Army Form C. 2118.

WAR DIARY
INTELLIGENCE SUMMARY.
(Erase heading not required.)

Instructions regarding War Diaries and Intelligence Summaries are contained in F.S. Regs., Part II. and the Staff Manual respectively. Title pages will be prepared in manuscript.

Place	Date	Hour	Summary of Events and Information	Remarks and references to Appendices
HAUTMONT	26/11/18	09.00	113 patients in D.R.S. Squad drill & fatigues. Chief Clerk & 2 men Sergt & 27 other ranks arrived.	
		18.30	133 Coat potential interviewed formerly Unit.	
	27/11/18	09.00	120 patients in D.R.S. All funeral & out of work perfect arrangements being made not situation & station commands, informs of a further increase to 1130. Staff Hatriels incomplete.	
		18.30	Full Dig of patients elating present this day	
	28/11/18	09.15	118 patients in D.R.S. Unit leaves HAUTMONT for [illegible] in motor van if route reveal. Rent furniture returned for HAUTMONT to unit. 2nd 4/2 team winning. 18 cat. admitted.	
	29/11/18	09.00	126 patients in D.R.S. Squad drill & fatigues to work. Forms arrived by post. A.D.M.S. inspected D.R.S. [illegible] any and their [illegible]. 15 cas. admitted.	
	30/11/18	09.15	119 patients in D.R.S. Unit cmb Transfers & letters from a [illegible] [illegible] and orderly other 16 cas. admitted.	

1/3rd EAST LANCASHIRE FIELD AMBULANCE

Appendix 84
3.11.18
3/4.11.18

1. Number admitted up to 8 pm   124
2. Number admitted after 8 pm.   4
3. Number of Patients in hospital by wards.

Wards	Accomodation	No of Patients	Orderlies available Day	Night
'A'	80	92	3	1
'B' (Pyrexia)	80	118	3	2
'C' (Scabies)	40	25	1	.
'D' (Convalescent)	100	76	.	.
'E' (Officers)	10	13	1	1
'F'	60	85	2	1
Detained	40	22	.	.
Totals	410	431	10	5

DIETS
  Ordinary 220
  Milk   107
  Light   104

COOKS to prepare diets
  2 by day
  1 by night.
  1 Cook for Officers.

BATH-HOUSE. Orderlies 1.

Copy No. 5

1/3rd E.Lancashire Field Ambce.

Order No. 59

Reference Maps. 57.B.,51.A.,51.
A.D.M.S. 42nd Division Med. Arrangements No.15.

16th.Nov.1918.

1. The Divisional Rest Station is closing down at CAUDRY and re-opening at HAUTMONT. All area stores will be conveyed to new site in motor lorries and all mobilisation equipment in Horse Transport.

2. The 1/3rd E.Lancashire Field Ambce with band, less Headquarters, advance party under Capt.F.C.PRESTWICH already at HAUTMONT; and rear party under Major JOHNSON.M.C. will proceed by march route under command of Major HASKINS.M.C. on 17-11-18, will bivouac for that night at LE QUESNOY and arrive at HAUTMONT on 18-11-18. Orders for parade and for the march will be issued separately by Major HASKINS, who will make all necessary arrangements for billeting the unit on the night of 17-11-18, one Daimler Ambce will be at his disposal for this purpose.
Capt.F.C.SERGEANT and Surgeon R.C.W.STALEY R.N. will proceed with the unit, S/Sgt J.H.ASHTON.M.M. will be senior N.C.O.

3. Headquarters will proceed by Motor Ambulance to HAUTMONT on 17-11-18.

4. All Section equipment will be loaded on Section Transport by evening of 16-11-18.
All Headquarters equipment will be loaded on Headquarters Transport by evening of 16-11-18.
Transport will be parked and guards detailed by Major HASKINS M.C.

5. Eight motor lorries will report at CAUDRY at 0800 on 18-11-18. The rear party under Major JOHNSON.M.C. and the QUARTERMASTER will load all area stores on these lorries and proceed direct to HAUTMONT.
O.C. Rear Party will hand over all billets comprising the present D.R.S. to the Town Major, clean and tidy and obtain the necessary certificates.
One Motor Ambce will be at the disposal of this party, S/Sergt F.W.RITCHIE will be senior N.C.O.

6. All patients fit to march and attached men will march with the Main Body.

7. The Foden Thresh Lorry will proceed independently to the new D.R.S. site at HAUTMONT on 18-11-18.

Lieut-Colonel,
Cmdg 1/3rd E.Lancashire Field Ambulance.

Issued at 12.20.
Distribution:-
Copy No.1. Major N.H.H.Haskins M.C.
" 2. Major A.M.Johnson.M.C.
" 3. Capt.F.C.Prestwich.
" 4. Quartermaster.
" 5&6. War Diary.
" 7. File.

Confidential

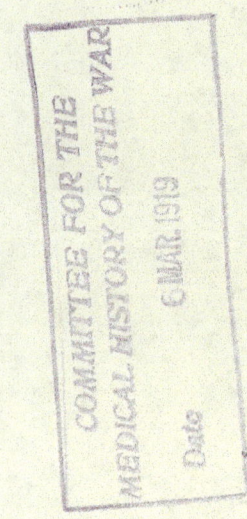

WAR DIARY

OF

1/3rd EAST LANCASHIRE FIELD AMBULANCE

FROM :- DECEMBER 1st 1918   TO :- DECEMBER 31st 1918.

(V O L U M E   XII)

WAR DIARY
INTELLIGENCE SUMMARY

Army Form C. 2118.

Place	Date	Hour	Summary of Events and Information	Remarks and references to Appendices
HAUTMONT	1-12-18	0915	116 Cases in D.R.S. Field Ambulance paraded in walking out dress with band & proceeded to where H.M. Divisional Band was, & were inspected by H.M. The KING. Captain FARMSTONE attended funeral of Driver WOOD in Belg: pleasg. 9, 9.5. Divisional Cemetery. 14 cases admitted	
	2-12-18	0900	113 Cases in D.R.S. Sergeant Drill to men of "D" in duties Bugler STALEY attd. t/c 2nd Div. R.F.A. & Dism'd Communication between columns 19 Cases admitted	
	3-12-18	0900	Captain PRESTWICH proceeded to D.H.Q of Tempary chief as acting D.A.D.M.S. 111 Cases in D.R.S	
		0915	RAMC paraded excluding duties proceeded to route march in marching order All ranks less H.D. on Chg. of Units instructed by Hon. Brusley Corporation on salute	
		1445	Surgeon Lieutenant STALEY R.N. detailed to temporary extended duty. Field Ambulance takes N°60	
		1815	88 patients admitted	
	4-12-18		120 Cases in D.R.S. Wet day. Period cleaning kit & quarters 16 Cases admitted	
	5-12-18	0900	111 Cases in D.R.S. RAMC paraded excluding duties proceeded to route march in marching order Major JOHNSON MC. returned from school leave to PARIS 9 patients admitted	

Army Form C. 2118.

WAR DIARY
INTELLIGENCE SUMMARY.
(Erase heading not required.)

Instructions regarding War Diaries and Intelligence Summaries are contained in F. S. Regs., Part II. and the Staff Manual respectively. Title pages will be prepared in manuscript.

Place	Date	Hour	Summary of Events and Information	Remarks and references to Appendices
HAUTMONT	6.12.18	09.00	106 Patients in D.R.S. RAMC personal paraded for route to guard duty. All fatigue parties & limit checks to all quarters of our troops. 4 G.S.Wagons admitted 4 G.S. Wagon pieces & mail notices CHARLEROI convoy been run of Division	
	7.12.18	09.00	99 Patients in D.R.S. RAMC marched with hard hospital of route march in meekly order. 5 cases admitted	
	8.12.18		102 Patients in D.R.S. Church service of common demonstration Fine day. May all personal attend Divinity refused All three motor cars refused & painted. Motor ambulance traveling left in direction of CHARLEROI to collect mail from divisional collecting point. Details of day's convoy march (rating taken) & working order. 11 Cases admitted	
	9.12.18	09.00	101 Patients in D.R.S. RAMC personal parade & squad drill 14 cases admitted	
	10.12.18	09.30	103 Patients in D.R.S. RAMC & personal parade & route march in meekly order	

Army Form C. 2118.

WAR DIARY
or
INTELLIGENCE SUMMARY.
(Erase heading not required.)

Instructions regarding War Diaries and Intelligence Summaries are contained in F. S. Regs., Part II. and the Staff Manual respectively. Title pages will be prepared in manuscript.

Place	Date	Hour	Summary of Events and Information	Remarks and references to Appendices
CHARLEROI	15.12.18	1830	Told A Section Tented divison arrive 3 day	
"	16.12.18		Staff of Division billeted dans l'hôtel St. D.R.S. HAUT(?) Advance party to CHARLEROI unable to commence work owing to units still moving to D.R.S. City	
"	17.12.18	0930	32 S Patients in D.R.S. HAUTMONT. Captain DELAFIELD arrived at CHARLEROI from B Section previously with Division and commenced own D.R.S. as far as possible owing to details still emerging ... R.E. given details of purchase from them.	
"	18.12.18	1240	A.D.M.S. visited site of D.R.S. Details of Schools (buildings) arrived to come to an arrangement for telephone attached it being of the accommodation in place to arrange a room to make details. He has found in unity to limit as that	
		1610	150 sick from D.R.S. HAUTMONT arrived accommodated in them attendance as Army ? Corps Troops hand not yet arrived only School of B Section to afford under command of Captain ... arrived. I would revert from HAUTMONT having maintained, and a man fellow en route	
"	19.12.18	1500	Army & Corps Troops moving out of D.R.S. sit commenced is conduction of B ... of fellow who of quarters. Remainder of Patients from HAUTMONT arrived. 70 in addition A.S.C. Rerant of horses completed known at all. C Section with Major HASKINS M.S. arrived from HAUTMONT.	
		1615		

WAR DIARY

INTELLIGENCE SUMMARY

(Erase heading not required.)

Army Form C. 2118.

Instructions regarding War Diaries and Intelligence Summaries are contained in F. S. Regs., Part II. and the Staff Manual respectively. Title pages will be prepared in manuscript.

Place	Date	Hour	Summary of Events and Information	Remarks and references to Appendices
HAUTMONT	10-12-18		nil on leaving. The 2nd ambulance attached to H.Q. with this 18 cases admitted	
"	11-12-18		105 patients in D.R.S. Wet windy day	
		11.20	Ambulances to move of units. D.R.S. moves Field Ambulance lost No. 31+ conveyance	Memo 20.
		19.30	Telephone message received ordering Major Johnson MC to England to relieve... Seven officers returned 13 Cases admitted Centuriat.	
	12.12.18		104 patients D.R.S. dry with a dusty day	
		11.00	H.Q. moved to CHARLEROI. Told money for D.R.S. Major Hawkins meets us at D.R.S. HAUTMONT. Arrangements made for ASection Inhaming Bury 11 Cases admitted.	
	13.12.18		B Section of D.R.S. Total Invalids accommodated. Passing of Public Holidays. ADMS Division came and Inspected also D.R.M.S Corps accommodation [?] patients of D.R.S. Transferred. Bad cases with bad constipation enemas + long 17 ...	
		14.45	D.R.S. at HAUTMONT filling up not letters accommodate rapidly Action on 205 attached D.R.S. rations	
CHARLEROI	14.12.18	17.10	Suspect Mjr Isled down Sergeant Siddaman a boy's Cook arrived Instrmn Questions arrived from our train general arrival of the Battalion belongings. N.C.O.s now a hrs unfit service	
"	15.12.18		AAA AN.C. of ADMS visits ECOLE MOVENNE until arrival into the building and D.R.S. ...	

Army Form C. 2118.

WAR DIARY
INTELLIGENCE SUMMARY.
(Erase heading not required.)

Instructions regarding War Diaries and Intelligence Summaries are contained in F. S. Regs., Part II. and the Staff Manual respectively. Title pages will be prepared in manuscript.

Place	Date	Hour	Summary of Events and Information	Remarks and references to Appendices
CHARLEROI	20.12.18		C.O. hands on command of the Units temporarily to Major H.J. KIRK M.C. on arriving duties / acting A.D.M.S. Division during absence on leave of A.D.M.S. 13 patients admitted	MXL
Do	21.12.18		Major H.H. HASKINS M.C. arrived rejoined as above. 13 patients in D.R.S. C. Section have transport arrived from HAUMONT 1/2 movements 12 patients admitted	MXLII
	22.12.18		105 patients in D.R.S. Wards provided with - tasks erected - system of bath-house & trestles & canteen in YARD rooms indents in continual 7 patients admitted	MXLVII
	23.12.18		95 patients in D.R.S. Demonstration from A.D.M.S 21.15 +16 fell in front - P Quality by outsides Patients admitted 6.	MXLII

D. D. & L. London, E.C.
(A10266) Wt W5300/P7713 750,000 2/18 Sch. 52 Forms/C2118/16.

Army Form C. 2118.

WAR DIARY
INTELLIGENCE SUMMARY.
(Erase heading not required.)

Instructions regarding War Diaries and Intelligence Summaries are contained in F. S. Regs., Part II. and the Staff Manual respectively. Title pages will be prepared in manuscript.

Place	Date	Hour	Summary of Events and Information	Remarks and references to Appendices
CHARLEROI	24/12/8		76 patients in D.R.S.	
		10.01	D.D.M.S. & A.D. inspected the D.R.S.	
		12.30	Photograph of unit (outdoors) taken by D.A.D.M.S., afterwards group of officers + men who left ENGLAND in 1914, until the unit (about 40) 13 patients admitted	
do	25/12/8		61 patients in D.R.S. — Xmas concept nursing sisters etc — the G.O.C. Division and A.D.M.S. visited the unit at 13.00 during the main dinner & visited them. The comforts of the men. The decoration and grub and the meals excellent. 5 patients admitted	
	26/12/8		51 patients in D.R.S. Only work during christmas formed — except in return pain in severing by one of the work — consolidation? 4 patients admitted	

D. D. & L., London, E.C.
(A10260) Wt.W5100/P715 750,000 2/18 Sch. 52 Forms/C2118/16.

WAR DIARY
INTELLIGENCE SUMMARY
(Erase heading not required.)

Army Form C. 2118.

Place	Date	Hour	Summary of Events and Information	Remarks and references to Appendices
CHARLEROI	27/12/18		63 patients O.R.S.	
		8900	Unit reconnoitred, informed that O.R.S. would be moving to another site — 30 min search in BACKSTREETS and only existing unit in BHTPS contacted.	XXII
			Proceeded with unloading of offices surrounded with furniture — O.S. began to dump at O.R.S.	
			9 patient admitted	
	28/12/18		58 patients O.R.S.	XXIII
		8900	Unloading of large contents — commenced very quietly — German beds and ward fittings in hospital	
			I. the EARLY TREATMENT centre approximately 250 men treated in 5 hrs. —	
			Work in O.R.S. continued	
			Patients admitted 11	
	29/12/18		63 patients in O.R.S.	XXIV
			51 men treated in EARLY TREATMENT CENTRE	
			Patients admitted 11	

WAR DIARY
INTELLIGENCE SUMMARY.
(Erase heading not required.)

Army Form C. 2118.

Place	Date	Hour	Summary of Events and Information	Remarks and references to Appendices
CHARLEROI	30/1/19	11.10	Patients in D.R.S. 60	
			C.O. visited the Main Transport lines – attn. Horse stopping last tee recommenced – now the saddle plates left firmly disinfected	
		1.15	to be clipped by D.A.D.V.S. 42nd Division	
		13.00	D.D.M.S. visited the D.R.S. that took –	NMNN1
		18.30	Came by walks keep THE SWABS. B.O.C. 42 Division and good number of Div STAFF et the evening staff – Excellent show	NMN321
			and Moves of 20, 53 and 53 C.C.S.s. –	
			Patients treated in EARLY TREATMENT CENTRE 69. 1. 2. Venereal cases admitted (mild & below) the list not transmitted punctually	
			Patients admitted 20.	
CHARLEROI	31/1/19	0900	Patients in D.R.S. 77.	
			Patients treated in EARLY TREATMENT CENTRE 54	
		19.00	Admitted by the unit – any Belgian civilians attended –	1111111F
			Patients admitted 14.	

1/3rd East Lancashire Field Ambulance.   Copy No. 3.

Order No. 60.

Reference Map Sheet. 51.
A.D.M.S. 42nd Division. 165 dated 3-12-1918.   3rd December 1918.

1. Surgeon Lieut. R.C.W. Staley. (R.N.) is detailed to proceed to 211th Brigade R.F.A. for temporary duty vice Capt. F.G. Sergeant (on leave to U.K.)

2. He will report to O.C. 211th Brigade R.F.A. forthwith.

3. Necessary transport will be provided.

                                                                  Lieut-Colonel,
            Commanding 1/3rd East Lancashire Field Ambulance.

Issued at 1815.

Distribution:-

Copy No. 1. Surgeon Lieut. R.C.W. Staley. (R.N.)
Copy No. 2. O.C. 211th Brigade R.F.A.
Copies Nos. 3 & 4. War Diary.
Copy No. 5. File.

1/3rd East Lancashire Field Ambulance.   Copy No.........

Addendum & Corrigendum No.1 to Field Ambulance Order No. 61.

Reference Map:- N.W. Europe, Parts of Sheets 1 & 4 Combined.
42nd Divisional R.A.M.C. Order No. 63.   11th December 1918.

1. Dress.   Marching order with helmets, box respirator, one blanket and one groundsheet.   Jerkins to be carried in pack.

2. One bicycle (ordinary) will accompany "B" Section.

3. As soon as possible after arrival in a billeting area O.C. "B" Section will arrange to send two orderlies who know their own Headquarters to the Brigade Headquarters; one orderly will then return to the Section the other remaining at Brigade Headquarters.

4. During halts, charges and pack animals must be well on the right hand side of the road facing inwards.

5. On no account is any man (except drivers and brakesmen) to be allowed to ride on any cart, G.S. Wagon, or limber.

   Men marching with transport must march immediately in rear of the wagons and not fill up the road on either side of them.

6. Men must be taught to refrain from smoking and drinking during the march.

7. O.C. "C" Section will arrange to collect 42nd Divisional Artillery, 93 A.F.A. Brigade and 19th Mobile Veterinary Section sick from HAUTMONT at 11.00 hours on the 14th, from MARPENT and JEUMONT at 09.30 on 15th and from PEISSANT and MERBES STE MARIE at 09.30 on 16th.

   O.C. "A" Section will arrange to collect sick of this group from LOBBES and THUIN at 09.30 on 17th, and from LOBBES and THUIN at 09.30 on the 18th

8. The Divisional Reception Camp will move to LE QUESNOY, so sick parade will not be held at the D.R.S. HAUTMONT.

9. "A" & "B" Sections will carry sufficient fuel for two days.

Continuation of Addendum & Corrigendum No 1 to F.A. Order No. 61
---

10. As the Reception Camp will not be located in HAUTMONT each Infantry Brigade and Field Artillery Brigade will detail one Officer and not less than two other ranks per unit to remain in charge of surplus baggage dump. R.E., R.A.S.C., R.A.M.C., Northumberland Fusiliers and M.G.Bn. will detail not less than two men per unit to remain in charge of the dump.

    All parties to be rationed up to and for 15th inst.
    They will be attached to 42nd Divisional Rest Station for rations on and after that date. Actual numbers remaining at the dump will be reported to Division "Q" by 18.00 on 12th inst.

11. Reference para 6 of Field Ambulance Order No 61 for:-
    One daimler will proceed to CHARLEROI on 14-12-18.
    read   "   "   "   "   "   "   " 16-12-18.

    For   One Ford will proceed to CHARLEROI on 16-12-18.
    Read M.A.C.Car attached etc., "   "   " 16-12-18.

    For   M.A.C.Car attached to "C" Section etc.,
    Read One Ford   "   "   "   "   "

12. All patients discharged to duty from 14th inclusive will be sent to Divisional Reception Camp at LE QUESNOY.

                                                Lieut-Colonel,
                                    Cmdg 1/3rd East Lancs Field Ambulance.

Copy No. 8

1/3rd East Lancashire Field Ambulance.

Order No 61.   Appendix 90

Reference Map :- N.W.Europe, Parts of Sheets 1 & 4 Combined.
A.D.M.S. 42nd Division.

11th December, 1918.

1. The Field Ambulance will move to CHARLEROI and establish a new Divisional Rest Station there, after which that in HAUTMONT will close down.

2. "A" Section (Approximate strength:-Officers 3, Other Ranks 66, H.D.Horses 10, L.D.Horses 11.) will proceed as an advance party by lorries on 12-12-18 to prepare a new D.R.S. O.C."A" Section will ensure that a sufficient supply of blankets and stores are taken for the purpose.
    Headquarters and "A" Section Transport, less 1 H.D.Ambulance Wagon, 1/c of S.S.M.Halsey will, proceed by march route on 12-12-18, halting on night 12/13 at ESTINNE-AU-MONTI, on night of 13/14 at ANDERLUES, and night 14/15 at CHARLEROI.

3. "B" Section (Approximate strength:-Officers 1, Other Ranks 60, H.D.Horses 6, L.D.Horses 7.) with transport, including "A" Section H.D.Ambulance Wagon, will proceed by march route on 14-12-18 under the orders of G.O.C. 125 Infantry Brigade.

4. "C" Section (Approximate strength:-Officers 1, Other Ranks 60, H.D.Horses 5, L.D.Horses 7.) will form rear party and form personnel for D.R.S.HAUTMONT, until it is closed down, when the R.A.M.C. personnel and patients (Approximate strength 120) will proceed by lorries to the new D.R.S. at CHARLEROI. The Section Transport moving by march route.

5. Headquarters will move to CHARLEROI on 14-12-18.

6. Detail of Mechanical Transport :-
    1 Ford Car will proceed to CHARLEROI on 12-12-18.
    1 Daimler   "   "   "   "   " 14-12-18.
    1 Ford   "   "   "   "   " 16-12-18.
    1 M.A.C.Car attached "C" Section will proceed with the Section.
    Motor Cyclist will proceed on 12-12-18.

7. The Bandsmen will proceed with their respective sections.

8. O.C."C" Section will arrange to collect sick of 125 Brigade from MAUBEUGE at 0900 hours on 15-12-18, from ESTINNE-AU-MONTI at 0830 hours on 16-12-18.
    O.C."A" Section will arrange to collect the sick of 125 Brigade from ANDERLUES at 1030 hours on 17-12-18, and from ANDERLUES at 0845 hours on 18-12-18.

9. Sick of Divisional Reception Camp will parade at the D.R.S.HAUTMONT, on 14th, 15th, 16th, 17th, and 18th December.

10. O.C."C" Section will ensure that D.R.S.HAUTMONT, is left in a clean and sanitary condition and that all stores are sent forward to the new D.R.S.CHARLEROI.

Issued at 1120.
Distribution:-
Copy No 1. O.C."A" Section.
 "   " 2. O.C."B"   "
 "   " 3. O.C."C"   "
 "   " 4. Quartermaster.   Copy No 5. S.S.O. 42nd Division.
 "   " 6. A.D.M.S. 42nd Division. "   " 7. 125 Brigade.
 "   " 8&9. War Diary.   "   " 10. File.

Lieut-Colonel,
Cmdg 1/3rd E.Lancs Field Ambulance.

42nd DIV

Box 2475

WAR DIARY

OF

1/3rd EAST LANCASHIRE FIELD AMBULANCE

FROM :- January 1st, 1919   TO :- January 31st, 1919.

(VOLUME 1)

Army Form C. 2118.

WAR DIARY
or
INTELLIGENCE SUMMARY.
(Erase heading not required.)

Instructions regarding War Diaries and Intelligence Summaries are contained in F. S. Regs., Part II. and the Staff Manual respectively. Title pages will be prepared in manuscript.

Place	Date	Hour	Summary of Events and Information	Remarks and references to Appendices
CHARLEROI	1/1/19	0900	Patients in D.R.S. 77	
			Provided with voluntary party — filled with German Patients, etc — being inspected weekly.	
			70 patients treated in EARLY TREATMENT CENTRE	
			9 patients admitted	
	2/1/19		86 patients in D.R.S.	
		0900	C.O. inspected new site for D.R.S. in hospital for women (hotel). Relieving recommended, intention but — unknown upon front — getting in with hospital front — Find new building.	
			61 new patients in EARLY TREATMENT CENTRE	
			11 patients admitted	
	3/1/19		91 patients in D.R.S.	
			2 O.Rs reported from 1/0 but from 7td that I issued is ready on S	
			Been removed to take down both men to D.R.S. BLUES HOTELS.	
			Contact given last few days = 150.	
			164 new patients in EARLY TREATMENT CENTRE	
			2 patients admitted	

(A10256) Wt W5900/P713 750,000 2/18 Sch. 52 Forms/C2118/16. D. D. & L., London, E.C.

Army Form C. 2118.

WAR DIARY

INTELLIGENCE SUMMARY.
(Erase heading not required.)

Instructions regarding War Diaries and Intelligence Summaries are contained in F. S. Regs., Part II. and the Staff Manual respectively. Title pages will be prepared in manuscript.

Place	Date	Hour	Summary of Events and Information	Remarks and references to Appendices
CHARLEROI	4/1/19		110 patients in D.R.S.	
		14:00	A.D.M.S. & C.O. met O.R.E. Officer who says D.R.S. is not prepared to take in civilians	Appx
			Shew a meeting point	
			84 men billeted in EARLY TREATMENT CENTRE	
			22 patients admitted	
	5/1/19		128 patients in D.R.S.	
		10:30	acting C.O. attended conference at A.D.M.S.	Appx
		11:00	No. 59 Sanitary Section arrived and were billetted in D.R.S.	
			15 patients admitted	
	6/1/19		123 patients in D.R.S.	
		11:00	C.O. visited new D.R.S. site - R.E. meeting the A. hta. but wishes not working in flooring	Appx
			6-9 men billeted in EARLY TREATMENT CENTRE	
			15 patients admitted	

Army Form C. 2118.

WAR DIARY
INTELLIGENCE SUMMARY.
(Erase heading not required.)

Instructions regarding War Diaries and Intelligence Summaries are contained in F. S. Regs., Part II. and the Staff Manual respectively. Title pages will be prepared in manuscript.

Place	Date	Hour	Summary of Events and Information	Remarks and references to Appendices
CHARLEROI	7/1/19	09.00	128 patients in D.R.S. Work proceeded with in new D.R.S. with 63 men treated in Early Treatment Centre 15 patients admitted	MMM
"	8/1/19	09.00	130 patients in D.R.S. 4 men class sent to Corps Concentration Camp for investigation. Nos 5754, 15 61 men treated at Early Medical Centre 13 men admitted	MMM
"	9/1/19	09.00	134 patients in D.R.S. Work proceeded with — progress in new D.R.S.	MMM
		09.30	14 men treated for H.F. Came to visit 2/3 of Ent. Zone Field Amb at 11:15 Staff visited in Early Treatment Centre 17 patients admitted	

Army Form C. 2118.

WAR DIARY
INTELLIGENCE SUMMARY.
(Erase heading not required.)

Instructions regarding War Diaries and Intelligence Summaries are contained in F.S. Regs., Part II. and the Staff Manual respectively. Title pages will be prepared in manuscript.

Place	Date	Hour	Summary of Events and Information	Remarks and references to Appendices
CHARLEROI	10/1/19		139 patients in R.R.S.	
		11.00	Actg C.O. visited the 125 Belt Barracks - attempt is restarting in central Protection Room	MM
			52 men listed in Early Treatment Centre	
			Patients admitted to RS 22	
"	11/1/19		136 patients in D.R.S.	
		0900	Parties under own O.R.S. investigates 22 men formerly attached from 1/1 East Lancs Field Amb. 8.3 negative reports on no patient - many to R.E. C.R.6, 442nd Division sick and suffering fatigues	MM
			150 German inmates billets moved from School HOUSE, MONTIGNY.	
			Patients treated in EARLY TREATMENT CENTRE = 59	
			9 patients admitted to D.R.S.	
"	12/1/19		136 patients in the D.R.S.	
			The R.A.M.C officers attached to the 125 Bde - from which these not collect sick and allotted to the Field Amb for today - The arrangement being a central Medical Inspection Room for the Bde proct and Corps troops.	

WAR DIARY
or
INTELLIGENCE SUMMARY.
(Erase heading not required.)

Army Form C. 2118.

Place	Date	Hour	Summary of Events and Information	Remarks and references to Appendices
CHARLEROI	12/1/19		At what seek he considered at 09.00 hr — 148 sent sick by the orderly Officer to D.R.S. Sub-totals of admin. C.O., Suffern Samuel i/c weight D.R.S. 1st/Lt i/c M.I. Room at Bde and met in Sanitary duties of all units in the area A.D.M.S. Held Board re D.R.S.	W/M/I
	13/1/19	11.00	45 men admitted to D.R.S. inspected new O.R.S. with CRE 8 patients admitted in EARLY TREATMENT CENTRE	
		14.00	135 patients in D.R.S. Position work on new D.R.S. continued 53 men treated at EARLY TREATMENT CENTRE 5 patients admitted to D.R.S.	W/M/I
"	14/1/19		135 patients in D.R.S. Routine. D.A.N.S. to trips called but did not inspect D.R.S. 47 men treated in EARLY TREATMENT CENTRE S Loose & putter D.Q.S.	W/M/I

Army Form C. 2118.

WAR DIARY
or
INTELLIGENCE SUMMARY.
(Erase heading not required.)

Instructions regarding War Diaries and Intelligence Summaries are contained in F. S. Regs., Part II. and the Staff Manual respectively. Title pages will be prepared in manuscript.

Place	Date	Hour	Summary of Events and Information	Remarks and references to Appendices
CHARLEROI	15/9/19	0900	142 patients = 325	11/11/22
		1400	Work on new D.R.S. progress. Progress reported in R.S. III Work done well, most meaningful, many workers. New hosted in EARLY TREATMENT CENTRE = 92. Admission to D.R.S. 17	
	16/9/19		147 patients in D.R.S. Quarters — 50 patients treated in EARLY TREATMENT CENTRE III reports submitted Patients in D.R.S. 146	11/11/22
,,	17/9/19	0900	Went to new O.R.S. as chauffeur about official name. CHARLEROI DE SERVICE INTER COMMUNAL DES MOEURS Section sea, shafts and personnel round. So registered in EARLY TREATMENT CENTRE	""

(A10256) Wt W3500/P713 750,000 2/18 Sch. 52 Forms/C2118/16.
D. D. & L., London, E.C.

Army Form C. 2118.

WAR DIARY
or
INTELLIGENCE SUMMARY.
(Erase heading not required.)

Instructions regarding War Diaries and Intelligence Summaries are contained in F. S. Regs., Part II. and the Staff Manual respectively. Title pages will be prepared in manuscript.

Place	Date	Hour	Summary of Events and Information	Remarks and references to Appendices
CHARLEROI	18/19	0900	145 patients in D.R.S.	
			Now complete — also employed in general — tents after midday meal	MMVII
			Men employed with clearing of the field ambulance	
			113 patients treated in EARLY TREATMENT CENTRE	
			147 patients admitted to D.R.S.	
	19/19		Men employed by midday.	
			The new D.R.S. not being complete — patients and personal having to use one room leaving room between out	MMVIII
			slender tents.	
			437 patients treated in the EARLY TREATMENT CENTRE	
			147 patients admitted + transferred to O.R.S.	
	20/9.		147 patients in D.R.S.	
			Personal paid —	MMIX
			46 men treated in EARLY TREATMENT CENTRE	
			26 patients admitted + transferred to D.R.S	

Army Form C. 2118.

WAR DIARY
or
INTELLIGENCE SUMMARY.
(Erase heading not required.)

Instructions regarding War Diaries and Intelligence Summaries are contained in F. S. Regs., Part II. and the Staff Manual respectively. Title pages will be prepared in manuscript.

Place	Date	Hour	Summary of Events and Information	Remarks and references to Appendices
CHARLEROI			15.9 patients in D.A.S.	
	21/1/19	12.00	G.O.C. Down with A.D.M.S. inspected the D.R.S. – officers to think seriously of rally + take a rest	MMM
			3 men of D.R.S. sent on a bit of work to the a few select musicians	
			4 U men treated in EARLY TREATMENT CENTRE	
			24 patients admitted + transferred to D.R.S.	
	22/1/19		160 patients in D.R.S	MMM
			Battalion meet – chair not quite finished.	
			Routine	
			34 new men treated in EARLY TREATMENT CENTRE	
			Patients admitted and transferred to D.R.S. = 17	
"	23/1/19		Patients in D.A.S. 163.	MMM
			40 patients treated in EARLY TREATMENT CENTRE	

WAR DIARY
INTELLIGENCE SUMMARY
(Erase heading not required.)

Army Form C. 2118.

Instructions regarding War Diaries and Intelligence Summaries are contained in F. S. Regs., Part II. and the Staff Manual respectively. Title pages will be prepared in manuscript.

Place	Date	Hour	Summary of Events and Information	Remarks and references to Appendices
CHARLEROI	24/4/19		Patient admitted & transferred to D.R.S. 23	XXXIV
			106 patients in D.R.S.	
			Bathhouse almost completed — German hut completed except for stoves and glass in windows.	
			The various features in Bathing bing or RECEPTION ROOM — patients & personal washing and dressing in the rear quarter i.e. While hut and dining ROOM. We are trying very hard now to bring of R.E. proved hut to Barlington estimate took weeks of work.	XXXV
			53 men treated in EARLY TREATMENT CENTRE	
			23 patient admitted and transferred to D.R.S.	
	25/4/19		170 patients in D.R.S.	LXXXVI
			Work in D.R.S. continued	
			85 patients treated in EARLY TREATMENT CENTRE	
			22 patient admitted & transported to the D.R.S.	

Army Form C 2118.

WAR DIARY
or
INTELLIGENCE SUMMARY.
(Erase heading not required.)

Instructions regarding War Diaries and Intelligence Summaries are contained in F. S. Regs., Part II. and the Staff Manual respectively. Title pages will be prepared in manuscript.

Place	Date	Hour	Summary of Events and Information	Remarks and references to Appendices
CHARLEROI	26/1/19		179 Patients in D.R.S. 95 men Posted to Early Treatment Centre Admissions + Transfers to D.R.S. 13	
	27/1/19		Lt Colonel H.H.B. CUNNINGHAM resumed command on return from D. of Q. 193 Patients in D.R.S. 21 Cases admitted	
	28/1/19		191 Patients in D.R.S. 16 Cases admitted Major GIBSON proceeded 1/2 last term Field Ambulance on being ordered to the King. Lieutenant CARR (T.C.) posted (unit for duty) New isolation ward [illegible] into use.	
	29/1/19		161 Patients in D.R.S. 16 Cases admitted	

Army Form C. 2118.

WAR DIARY
INTELLIGENCE SUMMARY.
(Erase heading not required.)

Instructions regarding War Diaries and Intelligence Summaries are contained in F. S. Regs., Part II. and the Staff Manual respectively. Title pages will be prepared in manuscript.

Place	Date	Hour	Summary of Events and Information	Remarks and references to Appendices
CHARLEROI	30.1.19		156 Patients in DRS. All ward now in working order. Isolation wards operation are in the course of being constructed. Many field cases have better room use. 16 patients admitted	MM
"	31.1.19		153 Patients in DRS. Personal quarters are now fit and a working arrangement made to ensure their comfort. Personal Cook house ablution houses & latrines completed. DRS incinerator completed.	MM

W M Cunningham Col.

WAR DIARY.

1/3RD EAST LANCASHIRE FIELD AMBULANCE.

Vol.II

FEBRUARY 1 - 28th. 1919.

Army Form C. 2118.

WAR DIARY
or
INTELLIGENCE SUMMARY.
(Erase heading not required.)

Instructions regarding War Diaries and Intelligence Summaries are contained in F.S. Regs., Part II. and the Staff Manual respectively. Title pages will be prepared in manuscript.

Place	Date	Hour	Summary of Events and Information	Remarks and references to Appendices
CHARLEROI	1.2.19		136 patients in D.R.S. 6 cases admitted	
	2.2.19		131 patients in D.R.S. 4 cases admitted. Consultation this a.m. with our orders of admission from D.M.S.	
	3.2.19		125 patients in D.R.S. 6 cases admitted	
	4.2.19		126 patients in D.R.S. 10 cases admitted	
	5.2.19		119 patients in D.R.S. Col. Ashford flying visit, would not wait a min. to stay. Wrote mid. 18 cases admitted	
	6.2.19		Very bad snow during Tuesday night. Wrote emphatic snow plough at end. Clarify orders to D.R.S. this return. 123 patients in D.R.S. 10 cases admitted	

Army Form C. 2118.

WAR DIARY
— or —
INTELLIGENCE SUMMARY.
(Erase heading not required.)

Instructions regarding War Diaries and Intelligence Summaries are contained in F. S. Regs., Part II. and the Staff Manual respectively. Title pages will be prepared in manuscript.

Place	Date	Hour	Summary of Events and Information	Remarks and references to Appendices
CHARLEROI	7.2.19		108 patients in D.R.S. Very cold weather freezing hard. One man dispatched previous day to England as an Army Road man. A.S.C. Cadre strength of Unit made up today. 11 cases admitted. D.M.S. Army visited D.R.S.	
"	8.2.19		94 patients in D.R.S. Still freezing hard. 14 cases admitted	
"	9.2.19		86 patients in D.R.S. 9 cases admitted	
"	10.2.19		76 patients in D.R.S. 12 cases admitted	
"	11.2.19		91 patients in D.R.S. Captain LEACH M.O.R.C. U.S.A. reports his arrival as a reinforcement to this Unit. 11 cases admitted	

Army Form C. 2118.

WAR DIARY
INTELLIGENCE SUMMARY.
(Erase heading not required.)

Instructions regarding War Diaries and Intelligence Summaries are contained in F. S. Regs., Part II. and the Staff Manual respectively. Title pages will be prepared in manuscript.

Place	Date	Hour	Summary of Events and Information	Remarks and references to Appendices
CHARLEROI	12-2-19	1502	70 Patients in D.R.S. The General Commd'r visited the D.R.S. today inspecting all wards, Officers & Billets. 9 Cases admitted.	
"	13-2-19		65 patients in D.R.S. 11 Cases admitted	
"	14-2-19		61 patients in D.R.S. 18 Cases admitted	
"	15-2-19		55 patients in D.R.S. 12 home sent to England. 16 Cases admitted	
"	16-2-19		51 patients in D.R.S. 10 Cases admitted	
"	17-2-19		53 patients in D.R.S. 10 Cases admitted	

Army Form C. 2118.

WAR DIARY
INTELLIGENCE SUMMARY.
(Erase heading not required.)

Instructions regarding War Diaries and Intelligence Summaries are contained in F. S. Regs., Part II. and the Staff Manual respectively. Title pages will be prepared in manuscript.

Place	Date	Hour	Summary of Events and Information	Remarks and references to Appendices
CHARLEROI	18.2.19		54 Patients in D.R.S. 11 Cases admitted.	
	19.2.19		57 Patients in D.R.S. 19 Cases admitted.	
	20.2.19		68 Patients in D.R.S. 21 Cases admitted	
	21.2.19		43 Patients in D.R.S. 12 Cases admitted	
	22.2.19		Warning notice received that D.R.S. would be closed & buildings & grounds handed in to C.C.S.	
	23.2.19	0930	74 Patients in D.R.S.	
		1000	Telephone message received that 55 C.C.S. would take over D.R.S. fixtures & maintenance of 55 C.C.S. arrd ascertained to take on bed blankets attachments	
		1200	all patients in D.R.S. (64 in number) handed over to 55 C.C.S.	
		1230	O.C. 55 C.C.S. arrd & handed back over groups admitting.	
			Personnel remain in their billets in the town on night room fixed up in a room at the town Field Ambulance now closed, & maintaining a Medical Inspection room in the Barracks a L.P.of(?) treatment room in the town	

Army Form C. 2118.

WAR DIARY
or
INTELLIGENCE SUMMARY.

(Erase heading not required.)

Instructions regarding War Diaries and Intelligence Summaries are contained in F. S. Regs., Part II. and the Staff Manual respectively. Title pages will be prepared in manuscript.

Place	Date	Hour	Summary of Events and Information	Remarks and references to Appendices
CHARLEROI	24.2.19		Fine day. Some good fatigues today done generally of [illegible] prisoners of war of writing and clearing of mobilization stores. Ground site allotted for parking wagons.	
	25.2.19		Orderly Room established in a Billet in town	
	26.2.19		New Medical Inspection Room established in a billet in town	
	27.2.19		7 Horses sent to Depot for disposal	
	28.2.19	1100	Demobilisation of A.S.C. personnel of Unit commenced. C.O. attended a Committee meeting at H.Q. IV Corps of DMS [illegible] giving of [illegible] evidence on return of Field Ambulance i.e. medical ordnance equipment etc returned	
		1945	When [illegible] to a [illegible] of Lieutenant CARROLL returned to return to No. 2 General Hospital for duty with Chinese Field Ambulance No. 63	Appendix 9.

[signature]

Copy No. 3

1/3rd East Lancashire Field Ambulance.

Order No. 62

D.C.M.S. No P1371 dated 22-2-19.
D.M.S. IV Army P19/146.
A.D.M.S. 42nd Divn M14/ 281.

28th February, 1919.

Temp. Lieut. P.Carroll, R.A.M.C. T.C. 1/3rd East Lancashire Field Ambulance is detailed to proceed forthwith and report to O.C. No. 3 Native Labour General Hospital, NOYELLES, for duty in connection with repatriation of Chinese Labour Corps.

Lieut-Colonel,
Commanding 1/3rd East Lancashire Field Ambulance.

Issued at 1945

Distribution:-
Copy No. 1. Lieut. P. Carroll.
"   2. O.C. No. 3 Native Labour General Hospital.
"   3 & 4 War Diary.
"   5. File.

140/3551

21 JUL 1919

11/3/1 Cert Cause F.C.

Jun 1919

Army Form C. 2118.

14 WAR DIARY or INTELLIGENCE SUMMARY.

(Erase heading not required.)

Instructions regarding War Diaries and Intelligence Summaries are contained in F. S. Regs., Part II. and the Staff Manual respectively. Title pages will be prepared in manuscript.

April 26
Closed

Place	Date	Hour	Summary of Events and Information	Remarks and references to Appendices
CHARLEROI	1.3.19		All wagon parks up in Shivenwil Park.	MMM
	3.3.19		8 Horses cast to Mobile Veterinary Section of local sale. Captain F.G. PRESTWICH ordered to this Unit ex above 2nd Sengl. 2 Troop 10th BR to proceed with orders of Maritime Medal, Sngt. ALGER placed with orders of Maritime Service Medal.	MMM
	4.3.19		Orders received of Captain FANSTONE transfer to 47 G.S. 4. footing etc 7 Field Ambulance Index No. 63	MMM April 92
	5.3.19		Routine	MMM
	6.3.19		O/C C.O. A/M. Captain LEACH M.C. U.S.A. on duty with Field Ambulance Orders received to return to USA to be down to us establishment, the 10% previously allowed remains to remain.	MMM
	7.3.19		Whole of Riding horses cast to Mobile Veterinary Section of sale closing, my four changes Hy horses remaining in Unit.	MMM
	8.3.19		Routine	MMM
	9.3.19		Routine	MMM
	10.3.19		C.O. assumed territory during DD.M.S. in addition to ordinary advance medical orderly made out to compete observer regarding Mobilization	MMM
	11.3.19		Routine, drafts Office work	MMM

Army Form C. 2118.

WAR DIARY
or
INTELLIGENCE SUMMARY.
(Erase heading not required.)

Instructions regarding War Diaries and Intelligence Summaries are contained in F. S. Regs., Part II. and the Staff Manual respectively. Title pages will be prepared in manuscript.

Place	Date	Hour	Summary of Events and Information	Remarks and references to Appendices
CHARLEROI	12-3-19	0900	A.D.M.S. returned & resumed duties, as S.O. i/c med stations of officers/ABIES	
	13.3.19		Routine.	
	14.3.19		No demobilisation to-day, prisoners of all ranks plus R.F.S. & N.Z. forces returned to train	
	15.3.19		Routine	
	16.3.19		Routine	
	17.3.19		Major FABRIS returned from leave in U.K. Lt Col Crompton proceeded on leave to U.K. Major Watkin assuming command	
	18.3.19		" Routine	
	19.3.19		Routine. Orders from D.A.D.O. received & 1 field amb. to move in approx 24 hrs to ANTWERP - on leave & thence by boat to IMMINGHAM.	
	20.3.19		Unit paid, 1 Capt and 4 O.R. proceeded for duty to 46 Sanitary section	
	23.3.19		Routine	
	24.3.19		Routine. Orders of move cancelled	
	25.3.19		Routine	

Army Form C. 2118.

WAR DIARY
or
INTELLIGENCE SUMMARY.
(Erase heading not required.)

Instructions regarding War Diaries and Intelligence Summaries are contained in F. S. Regs., Part II. and the Staff Manual respectively. Title pages will be prepared in manuscript.

Place	Date	Hour	Summary of Events and Information	Remarks and references to Appendices
CHARLTON	27.3.19		MORE Capt Lock proceeded to Bayfort where he effected the distribution for ceremony on 30th	Neal
"	28.3.19		" Wigan hunted as WESTRA to Remaining 5 horses rendered over to R.G.A.	WNN
"	29.3.19		Orders Orders received that cadre strength of Offrs reduced from 3 to 2 — n.c.o's. and rank/file 	WNN
"	29.3.19		Marched via WEBB	
"	30.3.19	19.00	Details returned outside station of VILLE HAUTE CNAFE 51701 — Swing Load Supplemented 17.3.R. transferred to strength of 65 C.C.S Cadre 2 officers 61 O.R. with 14 vehicles and equipment retained for Details Weather Snowy & foggy Capt PARTON CO applied to 1/1st Cost their Field Ambulance	NNN

(A7092). Wt. W28/39/M1293. 73,000. 1/17. D. D. & L., Ltd. Forms/C.2118/14.

Army Form C. 2118.

WAR DIARY
or
INTELLIGENCE SUMMARY.
(Erase heading not required.)

Instructions regarding War Diaries and Intelligence Summaries are contained in F.S. Regs., Part II. and the Staff Manual respectively. Title pages will be prepared in manuscript.

Place	Date	Hour	Summary of Events and Information	Remarks and references to Appendices
ANTWERP	31/8/19	0730	Arrived Antwerp at siding at SIBERIA DOCK	
			Company aids in adjoining EMBARKATION CAMP assigned quarters for the day hots — relocating horses out to hay	
		16.30	Horses taken to the dock	
		18.00	Had rations on Canadian Pacific Ocean Service S.S. SICILIAN	
			Orders issued to entrain in above steamer of the following troops — proceeding on arrival at OCEAN.	
	1/9/19	0700	Embarking on S.S. SICILIAN.	
			H.Q. 2nd Bn R.E.Inf.Brig. Bde. i/c EMBARKATION CAMP including full firm of dept	
			Capt. Winterbotham 2129 Falg. R.E. 1/6th Norfolk R.E. 1/4 H.Q. 171st Brigade 1/2 dk. Fd. Lab.	
			No.H. Coy 42nd Div A.S.C. 1/2 2nd two Batt. Staff	
		6800	SAILED. Disembarked the above Bde. Royal 19th 14th at 19 am 14.23.	
			This closes the WAR DIARY for B.E.F.	

www.ingramcontent.com/pod-product-compliance
Lightning Source LLC
Chambersburg PA
CBHW080919230426
43668CB00014B/2159